Ground Truth

Ground Truth

The Moral Component in Contemporary British Warfare

Edited by

Frank Ledwidge, Helen Parr & Aaron Edwards

BLOOMSBURY ACADEMIC

LONDON • NEW YORK • OXFORD • NEW DELHI • SYDNEY

BLOOMSBURY ACADEMIC
Bloomsbury Publishing Plc
dford Square, London, WC1B 3DP, UK
Broadway, New York, NY 10018, USA
Earlsfort Terrace, Dublin 2, Ireland

SBURY ACADEMIC and the Diana logo are trademarks of
Bloomsbury Publishing Plc

rst published in Great Britain 2024

nk Ledwidge, Helen Parr, Aaron Edwards, 2024

Aaron Edwards have asserted their right under the Copyright,
s Act, 1988, to be identified as Authors of this work.

cknowledgements on p. xii constitute an extension of this
copyright page.

Series design by Adriana Brioso
er image © John Moore/Getty Images

ord for this book is available from the British Library.

of Congress Cataloging-in-Publication Data

k, editor. | Parr, Helen, 1974- editor. | Edwards, Aaron, editor.
the moral component in contemporary British warfare /
r: Frank Ledwidge, Helen Parr, Aaron Edwards.
Moral component in contemporary British warfare
New York: Bloomsbury Academic, 2024. | Series: Studies in
varfare | Includes bibliographical references and index.
368 (print) | LCCN 2023052869 (ebook) | ISBN 9781350335523 (hb)
b) | ISBN 9781350335547 (epdf) | ISBN 9781350335530 (ebook)
ethics–Great Britain. | Military art and science–Moral and ethical
| Military art and science–Great Britain–History–21st century. |
3ritain. | Afghan War, 2001-2021–Participation, British. | Iraq War,
2003-2011–Participation, British.
on: LCC U22 .G77 2024 (print) | LCC U22 (ebook) |
DDC 172/.420941–dc23/eng/20240128
rd available at https://lccn.loc.gov/2023052868
record available at https://lccn.loc.gov/2023052869

ISBN: HB: 978-1-3503-3552-3
PB: 978-1-3503-3551-6
ePDF: 978-1-3503-3554-7
eBook: 978-1-3503-3553-0

Series: Studies in Contemporary Warfare

y Deanta Global Publishing Services, Chennai, India
Printed and bound in Great Britain

bout our authors and books visit www.bloomsbury.com and
sign up for our newsletters.

Contents

Foreword

Professor Sir Lawrence Freedman

I got to know David Benest when I was writing *The Official History of the Falklands Campaign*. David's detailed history of the Battle of Goose Green, written on the journey home from the South Atlantic after talking to his comrades from the 2nd Battalion, The Parachute Regiment (he had been regimental signals officer), informed every subsequent account. His history was moving, as he described the deaths of young soldiers he knew, but also unsparing in his determination to avoid myth-making and glossing over the more awkward aspects of the battle. Time and again in our conversations we discussed the role of Colonel 'H' Jones, who lost his life urging his men forward. There was no doubting his brave leadership, but had his actions been appropriate for a commanding officer? And this led us back to a discussion of the challenges of command. How much was it possible to control the course of a battle when it was not unfolding as hoped and expected? How much could and should tactical decisions be left to company commanders? I was last in touch with David not long before he died, hoping to meet up to discuss the book I was just starting to write on command,[1] in which I would be returning to Goose Green.

David's important role as a practitioner-historian provides a vital inspiration for the essays in this volume, but so too does his conviction that the military profession required a firm moral compass. It was here that he made an important contribution to contemporary military thought. An ethical approach to soldiering was essential not only because unethical behaviour could be strategically counterproductive but also because it was inappropriate for a liberal-democratic society at war. He had little time for the argument that soldiers should be allowed to operate in a different moral universe because of the extreme conditions in which they might find themselves. He understood

---

[1] Sir Lawrence Freedman, *Command: The Politics of Military Operations from Korea to Ukraine* (London: Allen Lane, 2022).

why the reactions to allegations of excessive violence were so defensive. Young soldiers could find themselves in threatening situations where restraint appeared hazardous. He had done his tours in Northern Ireland and had no illusions about the IRA, but it was precisely because of the moral murk surrounding terrorist operations that it was imperative to insist on moral clarity for those acting for the government. This was especially the case when soldiers were in positions to act with impunity, able to use violence against vulnerable civilians or prisoners. It was incumbent on the professional to behave appropriately, in accord with the Geneva Conventions.

This was the official view, yet breaches had occurred all too often. In his contribution on British atrocities in counter-insurgency for the *Encyclopedia of Military Ethics*,[2] David was meticulous in chronicling each episode where UK forces had been responsible for unlawful killings that could not be excused on any grounds of military necessity. While optimistic that the British Army was now better educated and less likely to resort to campaigns that depended on atrocities, he was under no illusions that unacceptable acts still occurred. There were several possible explanations as to why this might happen. Perhaps the perpetrators were in the grip of some psychosis, or else reflecting factors in their upbringing, such as growing up in a violent neighbourhood. David was most troubled by those instances where these acts emerged out of a distinctive military culture, which seemed to sanction extreme violence as a way of imposing authority and punishing infractions. Should such cultures develop then that was a failure of command. Had he lived to see the Russian invasion of Ukraine he would no doubt have been appalled not only by the evidence of random killing, torture, rape, abductions and looting but also by how much this was sanctioned by the Russian state and high command.

The essays in this volume reflect these concerns. Unlike other collections prepared to honour individuals, this book has a strong focus and will be a valuable addition to the library on military ethics and contemporary warfare. It provides candid and uncompromising analyses of where things have gone wrong as well as what can be done to prevent them in the future. It considers the role of commanders in maintaining professional values even under the extreme stress of changing and dangerous operations.

Yet, it also asks about the decisions that led to these operations. The first two decades of this century posed special challenges because of counter-insurgency campaigns in Iraq and Afghanistan that were controversial in their origins (Iraq

---

[2] https://www.militaryethics.org/British-Atrocities-in-Counter-Insurgency/10/.

more than Afghanistan) and in their conduct. Victory became an ever more elusive concept that raised questions about what purposes were being served. With regular casualties and little to show for them, civilians could respect the military for their service while wondering about the tasks they were asked to fulfil. For a small volunteer force, this was a frustrating and difficult time.

For now there is little appetite for further military interventions of this sort. The focus is more on conflicts between great powers, and Britain has been content to support Ukraine in its war against Russia with equipment, training and advice instead of committing its own forces. But the issues raised by David and explored in this book will continue to be important and should be an essential part of officer education. Instead of having to be relearnt during the next campaign, it would be advisable if they were understood at the start.

Acknowledgements

The editors would like fulsomely to thank our authors, who have all delivered on time and without complaint, and Genevieve Benest for her support. We would also like to express our appreciation to all of our editors at Bloomsbury, particularly the series editor, Professor Andrew Mumford, who kept everything on track.

Introduction

Frank Ledwidge

David Benest, who died in August 2020, was a former commanding officer of the 2nd Battalion of The Parachute Regiment, a Falklands and Northern Ireland veteran, and a brave defender of the laws and customs of the British military profession. He was an ever-loyal friend and inspiration for anyone dealing with the essential process of constructive criticism of our military services. At his funeral, some of us decided that he should be commemorated in the form of a collection of essays, written by some of his friends and other experts in military ethics and professionalism. This book is the result; not only is it dedicated to his memory, but his thinking suffuses almost every chapter.

Before going any further, one point needs to be made, and made strongly. The norm of UK and, indeed, US operations has not been disgrace and transgression. In most places, and at almost all times, we have done military ethics well, by any reasonable standards. We have good soldiers and good commanders at the tactical level, who do their very best, often in almost impossible circumstances. Such soldiers take their professionalism seriously.

Consequently, even ten years after the end of UK combat operations in Afghanistan, and considerably longer since we left Iraq, it can be very difficult to raise and discuss the ethical and professional aspects of our activities in those places. For example, those of us involved with the campaign to ensure proper investigation into alleged war crimes committed by British special forces (three of whom have written chapters in this book) can attest that some responses were negative to, and beyond, the point of hostility. Nonetheless, there is no doubt whatsoever that in every corner of the armed forces and the British military world more widely, such hostility is rare.

Any account of deviation from high standards not only implies but states outright the existence of these standards and the fact that they are accepted and obeyed by the vast majority. There is no dispute whatsoever about what constitutes the laws and customs of war from a British perspective. They have been practised for centuries – and continue to be so. No one who has ever served in or with our armed services on operations can be anything other than moved by the humanity and moral strength of the men and women involved. Compliance with basic military ethical and professional behaviour is 'what we do'. Perhaps this is why being faced with allegations of failure is so painful to the British military professional. It, almost literally, hurts.

We've decided to divide this short collection of essays into four sections. These move from the more personal tributes to David Benest's thinking to wider perspectives on legal and moral accountability and accounts of the realities and myths of war. As you will see, there is some overlap in the authors' focus on Northern Ireland, Iraq and Afghanistan, but each chapter stands alone so that the reader can dip in and out.

Aaron Edwards opens Part One, *David Benest's legacy*, with an examination of the question of ethics in combat, most specifically in Northern Ireland and Iraq. He argues, echoing David Benest, that the successful use of force depends on its ethical application.

Simon Anglim, who knew David Benest well, considers why soldiers commit war crimes and what can be done about it. He does so by examining the perspectives of David Benest himself and his friend, the moral philosopher David Fisher. David Benest's central tenet was that identifying poor leadership, derived from and contributing to a defective command culture, is the key to understanding and therefore preventing criminal behaviour on operations. David Fisher stressed the importance of soldiers having a moral core, driven by what he called 'practical wisdom'. Of course, the approaches of 'the two Davids', as Anglim calls them, are complementary, applying as much or even more to senior officers as to junior soldiers. I remember David Benest stressing the vital and continuing nature of the obligations contained in the Sovereign's commission to officers.

Nicholas Mercer outlines what happened when the British government tried to enact a Bill that would have effectively provided amnesties for some serious breaches of the laws and customs of war and describes the arguments that he, David Benest and others deployed to defeat its most egregious terms.

Compliance with ethical obligations of command is one thing, legal consequences in the form of war crimes proceedings are quite another, and Part Two, *Legal and moral accountability*, presents three perspectives on this.

Andrew Williams reflects on the British government's lack of timely and effective investigation of allegations of war crimes, as determined by the International Criminal Court – the same government that has rightly committed significant resources to ensure timely and effective investigation of Russian crimes in Ukraine. He examines several options for improving the British military approach to what he clearly sees as a serious cultural problem.

Matthew Ford examines how the British Army learns or, more accurately perhaps, doesn't learn, from mistakes, negligence and failure. The most immediately obvious examples are Iraq and Afghanistan but, as Dr Ford shows, there is nothing new about the British military establishment avoiding lessons delivered by defeat in combat. While Ford focuses on 'forgetting to remember', Frank Ledwidge goes on to argue that, whether on the battlefield or off it, there is a chronic and highly damaging lack of the kind of accountability the British people expect from people in charge. Senior officers are all too willing to take the benefits of their roles while evading the attendant obligations for often catastrophic failures of leadership.

Colonel Oliver Lee starts Part Three, *Combat realities*, with a description of how professionalism looks in practice and the effects of getting it right. He gives us a rare insight into the perspective of a senior retired Royal Marine officer planning an operational tour – someone who was well aware that the laws and customs of war are central to successful performance and professional efficiency.

On the other hand, Chris Green illustrates how potentially serious breaches of the laws and customs of war, in this case by special forces in Afghanistan, not only damage the campaign on the ground but also have a long afterlife. It is this alleged behaviour that partly gave rise to the inquiry being conducted by Lord Justice Haddon-Cave into 'matters arising' from the United Kingdom's deployment to Afghanistan, which, at the time of writing, is ongoing. Next, Louise Jones asks whether we should be fighting such wars at all. If we are to do so, how should we go about it, taking into account the lessons of other nations and our own recent past.

In Part Four, *Myths, stories and memory*, we look at stories and how they differ from reality – myths, in other words. Ed Burke examines the tragic case of Highlander Scott McLaren, murdered in Afghanistan by Taliban fighters in July 2011. Inaccurate stories about what exactly happened to McLaren fed the narrative of those seeking to justify another unlawful killing – of a Taliban fighter captured by a Royal Marine patrol two months later. John Wilson's essay on 'military myths' addresses such evergreen stories as systematic collusion between the British Army and loyalist terrorists in Northern Ireland, the importance of 'robust' behaviour in counter-insurgency and the perennial idea that the British 'do' counter-insurgency well. Myths, of whatever kind, can be deeply constructive but 'it is when these stories turn rancid that intervention is needed'.

Finally, we return to the character at the core of all of our reflections. Helen Parr writes about how we, the public, have seen the British soldier over the period of the 9/11 wars.

As we move out of the era of 'small wars' and back into what appears to be a time of conventional great-power conflict, questions of military ethics become even more important. Casualties among combatants and non-combatants in such wars will be far greater. Combat will be more intense by orders of magnitude, and there is a danger that ethical issues will fall even further down the agenda. Only one day at the United Kingdom's Advanced Command and Staff College – a course for those nominated for senior command – is currently dedicated to the ethics of combat. Far less is set aside in all arms of the service during the earlier phases of training of UK officer and non-commissioned ranks. Another indication of the priority placed upon the laws and customs of war more widely is that in the five-week infantry training course given to Ukrainian trainees by UK personnel (Operation INTERFLEX), no more than an hour of instruction in basic Law of Armed Conflict is given and then only to officers.

This book seeks to contribute to the considerable ongoing effort to bring the discussion of practical combat ethics and professionalism back to the centre of military education where it belongs. It also honours all those who, like David Benest himself, have spoken up for their crucial role in reinforcing the high standards for which the British Armed Forces are rightly respected throughout the world.

Part One

David Benest's legacy

1

'Not the British way of doing business'

Atrocities in military operations and how to avoid them

Aaron Edwards

Introduction

This chapter examines the writings of David Benest on the nature of military leadership in UK military interventions, with particular focus on the historical case studies of Northern Ireland and Iraq and related allegations of abuse and the unlawful killing of civilians. Benest grounded his critical analysis on a humanist approach to morality, ethical leadership and human rights, rather than on explicitly Christian values, identifying shortcomings in the British Army that had led to high-profile atrocities. His approach placed the spotlight not only on those individual soldiers responsible for carrying out abuses and atrocities but also 'in many cases [where] they have been the result of leadership and policy sanctioned at the highest level'.[1] Benest was motivated to act out of a strong sense of moral duty to safeguard the United Kingdom's reputation as a champion of liberal-democratic values, human rights laws and norms. To that end, this chapter considers Benest's claim that a subculture of 'put up, shut up, cover up' pervaded the highest levels of government and the armed forces in the wake of atrocities, which, he believed, was intended to influence both the judicial process and, ultimately, the historical record. It evaluates these claims in light of Benest's views that war and ethics were two sides of the same coin, and that success could only be guaranteed by a very high priority placed upon adherence to the law. Only by doing so could soldiers and their officers avoid repeating the mistakes of the past and, thereby, avoid such *jus post bellum* charges.

---

[1] David Benest, 'Atrocities in Britain's Counter-Insurgencies', *The RUSI Journal*, 2011, 156(3), p. 80.

The British way of countering insurgency

The British Army has been involved in operations short of war for hundreds of years.[2] As an institution operating across Britain's sprawling empire in the twentieth century, the military encountered a considerable constellation of armed challenges to London's imperial rule, from riots and subversion to armed insurrection, guerrilla warfare and terrorism. According to one noted authority, Major General Sir Charles Gwynn, there were three scenarios wherein the army might be required to deploy to counter violent challenges on behalf of British interests. In the first scenario were 'small wars', which he defined as 'deliberate campaigns with a definite military objective . . . undertaken with the ultimate goal of establishing civil control'.[3] In the second were 'cases when the normal civil control does not exist, or has broken down to such an extent that the Army becomes the main agent for the maintenance of or the restoration of order'.[4] In the third the military might be required to intervene on 'those occasions when the civil power continues to exercise undivided control but finds the police forces on which it normally relies insufficient'.[5] In the United Kingdom, the latter scenario has been referred to as 'military aid to the civil power', whereby troops were placed at the disposal of the local civilian authorities. In the latter two cases, which suggest some form of policing or gendarme role, Gwynn believed that the army was 'bound to exercise the minimum force required to attain its objective'.[6]

As Rod Thornton has illustrated in his work on the British tradition of minimum force, it was a principle forged in restraint or 'the sense that force be turned to only with extreme reluctance'.[7] The tradition itself can be traced back to the Amritsar massacre on 13 April 1919 when Major General Reginald Dyer ordered his troops to fire on a crowd of 5,000 Indian protestors in the Punjab. Approximately 500 people were killed and three times as many wounded. The Secretary of State for War at the time was Sir Winston Churchill who regarded Amritsar as

> an episode which appears to me to be without precedent or parallel in the modern history of the British Empire. It is an event of an entirely different order from any of those tragical occurrences which take place when troops are brought

---

[2] Hew Strachan, *The Politics of the British Army* (Oxford: Oxford University Press, 1997).
[3] Major General Sir Charles Gwynn, *Imperial Policing* (London: Macmillan and Co, 1934), p. 3.
[4] Ibid.
[5] Ibid., p. 4.
[6] Ibid.
[7] Rod Thornton, 'The British Army and the Origins of its Minimum Force Philosophy', *Small Wars & Insurgencies*, 2004, 15(1), p. 83.

into collision with the civil population. It is an extraordinary event, a monstrous event, an event which stands in singular and sinister isolation.[8]

Churchill did 'not think it is in the interests of the British Empire or of the British Army, for us to take a load of that sort for all time upon our backs' [by justifying the turn towards a disproportionate use of force against civilians] . . . We have to make it absolutely clear, some way or other, that *this is not the British way of doing business*.'[9]

For Thornton, the minimum force tradition was initially forged out of Victorian values held by establishment figures like Churchill and grounded in a certain pragmatism where soldiers and other servants of the state adhered to English Common Law, whether at home or in Britain's colonial empire.[10] Indeed, Thornton suggests that Churchill would have imbibed a very strong code of chivalric values like bravery, loyalty, courtesy and modesty from his time as a gentleman cadet at the Royal Military College at Sandhurst. It was this code that underpinned the British way of doing business.[11] Moreover, like other members of the ruling class, Churchill came to believe in the lightness of the imperial yoke and working in partnership with the people Britain ruled over.[12] Massacring them did little for this partnership.

Relations between colonial rulers and their subject peoples began to break down in the 1920s and 1930s, with uprisings in several colonies, Palestine and Cyprus being among the most violent. 'In her own imperial sphere,' argued H. J. Simson, 'Britain has adopted a bewilderingly easy-going attitude towards factions or races that take up arms and appeal to force in their own interests.' In Simson's influential book *British Rule, and Rebellion* (1937), he thought the tradition of minimum force positively encouraged a 'resort to force [by dissidents] where she governs'. Simson continued, 'One can hear it said today, all the way from the Far East right home to the front door, that if you want to get something out of the British, the best and quickest way to get it is to start shooting.'[13] Notwithstanding the shooting, the British Army, in particular, 'developed methods and, more importantly, principles upon which the methods were based "for conducting internal security operations"', according to Thomas R. Mockaitis.[14]

---

[8] House of Commons Debates (Hansard), 8 July 1920, Vol. 131, Col. 1725.
[9] Ibid., Col. 1730. My emphasis.
[10] Thornton, 'The British Army and the Origins of its Minimum Force Philosophy', pp. 85, 95.
[11] Ibid.
[12] Ibid., pp. 87–9; see also House of Commons Debates (Hansard), 8 July 1920, Vol. 131, Col. 1731–2.
[13] H. J. Simson, *British Rule, and Rebellion* (London: William Blackwood & Sons, 1937), p. 14.
[14] Thomas R. Mockaitis, *British Counterinsurgency in the Post-Imperial Era* (Manchester: Manchester University Press, 1995), p. 1.

As the guns fell silent in the Second World War, the shooting against Britain's colonial rule became more audible.[15] Stirring memories of atrocities like Amritsar gave sustenance to the Indian independence movement under Mahatma Gandhi, even though he himself had urged Indians to avoid the turn towards violent protest. Immediately after independence was granted to India in 1947, Britain was confronted by further insurrection in Palestine, Malaya, Kenya and Cyprus.[16] In providing military aid to the civil power in these places, British troops found themselves in the firing line where, in some cases, law and order was sufficiently fragile for the military to be given the lead in suppressing revolt by more coercive means.[17] In some infamous cases, such as the Batang Kali massacre in Malaya in December 1948, British troops carried out the unlawful killing of civilians.[18] A generation after Amritsar, the armed forces' reputation for employing only a minimum use of force was again sullied. David French has gone further to argue that such brute force 'was always the basis of British counter-insurgency campaigns', in the post-war period.[19] Along with John Newsinger and Douglas Porch, French has challenged the 'Whiggish view of decolonisation that portrayed the way in which the British left their empire as having been an orderly and dignified process of planned withdrawal'.[20]

It was against this academic backdrop that David Benest sought to understand what could have led soldiers to perpetrate these abuses and atrocities during British military interventions. He operated from the perspective that the British experience of small wars and insurgencies was, notwithstanding the episodes cited earlier, on the whole, a record 'to be proud of', given 'the principle of "courageous restraint" [was] rarely emulated in other COINs [counterinsurgencies] such as at the hands of the French in Algiers, the Americans in Vietnam or the Russians in Afghanistan'.[21] In his writings Benest, therefore, sought to critically engage with high-profile incidents of abuse and unlawful killing of civilians on the

---

[15] Ibid.

[16] Hew Strachan, 'British Counter-Insurgency from Malaya to Iraq', *RUSI Journal*, December 2007, 152(6), pp. 8–11.

[17] Douglas Porch, *Counterinsurgency: Exposing the Myths of the New Way of War* (Cambridge: Cambridge University Press, 2013), pp. 264–5.

[18] Ian Ward and Norma Miraflor, *Slaughter and Deception at Batang Kali* (Singapore: Media Masters, 2009); Christopher Hale, *Massacre in Malaya: Exposing Britain's My Lai* (Stroud: The History Press, 2013).

[19] David French, 'Nasty Not Nice: British Counter-Insurgency Doctrine and Practice, 1945–1967', *Small Wars & Insurgencies*, 2012, 23(4–5), p. 757.

[20] Ibid., p. 758.

[21] David Benest, 'A Liberal Democratic State and COIN: The Case of Britain, or Why Atrocities Can Still Happen', *Civil Wars*, 2012, 14(1), p. 29.

basis that he believed 'high standards of discipline and leadership were found wanting' and that politicians, soldiers and police 'disregarded the common law basis for action, with terrible human consequences'.[22] In one notable scholarly article, Benest sought to illustrate his main working hypothesis that 'the attitude of senior leaders often is the critical determinant in whether or not the officers and men serving under them obey the laws of war and treat both non-combatants and captured enemy troops appropriately and humanely'.[23] Drawing on the ground truth he had witnessed first-hand in a long and distinguished military career, Benest believed abuses and atrocities were typically the result of a myriad of factors, from the psychological state of mind of those individual commanders who ordered them through to deliberate government policy and the cheerleading or complicity in brute force techniques.[24]

While Benest was keen to identify the specific role of individual military leaders who presided over the abuse and unlawful killing of civilians, he was also mindful of broader structural factors that gave rise to such agency. From an intellectual point of view, Benest regarded irregular war as having a timeless quality to it in so far as the methods for waging it may change, even if its nature remained essentially the same. Unlike Newsinger and others, Benest recognized that insurgents who directly participated in hostilities were willing combatants who could also employ force – sometimes indiscriminately – against their opponents. Nevertheless, what seemed to preoccupy Benest most in his work was the conduct of the state and its military forces when stabilizing a situation in which there was an evident breakdown in civil authority and law and order. As a clear advocate of operating within English Common Law in a way that held all belligerents to account, Benest came to share similar views to those promulgated by other warrior scholars, including US Army Colonel Dave Grossman, who observed how most people would prefer to revel in naive thinking on atrocities: that it was *an act or series of acts indulged in by other people and certainly not one's own troops*. Notwithstanding such denial, Grossman informs us that those who 'commit atrocity have made a Faustian bargain with evil. They have sold their conscience, their future, and their peace of mind for a brief, fleeting, self-destructive advantage.'[25]

---

[22] Ibid.
[23] Ibid. See also Chapter 2 in this volume.
[24] Ibid.
[25] Lieutenant Colonel Dave Grossman, *On Killing: The Psychological Cost of Learning to Kill in War and Society* (New York: Little, Brown, 1995), p. 222. Emphasis in original.

For Benest, the denial of crimes committed by the British military on operations was also attributable to a prevailing subculture he characterized as 'put up, shut up, cover up'. In Benest's words:

> The 'system' has long taken the view that, while it knows these crimes have been (and are) committed, it will not admit to them – until forced by sheer weight of incontestable evidence – if that admission would 'give aid and comfort' to the enemy.[26]

Denial of abuses and atrocities by British politicians in lieu of incontestable evidence must also be seen in light of the historical legacy of General Dyer's 'monstrous event' in Amritsar. In remaining aloof from the actions of their soldiers, however, Benest argued that the government invertedly committed moral offence to Britain's proud reputation of courageous restraint. He shared a similar ethical stance to that occupied by Dr David Fisher, a former Ministry of Defence (MOD) official who entered academia after a successful career as a civil servant (see also Chapter 2 in this volume). Fisher argued for a form of virtuous consequentialism in which 'our service people are good people who deploy the lethal force with which society entrusts them with for the sake of a good end and in ways of which they and the society whom they serve can be justifiably proud'.[27] The United Kingdom's virtuous mission was jeopardized when its military servants were 'bad people' who abused their positions, thereby 'using force for bad ends', with 'harmful consequences'.[28] Fisher advocated a radical overhaul in the way in which the moral component of British fighting power was disseminated to soldiers of all ranks. He believed, as did Benest, in the need to provide training and education to soldiers and their officers in morality and ethics so that they became 'an integral part of the very fabric of service life'.[29]

In setting out to reappraise the worst excesses of 'using force for bad ends' from the point of view of a military commander, Benest drew on several case studies, including the deployment of troops in Northern Ireland between 1969 and 2007, with which he was most familiar in his own career, and the British military intervention in Iraq between 2003 and 2009.

---

[26] Benest, 'A Liberal Democratic State and COIN', p. 85.
[27] David Fisher, *Morality and War: Can War be Just in the Twenty-First Century?* (Oxford: Oxford University Press, 2011), p. 129.
[28] Ibid., p. 127.
[29] Ibid., p. 130.

'Amritsar on the Foyle'? British troops and the Bloody Sunday massacre

British soldiers who deployed to Northern Ireland on 14–15 August 1969 were shocked at the intensity of the intercommunal confrontations they witnessed on the streets. The depth of enmity between Protestant unionists who wished to maintain the union between Great Britain and Catholic nationalists who wanted to see an end to the connection had been building steadily for over a year. Violence was most acute in the cities of Derry/Londonderry and Belfast where nationalists attacked local police officers from the Royal Ulster Constabulary (RUC) with bricks, bottles and petrol bombs. Local police officers were forced to protect themselves and their stations.[30] They were overstretched and exhausted. After fifty hours of non-stop rioting, troops were sent to the aid of the police. The County Inspector for Londonderry said the army were deployed, 'purely and simply because the situation in the rest of the Province has precluded adequate forces coming to this city to relieve the police already there'.[31] However, for nationalists caught up in the violence, it was the RUC who were 'running loose armed and in uniform'.[32] One local newspaper reported how it was the duty of 'all who believe in Northern Ireland and its future [to] . . . approve wholeheartedly action against those who seek its downfall'.[33]

Among the first troops deployed to Belfast were the 1st Battalion, The Parachute Regiment (1 Para). Their commanding officer (CO) at that time was Lieutenant Colonel Michael Gray who remembered:

> Operating in your own country was very strange. Equally you were working on old fashioned legal approaches. The magistrate had to read out the Riot Act if there was a confrontation between people. The police were always there in the front row but totally unprepared for what it was that was coming at them. And there were we who had to be behind them, the proverbial line on the ground that was drawn. And it seemed to me to be out of touch with reality as things were beginning to happen. In the early days when those sorts of scenarios were drawn up there weren't such things as petrol bombs. People were not using petrol bombs. It seemed to me that we the army were drawn in to be policemen, which is what we are not. We carry a rifle as part of our trade in the same way

---

[30] *Belfast Newsletter*, 14 August 1969.
[31] Ibid.
[32] Ibid.
[33] Ibid.

that a stone mason would carry his hammer. And we were being asked to take on police roles when in fact we should have been in support of the police.[34]

1 Para remained in Northern Ireland until February 1970, when they returned to England. The battalion was deployed again to Belfast for a second, two-year residential tour in September 1970 where it spent the next few months serving as the reserve battalion for the 39th Infantry Brigade, the formation responsible for military operations in Belfast.

In the summer of 1971, Mike Gray handed over command of 1 Para to Lieutenant Colonel Derek Wilford who had previously seen operational experience in Malaya and Aden. Wilford had also served for four years with the elite Special Air Service (SAS), before transferring to The Parachute Regiment in 1969. During his time as a company commander with 2 Para in Northern Ireland, Wilford claimed he 'developed ideas on training and deployment in regard to IS [Internal Security] operations in built up areas'.[35] Wilford recalled taking over command of 1 Para, a 'good battalion' where the men were 'well-disciplined and morale was high'.[36] Wilford pushed 1 Para to deploy onto the streets 'fast and in strength', with a more 'interventionist' or 'fast response unit' role, marked by its toughness and coercion, even though he believed his battalion enjoyed 'excellent community relations'.[37] There was something of an inherent contradiction in Wilford's thinking, as 1 Para spent more time on its aggressive tactical response to 'aggro' on the streets than on developing a firmer understanding of the socio-economic inequalities and sectarian structures that gave rise to the trouble in the first place.

When Wilford took command of 1 Para, much of the violent campaign waged by the Irish Republican Army (IRA) was being directed towards his unit's sister battalion, 2 Para, who were stationed in West, South and North Belfast. 2 Para's regimental history records how the IRA began to ramp up its bombing campaign across the city in the summer of 1971, with attempts 'made to mine patrols from the Battalion almost daily' and sniping at 2 Para soldiers becoming 'quite commonplace'.[38] One soldier, Private Richard Barton, had been killed in an ambush on his patrol vehicle on 14 July 1971. The next day the battalion

---

[34] Imperial War Museum Sound Archive, Interview with Michael Gray. Reel 28/52, https://www.iwm.org.uk/collections/item/object/80030368.

[35] Lieutenant Colonel Derek Wilford Statement to the Bloody Sunday Inquiry, dated 18 September 2002, https://webarchive.nationalarchives.gov.uk/ukgwa/20101017060841/http://report.bloody-sunday-inquiry.org/evidence/B/B944.pdf,.

[36] Ibid.

[37] Ibid.

[38] The National Archives (TNA), WO305/4411, Regimental History, 2nd Battalion, The Parachute Regiment for the period 1 April 1971 to 31 March 1972.

conducted a large-scale cordon and search operation in which they obtained 'more information about the IRA'.[39] 2 Para noted how the 'information gained during these searches' was used substantively to help draw up the 'lists for internment'.[40] An officer from the battalion was later wounded in an attack, and on 6 August the IRA carried out an audacious gun attack on a platoon post on the Springfield Road where two gunmen fired at soldiers from the upper deck of a public bus. After a van backfired outside the local police station, soldiers stationed there on guard duty nervously opened fire, killing the driver, Henry Thornton. The incident sparked extensive rioting along the Springfield Road and in adjoining nationalist estates.

Simultaneously, troops were deployed on a large-scale internment operation, code-named Demetrius, to detain terrorist suspects on 9 August. Unsurprisingly, violence again escalated. In response, 39th Infantry Brigade commander Frank Kitson immediately ordered two companies, Alpha and Charlie in 1 Para, which acted as his reserve battalion in the city, into West Belfast on 11 August to relieve their embattled comrades in their sister battalion, 2 Para.. His orders were to 'clear all barricades erected on the entry roads to Turf Lodge, New Barnsley and Ballymurphy' and to 'clear the area of Irish Republican Army ("IRA") gunmen'.[41] In the ensuing operation, which was marked by considerable gunfire from within these districts, 1 Para soldiers shot dead two civilians, twenty-year-old Eamon Lafferty and forty-three-year-old Joseph Corr.

Following an escalation of serious rioting in late January 1972, the Commander of Land Forces, Major General Robert Ford, turned to 39 Brigade and ordered them to reinforce 8 Brigade in Londonderry.[42] 1 Para were in turn ordered to conduct an arrest operation in Derry on 30 January. For commentator Colonel Michael Dewar, 1 Para 'were ideal for the job at hand: they knew what to expect, they would be steady under fire, they would be able to identify any terrorists, they were, in short, the most experienced troops in Ulster at the time'.[43] Historian Douglas Porch suggests that this made 1 Para well disposed to react more aggressively than was the norm, thereby chiming with Wilford's 'interventionist'

[39] Ibid.
[40] Ibid.
[41] Judiciary NI, In the matter of a series of deaths that occurred in August 1971 at Ballymurphy, West Belfast – Incident 4, delivered 11 May 2021, https://www.judiciaryni.uk/judicial-decisions/2021 -nicoroner-6.
[42] General Sir Frank Kitson Statement to the Bloody Sunday Inquiry, dated 18 February 2000, https:// webarchive.nationalarchives.gov.uk/ukgwa/20101017060841/http://report.bloody-sunday-inquiry .org/evidence/CK/CK_0001.pdf. Kitson claimed he had no recollection of a conversation with Wilford and was probably on leave over that period.
[43] Michael Dewar, The British Army in Northern Ireland (London: Arms and Armour Press, 1985), p. 58.

ideas.[44] However, another historian, David Charters, makes the case, drawing inferences from a close reading of archival material, that the decision to deploy 1 Para on that day was out of step with the change in counter-terrorism policy that emphasized a low-key approach to military operations.[45] This appears to be borne out by the Army's chain of command in Lisburn ensuring that all soldiers were issued a copy of the Rules of Engagement (ROE), known locally as the Yellow Card, which detailed the circumstances in which soldiers could open fire.[46] Major Ted Loden, the Officer Commanding of 1 Para's Support Company, who took over command of his company on 6 December 1971, claimed that one of his first actions was to check that every member of his company had received a copy of the Yellow Card.[47] It was Loden's understanding that his soldiers could open fire only when ordered to do so by a superior commander or when they believed there was an imminent danger to their lives. The orders Loden received from Wilford made no mention of opening fire as the main aim of the tactical operation was to be prepared to arrest rioters. Loden claimed he immediately issued his own orders to his subordinate platoon commanders to arrest as many rioters as possible. There was no mention of being prepared to open fire or that there was intelligence regarding the IRA preparing an attack.[48]

Nevertheless, shortly after soldiers deployed onto the ground, Loden believed the IRA had opened fire on his company. The men under his command quickly and ruthlessly retaliated, killing thirteen unarmed men and boys, including one other man who subsequently died of his wounds. The massacre would later be labelled 'Bloody Sunday'. 'If the IRA had not opened fire on my company and tried to kill my soldiers, no-one would have been killed that day,' he later told the public inquiry into the massacre.[49] 'To the best of my knowledge, the men in my company returned fire within the ROE. As I have said already, I regret the loss of life.'[50]

Clearly, the way in which soldiers open fire in a hostile environment is meant to be controlled. 'Warn the crowd by all available means that effective fire will be opened unless it disperses at once,' read the ROE. 'The order to fire must

[44] Porch, *Counterinsurgency*, p. 277.

[45] David Charters, *Whose Mission, Whose Orders? British Civil-Military Command and Control in Northern Ireland, 1968–1974* (Montreal and Kingston: McGill-Queen's University Press, 2017), pp. 136–7.

[46] The Yellow Card had been revised for the fourth time and reissued to all soldiers in November 1971.

[47] Colonel Edward Loden Statement to the Bloody Sunday Inquiry, dated 28 September 2000, https:// webarchive.nationalarchives.gov.uk/ukgwa/20101017060841/http://report.bloody-sunday-inquiry .org/evidence/B/B2212.pdf. Accessed: 23 August 2022.

[48] Ibid.

[49] Ibid.

[50] Ibid.

be given by the military commander himself to the fire unit commander(s) concerned. He will indicate the target and the number of rounds to be fired, and will make certain that only the minimum amount of force necessary to achieve the immediate aim is used.'[51] The ROE were underpinned by the British philosophy of minimum force, which Major Loden would have been well acquainted with from his time as a junior officer in Aden. Loden also claimed Aden gave him 'substantial experience of active service in an urban setting . . . and in being under fire in an urban environment and commanding men in such circumstances'.[52] However, Loden contradicted himself by also saying that although he was 'an experienced soldier, having taken part in operations in Aden and the Middle East', he was 'relatively inexperienced in the tactics of modem urban warfare'.[53] Aden may have been a very different security environment than Northern Ireland, but as his citation for a Military Cross he earned for courage under fire on 1 June 1967 attested:

> Early that morning shooting broke out in Sheikh Othman and a violent battle was fought all day between a large number of terrorists and roof top Ops manned by 1 PARA. By early afternoon our positions were short of ammunition. Captain LODEN, who knew the best routes and entrances to all the Ops, immediately offered to take an armoured vehicle and replenish all our positions with ammunition and water. Regardless of his own personal safety and, often having to expose himself to sniper fire, he succeeded in his task.[54]

It was the first of two separate episodes where he demonstrated bravery in the face of heavy fire. On 22 June 1967 Loden recovered dead and wounded British soldiers who had been shot by mutinous Arab soldiers. He was further commended for his own 'considerable personal bravery and a high standard of leadership'.[55] A damaged gutter, shot apart by a republican sniper, was in no way comparable to the violent opposition Loden and other senior soldiers from 1 Para had already faced in Aden.[56]

Bloody Sunday was an indelible stain on the Army's reputation throughout the remainder of Operation Banner, the official code name for the deployment. The events of that day led to changes in how the army handled large-scale public

---

[51] Ibid.
[52] Ibid.
[53] Ibid.
[54] TNA, WO 373/138/55, Citation for the Military Cross awarded to Edward Charles Loden, 7 August 1967.
[55] Ibid.
[56] Andrew Sanders, 'Principles of Minimum Force and the Parachute Regiment in Northern Ireland, 1969–1972', *Journal of Strategic Studies*, 2018, 41(5), pp. 659–83.

order issues, with the permanent under-secretary (PUS) at the Northern Ireland Office at the time (who subsequently became PUS at the MOD) Sir Frank Cooper believing the army had learnt lessons from the episode. He recalled, 'I wasn't haunted by the fear that you might have another Bloody Sunday. I think wherever you get serious major civil disturbance you've always got to watch very carefully what people do and how they act and how they behave.'[57]

For Benest, however, who deployed to Northern Ireland a year later, the 'notion of ethical duty [was] almost completely absent from our training and teaching' with 'misguided notions of "loyalty" emanating from the "very top levels of command", ensuring that not a single officer . . . [was] held accountable for "Bloody Sunday"'.[58] By the mid-1970s the army had handed control of the security situation back to the RUC, except for highly dangerous areas where the police required military protection to carry out their duties. As the number of incidents of shootings, bombings and large-scale civil unrest subsided in the 1980s, an intelligence-led response aimed at deterrence rather than intervention emerged. By the time the British Army came to deploy in support of military operations in the Gulf in 2003, they had the experience of three decades of consecutive deployments in Northern Ireland.

'A closing of ranks'? A very British war crime in Iraq

The US-led invasion of Iraq in March 2003 saw British forces mobilized on a size and scale not seen since Operation Motorman, a major military manoeuvre launched on 31 July 1972 to dismantle barricades erected by the IRA. Op Motorman involved 20,000 troops but, while effective in meeting its strategic objectives, was short-lived, lasting only a matter of hours.[59] Thirty years on, the British Army now played second fiddle to the police and civil authorities in Northern Ireland. Its role by the time of the 1994 IRA and loyalist ceasefires was radically reduced, something reinforced when the IRA reinstated its ceasefire in July 1997, following a renewed eighteen-month-long paramilitary campaign. The downscaling in security commitments at home left the door open to the British Army to become more involved in peacekeeping operations worldwide,

---

[57] Liddell Hart Centre for Military Archives, King's College London, Sir Frank Cooper Papers, 4/1/2, Interview with Sir Frank Cooper, 2 April 1998.

[58] David Benest, 'Review of *An Army of Tribes* by Ed Burke', *British Army Review*, Summer 2019, 175, p. 136.

[59] M. L. R. Smith and Peter R. Neumann, 'Motorman's Long Journey: Changing the Strategic Setting in Northern Ireland', *Contemporary British History*, 2005, 19(4), pp. 413–35.

with soldiers being deployed to the Balkans and West Africa among other places. By the time international tensions had increased with Saddam Hussein's regime in Iraq over claims of his retention of weapons of mass destruction, most units in the British armed forces had some experience of operations in several small wars and on peacekeeping missions.

Following a decision in Washington and London to forcibly disarm the Iraqi regime, without United Nations Security Council authorization, British soldiers found themselves intervening in a country they did not understand, where there was no recognized authority and where there was no long-term plan. One of the units deployed to spearhead intervention was the 1st Battalion of The Queen's Lancashire Regiment (1QLR), which was deployed on the first iteration of Op Telic in March 2003.[60] The QLR's initial mission was to provide security to the residents of the south-western city of Basra. In late July, 1 QLR's CO, Lieutenant Colonel Jorge Mendonca, was forced to reinstate night-time patrols and raids on suspected black markets that traded in weapons and ammunition, among other illicit goods. Code-named Operation Ali Baba, the operation was designed to return law and order to a city that had fallen into the grip of extremist groups and criminal gangs after the fall of Saddam Hussein's regime. 'I would say the vast majority of the population are happy to see us, although how happy depends on how well we deliver on the essentials of security, followed closely by fuel, electricity and water,' Mendonca told a journalist accompanying his troops. 'I think we are on probation. I'm not sure how long the probation will last.'[61] Within a week so-called 'soft hat' patrols were coming under attack as violence began to escalate against British troops. Local information suggested it could either be a mix of Baathists, foreign terrorists or Shia militants 'trying to establish . . . control in southern Iraq.'[62]

Colonel Mendonca based many of his assumptions about the security dynamics at play in Basra on his previous deployments on Operation Banner. He therefore saw the deployment of his Quick Reaction Forces in Iraq's second city as 'meant to test reaction times and patterns of operation.'[63] As with Northern Ireland, he believed it was crucial to re-establish an effective Iraqi police force. 'There are 1.5 million people in Basra,' he emphasized, 'and I can push 430 bayonets on to the street at maximum effort. These figures do not look too pretty.'[64] Despite his lofty tactical ambition of reconstituting a police force,

---

[60] Operation Telic was the code-name given to British military deployment in Iraq between 2003 and 2009. There were thirteen Op Telic rotations in total.
[61] Stephen Farrell, 'Ducking Insults and Missiles on Night Patrol – Iraq', *The Times*, 28 July 2003.
[62] Stephen Farrell, 'Attacks on British Troops Rise – Iraq', *The Times*, 5 August 2003.
[63] Ibid.
[64] Ibid.

Mendonca's troops soon became the coalition's only *gendarme* for Basra in the absence of law enforcement structures in the summer of 2003.

It was while training Iraqi police recruits that one of Mendonca's officers, twenty-nine-year-old Captain Dai Jones, was killed in a roadside bomb.[65] Shortly afterwards, soldiers from a Royal Military Police (RMP) detachment were killed in a drive-by shooting of their soft skin Land Rover.[66] Along with its RMP detachment, 1 QLR was responsible for running a residential training camp for Iraqi police recruits, which one QLR officer told reporters was designed to take 'these guys to this next stage further' in their police training.[67]

One of those who encountered 1 QLR while training police officers was a senior policeman, Colonel Daoud Mousa. He had arrived to collect his son Baha Salim Mousa on the morning of 14 September two hours after 1 QLR soldiers had arrived at the hotel in a planned raid to search for weapons. Colonel Mousa later said he saw three or four British soldiers breaking into a safe at the hotel and stealing the money, which they stuffed into the pockets of their uniform. 'I thought that it was a violation of English dignity and honour, and the honour of English troops,' he claimed. After reporting the theft to a platoon commander inside the hotel, he saw his son lying in a prone position, face down on the floor with several other men. 'I pointed to my son. The soldiers were standing by,' he later told an inquiry. 'I think they knew the one I was pointing to was my son. Therefore, they wanted revenge against me.'[68]

Colonel Mousa's son, Baha, had been working as a hotel receptionist when he was detained by the soldiers. Along with seven other Iraqi men, Baha was taken to the Temporary Detention Facility at the British Army's headquarters in Basra. There he was subjected to 'shock of capture' tactical questioning by QLR soldiers. Over the next twenty-four hours, Baha Mousa was placed in stress positions and harshly beaten during what the soldiers called 'the choir', a kangaroo court designed to interrogate them for information. He sustained ninety-three different injuries, including fractured ribs and a broken nose, finally dying as a result of his injuries at 9.40 pm on 15 September 2003.[69]

---

[65] James Hider and Michael Evans, 'Officer was Killed after Being Hurt in Fuel Riot – Iraq', *The Times*, 16 August 2003.
[66] James Hider and Michael Evans, 'British Troops Back in Armour after Killings in Basra', *The Times*, 25 August 2003.
[67] 'Police prepare for Basra', *The Times*, 25 September 2003.
[68] Adam Gabbatt, 'Baha Mousa Inquiry: Father Alleges "Revenge" by UK Troops', *The Guardian*, 23 September 2009.
[69] Steven Morris, 'British Soldier Admits War Crime as Court Martial Told of Iraqi Civilian's Brutal Death', *The Guardian*, 20 September 2006.

Allegations of British atrocities and abuse of detainees in Iraq initially became public when the *Times* published an article on 4 October 2003 revealing how a British soldier was under investigation by the RMP following the death of an Iraqi in custody in Basra.[70] The soldier under investigation was Corporal Donald Payne of 1 QLR. Payne had joined the army in 1988 and saw tours of duty in Northern Ireland and the former Republic of Yugoslavia. He was regarded as a tough soldier who liked to play rugby in his spare time. The RMP investigation into Corporal Payne's involvement in the death of Baha Mousa eventually led to six other soldiers from 1 QLR being recommended for court martial proceedings. Following a successful lobbying campaign courtesy of the Conservative-leaning *Daily Telegraph*, no British officer was recommended for prosecution. Indeed, the newspaper even spearheaded a campaign to exonerate Lieutenant Colonel Mendonca for any complicity in the actions of his subordinates. 'I am convinced we were a force for good and that my soldiers were rightly very proud of what we achieved', the newspaper reported Mendonca as writing in leaked correspondence with Brigadier Robert Aitken, a senior army officer tasked by General Sir Mike Jackson, then Chief of the General Staff (CGS), to investigate the allegations of brutality.[71]

Payne's defence barrister at his trial, Tim Owen QC, said his client was merely following a 'conditioning regime' put in place by the chain of command by their failure to countermand any subordinate orders. Payne found himself in the dock charged with a crime that 'must in large part be said to have flown from failings higher up the chain of command', his defence counsel told the court. As Owen continued:

> There is, I suggest, something a little distasteful about the sight of Don Payne standing here alone before you as the man – the only man – to be singled out for punishment for this sorry episode . . . Corporal Payne was doing something which was known of and indeed approved by his superiors . . . Unless very clear rules are set and enforced from the top downwards, rules which ensure detainees are treated decently at all times, the danger surely . . . is that inadequately trained soldiers will regard what is in fact unlawful as acceptable and it that slippery slope which is really the danger which has been set out or made clear in this case.[72]

[70] Rosie Garthwaite and Michael Evans, 'British Soldier Questioned over Captive's Death', *The Times*, 4 October 2003.

[71] Thomas Harding, 'First he is Given Top Honour for Bravery then they Treat him Like a War Criminal', *Daily Telegraph*, 14 November 2005.

[72] Transcript of Sentencing of Corporal Donald Payne, https://www.asser.nl/upload/documents/DomCLIC/Docs/NLP/UK/PaineSentencingtranscript.pdf.

In Owen's view, 'There is something deeply unattractive, deeply unfair about a prosecution which applies one set of rules to the junior ranks, those operating at the sharp end, and a very different set of rules to those higher up the chain of command.'[73] The defence crumbled in the face of evidence leading the court to find him guilty of a war crime.

Tim Owen said that even though Payne was convicted, awaiting sentencing, he was 'far from being the only person with responsibility for it'. It was Mr Owen's observation:

> Much has been made, justifiably, of how hard it was for the SIB [Special Investigations Branch – the Army's CID] to investigate this incident. The army – perhaps like any other institution that is to some extent closed from the world in the way it operates, rather like the Police Service or the Prison Service, present great difficulties in terms of investigation of incidents such as this and the reason is obvious and it was highlighted or indicated by my Lord in his ruling at half time: a closing of ranks. That closing of ranks makes it hard for the Crown to call reliable testimony from those who either need to cover up their own misdeeds – and I submit that that was going on to an obvious extent in this case – but also from those who, while they have not committed crimes themselves, are simply unwilling to dump on colleagues.[74]

Corporal Donald Payne was subsequently sentenced to one year's imprisonment, demoted and dishonourably discharged from the army. He was the first British soldier to be convicted on the serious charge of committing a war crime.

In a separate incident at Camp Breadbasket in another part of Basra, soldiers from the Royal Regiment of Fusiliers were accused of inhumane and degrading treatment of detainees. One soldier had taken photos of the detainee abuses, which he sent to be developed in the United Kingdom and soon found their way into the media. Of the twenty-two photos taken, most showed Iraqi civilians in stress positions, being 'beasted' and forced to simulate sex acts. After their return from Iraq, the soldiers were promptly arrested by the RMP and held until the convening of a court martial in Germany. In their defence, the soldiers told the court that they were ordered by a superior officer to arrest looters who were then to be 'worked hard'.[75] However, the court found that even though their company commander, Major Dan Taylor, 'had broken the law he had acted with "well-

---

[73] Ibid. See also Steven Morris, 'Singling out of Junior Soldiers for War Crimes Charges "Deeply Unfair"', *The Guardian*, 26 September 2006.

[74] Transcript of Sentencing of Corporal Donald Payne.

[75] Audrey Gillan, 'Army Cleared Major Who Gave Illegal Order', *The Guardian*, 22 January 2005.

meaning and sincere but misguided zeal'",[76] and there was insufficient evidence to convict him too. In a letter sent to Taylor by his then brigade commander, Nick Carter, on 7 January 2005, subsequently published by the media, Carter wrote that there was 'no evidence to suggest you ordered or encouraged those actions for which the individuals referred to above will stand trial by courts martial' and that 'any actions you intended to preserve humanitarian aid [were] for the benefit of the Iraqi population by means of deterring future theft'.[77]

According to reporters who attended the court martial in Osnabruck in Germany, the soldiers' defence team accused Major Taylor of 'misleading his superiors about the "severity" of the orders' to protect his own future in the army.[78] 'So vague was your order that it was open to misinterpretation,' the defence counsel said. 'You are prepared to let these soldiers be the sacrificial lambs so your own career can be preserved.'[79]

In both the Baha Mousa and Camp Breadbasket cases, the soldiers involved were later judged by a British Army inquiry to have failed to live up to the institution's 'Values and Standards', the code of conduct by which they are expected to operate on and off operations. After succeeding General Sir Mike Jackson as CGS, General Sir Richard Dannatt received Brigadier Rob Aitken's report in which it was recognized how post-invasion Iraq presented a very fluid situation, with the lack of serious training in operational law meaning that soldiers were prone to making decisions that were not well thought through.[80]

David Fisher argued that the soldiers in Basra guilty of abusing and killing Iraqi civilians not only 'displayed a lack of virtue, including that of self-control and respect for others required by justice' but, in addition, by covering up for those directly involved in abuses, those indirectly involved indulged in 'misplaced loyalty' and consequently 'ignored the wider interests of the regiment and Army in which they served, whose reputation was besmirched by their mendacity, and of the society in whose service they were employed'.[81]

For David Benest, these abuses spoke to the breakdown in leadership. 'It cannot be emphasised enough that where leadership has been sound, the likelihood of misbehaviour by security forces appears to have been much diminished,' he wrote in an article in the *RUSI Journal*. 'It is when those lacking a "moral compass" gained the ascendency that trouble inevitably followed.' Benest

---

[76] Ibid.
[77] Ibid.
[78] 'British Officer Denies "Beasting" Order', *The Guardian*, 24 January 2005.
[79] Ibid.
[80] Aitken, *The Aitken Report*, p. 8.
[81] Fisher, *Morality and War*, p. 127.

questioned the conclusions reached by the Aitken Report, taking some comfort from the fact that training and education of officers, in particular, had much improved, reducing the likelihood of future atrocities. For Benest, 'courageous restraint has always been required over decades, although regrettably not always exercised'.[82]

Conclusion

David Benest was a sixth-form student at the Royal Grammar School, Guildford, when The Parachute Regiment was deployed on the streets of Northern Ireland in the early 1970s. As he later wrote in the *Guardian*, he had 'little understanding of events in Northern Ireland' and by the time he commissioned from the Royal Military Academy, Sandhurst, in 1973 he was 'none the wiser'.[83] He recalled that, as a young officer, he 'swallowed whole the regimental line that soldiers from our first battalion had been under attack during a civil rights march in Derry in 1972, on what became known as Bloody Sunday, and responded accordingly with lethal force',[84] and believed that the army chain of command escaped unscathed in subsequent inquiries into these events. As an army officer, Benest questioned the basis of everything he was told. 'At each level [of command] I attempted to make clear that the authority and power in the use of lethal force, at just 18 years old, was awesome,' he recalled.[85] 'In situations where life was endangered or lost, a young "tom" was in effect a witness, a prosecutor, jury, judge and, if required, executioner, all in a matter of a split second'.[86] For Benest, Christian values were not the only set of principles compatible with soldiering and so he would formulate his own ethical approach to leadership based on humanism.

Twenty-two years after Bloody Sunday and amid a wind-down in the major paramilitary campaigns, Benest was serving as the CO of 2 Para in Northern Ireland. By then he had built up a thorough understanding of the context in which military force was being used and was particularly interested in how leadership and command played a role in determining the course and consequences of the conflict. As CO, Benest placed a 'very high priority upon adherence to the Law of Armed Conflict' and drove home the point to his subordinates that they 'must

---

[82] Benest, 'Atrocities in Britain's Counter-Insurgencies', p. 85.
[83] David Benest, 'I Served in Northern Ireland. It's Clear that there should be No Amnesty for Veterans', *The Guardian*, 22 May 2019.
[84] Ibid.
[85] Ibid.
[86] Ibid.

be extremely well versed in the Emergency Powers Acts and interpretation of the "Yellow Card".[87] As Benest reflected in a review article for the *British Army Review*, 'My exact words were that "I have 1,000 men and women under my military command – in effect, they are under your command. Tell us what you want or do not want, provided your 'order' is legal'.[88] As he recognized then and argued until his death in 2020, the United Kingdom 'has never accepted anything other than that complete legal responsibility at all times underpins the morale and discipline of our armed forces'.[89] To jeopardize this reputation for the responsible and ethical exercise of lethal force by providing an amnesty to those tiny number of troops accused and/or convicted of abuses of civilians and/or war crimes would be 'akin to the US forces in Vietnam' who acted with impunity in My Lai, which, Benest argued, would ultimately, take the United Kingdom down a 'hazardous road'. Benest argued that the UK should 'never, ever, risk such a repetition'[90] of the events that led to Amritsar.

In the citation for an MBE awarded for this invaluable work in Northern Ireland, it was noted by his superiors how David Benest excelled in his dealings with others primarily because he was 'prepared to listen carefully and to discuss matters frankly'.[91] His frankness earned him the 'implicit trust of all those who do business with him', including those 'men and women on the ground who had to perform difficult and often dangerous tasks'.[92] Benest knew that it was only by adopting a moral and ethical approach, based on courageous restraint, could British soldiers avoid committing atrocities and risk damage to the country's reputation as effective and enlightened purveyors of the lethal use of force. Anyone with a strong belief in defending their country, its people and those serving alongside them had to place the greater good ahead of narrow personal decision-making. It is a code of ethics that all those who genuinely believe in the utility of force would find easy to agree upon.

---

[87]   TNA, WO 305/7876, Unit Historical Record, 2 Para Commanding Officer's Directive (96/97), dated 14 February 1996.

[88]   David Benest, 'Review of *Secret Victory: The Intelligence War that Beat the IRA*' by William Matchett, *British Army Review*, Winter 2018, 171, p. 138.

[89]   Benest, 'I Served in Northern Ireland'.

[90]   Ibid.

[91]   TNA, WO 373/181/310, Recommendation for the Award of the MBE to Major David Gareth Benest, 11 November 1988.

[92]   Ibid.

2

The military virtues

David Benest and David Fisher on when soldiers turn bad

Simon Anglim

Introduction: Friends and mentors

David Benest was a steadfast friend, supporter and mentor over thirty years – indeed, we planned to meet the week he died in August 2020. We first met in 1990 at Browning Barracks, Aldershot, when he was regimental adjutant of The Parachute Regiment (he always insisted on the capital 'T') and I was a lowly Ministry of Defence (MOD) civil servant curating the Airborne Forces Museum. He stood out even then: at a time when few missed opportunities to remind me of my lowliness, David treated me with unfailing kindness, consideration and interest in what I was doing. I was posted away in mid-1991 but we resumed contact in 2005 when, after a chance meeting at a conference in Oxford in his then capacity as Colonel, Defence Studies, British Army, he invited me to speak at a conference at Upavon.

For the next fourteen years, we met several times a year to talk about military matters over lunch and a pint or, in David's case, a glass of the very best red wine. I learnt a great deal from these conversations about how armies – the British Army in particular – work in reality, as opposed to the wishful thinking so often expressed in doctrinal manuals or official histories and this still informs my teaching and writing. Alongside this were his deeply valued contributions to my classes. After retiring from the Army in 2009, David spent several years, initially at Reading University and later at King's College London, lecturing and discussing with my undergraduates about the moral challenges facing commanders on the battlefield, based largely on his experiences in the Falklands War as well as his observations from Northern Ireland and of more recent episodes from the

'War on Terror', including the Baha Mousa and 'Danny Boy' incidents in Iraq, to which we will return. The issue of morality and battlefield leadership exercised David greatly and the theme of soldiers' bad behaviour as symptomatic of toxic or absent leadership runs through his published work, as we shall see.

These interests were shared by another much-missed friend and colleague from King's College London, Dr David Fisher, who died in 2014. Along with a third good friend and mentor, Professor Christopher Dandeker, he and I ran the War and Society class which David Benest addressed so memorably. David Fisher was a retired (very senior) civil servant who spent thirty-seven years in the MOD and Cabinet Office before completing a PhD in War Studies at King's College London, the basis of what I contend is the best one-volume introduction to military ethics currently available, *Morality and War: Can War be Just in the Twenty-First Century?* The two Davids hit it off immediately and subsequently sat together on several panels and seminars while carrying out an unofficial campaign for a greater ethical component in British Army training.

A pressing need?

This brings us to the subject of this chapter – the two Davids' views on some of the moral challenges facing soldiers on and off the battlefield and how they might be addressed. There is a pressing need for such discussion right now, given episodes occurring during Britain's involvement in the so-called 'War on Terror', which will be referred to several times in subsequent chapters.

Aaron Edwards has described the details of the Baha Mousa case in Chapter 1 of this volume. Following those events, a public enquiry, chaired by Sir William Gage, published its report in 2011, finding that Queens Lancashire Regiment, now incorporated into the Duke of Lancaster's Regiment, soldiers had violated the Geneva Convention and almost certainly lied to previous investigations. This included the battalion medical officer, Captain Derek Keillor, who treated the prisoners and claimed he found no signs of abuse – he had subsequently left the army and was working as a general practitioner, but was struck off the medical register after the findings.[1] David Benest touched on the Baha Mousa case in his entry on 'British Atrocities in Counter Insurgency' in the online *Encyclopedia of Military Ethics* alongside several others, including the potentially even more

---

[1] For a detailed account of this case, see Andrew Williams, *A Very British Killing: The Death of Baha Mousa* (London: Vintage, 2013) and also Chapter 7 of this volume.

serious allegations laid about operations around the 'Danny Boy' checkpoint on Route 6 in southern Iraq, that soldiers of the Princess of Wales' Royal Regiment (PWRR) tortured and murdered detainees and mutilated the bodies of insurgents killed in combat and that the British Joint Forward Interrogation Team had abused prisoners – amounting to torture – over a five-year period from 2003 to 2008.[2]

It was just after David Benest published this piece that the first news emerged of the case of 'Marine A', AKA Sergeant Alexander Blackman of the Royal Marines, who in Afghanistan on 15 September 2011 shot dead a badly wounded Taliban prisoner in front of two other marines. Blackman was subsequently found guilty of murder, dishonourably discharged and sentenced to life imprisonment with a minimum tariff of ten years, reduced on appeal to eight years for manslaughter due to diminished responsibility following a lengthy media campaign in his support involving retired senior officers and the right-wing tabloid press.

The two Davids' ideas on why these things happen arose from a lifetime's practical experience and it should be stressed that neither was a bleeding heart nor a middlebrow scribbler of the sort that is 'ten a penny' online. David Benest spent four decades in the British Army, an officer rising to senior rank in one of the world's great fighting regiments, participated in two significant conventional battles in the Falklands War and several tours of Northern Ireland, the last as commanding officer of his battalion; personal anecdotes suggest he could be a vigorous disciplinarian when necessary. David Fisher was a civil servant for almost forty years, served in several conflict zones, was Director of the 2001 Defence Training Review and ended his career in the Cabinet Office in the build-up to the invasion of Iraq in 2003.

Moreover, these issues matter for soldiers in real life. First, they should not do these things simply because they are wrong. It was through David Benest that I first learnt of moral trauma and its possible role – among other factors – in combat-induced post-traumatic stress disorder (PTSD), that the guilt and shame of witnessing or involvement in criminal or immoral acts can contribute to lifelong psychological injury.[3] Little work had been done on this in the United Kingdom until King's College London and the charity Combat Stress published the results of their joint study in 2019, indicating that moral injury could be

---

[2] David Benest, 'British Atrocities in Counter Insurgency', *Encyclopedia of Military Ethics*, 10 April 2011, https://www.militaryethics.org/British-Atrocities-in-Counter-Insurgency/10/.

[3] For a short introduction, see Victoria Williamson, Dominic Murphy, Andrea Phelps, David Forbes, and Neil Greenberg, 'Moral Injury: The Effect on Mental Health and Implications for Treatment', *The Lancet*, 17 March 2021, https://www.thelancet.com/journals/lanpsy/article/PIIS2215 -0366(21)00113-9/fulltext.

widespread among British veterans and that developing effective treatment needed further research.[4]

Such acts can also say things about the army and country that perpetrates them; David Benest was uncompromising on this, arguing consistently that the army of a liberal-democratic nation should uphold liberal-democratic values, above all the rule of law. To take his line of argument further, the United Kingdom has played a major part in extending the reach of international law and has made 'upholding the rules-based international order' a cornerstone of its defence and security policy; these rules include the laws of armed conflict, especially the Geneva and Hague Conventions and the Thomasine just war principles that underpin them, so it is betraying its own legacy and undermining this aim if these rules are violated by its own personnel. No country can aspire to global leadership, as 'Global Britain' still does, without setting a high moral example.[5] It also means that anything and everything soldiers do can have political impact – we have not just 'Strategic Corporals' but also 'Strategic Privates', as the Russians seem painfully unaware right now in Ukraine. David Benest certainly was aware of it, and this runs through his published thoughts on this issue.

David Benest on why soldiers go bad

These centre mainly on three papers: his chapter 'British Leaders in Irregular Warfare' in the 2009 edited volume *The Moral Dimensions of Asymmetrical Warfare*; his historical article 'Atrocities in Britain's Counter-Insurgencies' in the *RUSI (Royal United Services Institute) Journal* of July 2011; and his peer-reviewed paper 'A Liberal Democratic State and COIN: The Case of Britain, or Why Atrocities Can Still Happen', in *Civil Wars* of 2012, an abridged version of which forms his entry in the online *Encyclopedia of Military Ethics*.[6] These go alongside his correspondence with journals and the media and reviews of the works of others to give a good picture of his views on why British soldiers go bad, and how this might be prevented.

---

[4] Victoria Williamson, Neil Greenberg, and Dominic Murphy, 'Moral Injury in UK Armed Forces Veterans: A Qualitative Survey', *European Journal of Psychotraumatology*, 14 January 2019, https://www.kcl.ac.uk/kcmhr/publications/assetfiles/2019/williamson2019.pdf.

[5] For a detailed argument on these lines, see Peter Ricketts, *Hard Choices: The Making and Unbreaking of Global Britain* (London: Atlantic, 2021), pp. 154–7.

[6] David Benest, 'British Leaders and Irregular Warfare', in *The Moral Dimensions of Asymmetrical Warfare*, ed. Th. A van Baarda and D. E. M Verweij (Leiden: Brill, 2009), pp. 169–78; 'Atrocities in Britain's Counter-Insurgencies', *RUSI Journal*, June 2011, 156(3); 'British Atrocities', 2011, pp. 80–7, https://www.militaryethics.org/British-Atrocities-in-Counter-Insurgency/10/.

In the first of these papers, authored shortly after his retirement from the army, David laid out the historical and cultural context for this issue most clearly. He opened by challenging General Sir Rupert Smith's argument that armies now faced a 'new paradigm' of war among the people: rather, irregular warfare had always existed and probably always would.[7] Consequently, armies would still have to face situations where 'the media is ever present; the political aim is often obscure . . . [and] sometimes there is no political "solution" or exit strategy'.[8] Therefore, it is vital that leaders in irregular warfare have 'a strong ethical and moral "compass" as a guide to policies and action'.[9] This was mainly because soldiers are also citizens and therefore still subject to the rule of law, combining with the principle – central to the British approach to counter-insurgency – of minimum use of force, meaning the decision to open fire in counter-insurgency situations can have political repercussions:

> The issue facing leaders, therefore has been how to prosecute a war among the people without actually effecting their destruction, loss of civil liberty, humiliation or starvation and without incurring public vilification.[10]

Patience and restraint were essential if facing insurgents, who rarely abide by the laws of armed conflict and may try to provoke their regular opponents; it was principally the role of political and military leaders to impose these things on soldiers and abuses, of which David cited a lengthy list from British irregular wars over a hundred-year period, happened when they failed to do this.[11] Bad leaders 'must go' and, supporting this assertion, he named a number of figures he returned to repeatedly in print and conversation – Lord Kitchener in South Africa, Major General Sir Robert Hinde in Kenya and Lieutenant Colonel Colin Mitchell in Aden.[12]

This ties in closely with another of David's fields of investigation, the impact of leaders, particularly battalion commanding officers in the British Army, on operations. His interest here was passionate and personal: he deplored the tendency of the army to promote 'Alpha Male' types, big on presence but short on self-awareness and emotional intelligence, a type he saw epitomized by his CO from the Falklands, Lieutenant Colonel H. Jones VC. David

---

[7] Benest, 'British Leaders and Irregular Warfare', pp. 169–70; see also General Sir Rupert Smith, *The Utility of Force: The Art of War in the Modern World* (London: Allen Lane, 2005).

[8] Ibid., p. 170.

[9] Ibid., p. 171.

[10] Ibid.

[11] Ibid., pp. 171–2.

[12] Ibid., pp. 175–7.

remembered H. Jones as an excellent trainer and peacetime commander and a fundamentally decent man with a strong moral compass, but also impatient and with authoritarian traits militating against the building of an effective leadership team in his battalion, leading to near disaster at the Battle of Goose Green.[13] More darkly, David argued, there were other cases where putting such types in charge led to serious moral lapses including possible war crimes. He seemed to have developed a particular animus towards Mitchell, whose command of 1st Battalion, Argyll and Sutherland Highlanders, in the Crater area of Aden in summer 1967 and his imposition of 'Argyll Law' on the inhabitants David presented as a perfect example of how to transgress and get away with it. Mitchell became a national hero and, briefly, a Conservative MP despite allegations of brutality and outright criminal behaviour laid against the Argylls in Crater.[14]

The theme of bad leadership runs through David's RUSI article, where those same British officers are cited, but for the first time he touches on campaigns he was involved in personally, Northern Ireland in particular, and on his own regiment, dwelling at length on the Bloody Sunday incident in January 1972. According to David, the principal unit involved, 1st Battalion, The Parachute Regiment (1 Para), 'had already gained a reputation for ruthless violence and has [sic] been accused of reckless killings in West Belfast during internment'. This echoes the findings of Lord Saville's investigation that the killings originated in an unauthorized arrest operation initiated by 1 Para's CO, troops panicking after an officer fired warning shots (against rules of engagement) at the demonstrators, the sound then echoing through the streets and making them think they were under fire; more seriously, Saville ruled that many soldiers had made false statements to investigators.[15] In concluding, David stressed that it is a vanishing minority of British soldiers who transgress, the real issue being 'the manner in which senior military, government and civil service officials thought it expedient to steadfastly refuse to face the facts when atrocities took place'. He followed by expressing some optimism over the British Army now facing up to this issue, exemplified by the Aitken Report of 2008, published with the full endorsement of the Chief of the General Staff, General Sir Richard Dannatt, but notes that

---

[13] For more details, see Spencer Fitz-Gibbon, *Not Mentioned in Dispatches: The History and Mythology of the Battle of Goose Green* (Cambridge: James Clarke, 2001) – a book on which David B's opinion was consulted extensively. Also based on his lectures on 'Moral Challenges Facing Commanders' given to the War and Society module at King's College London.

[14] See in particular David B's Review of Aaron Edwards, *Mad Mitch's Tribal Law: Aden and the End of Empire* (Edinburgh: Mainstream, 2014) in *RUSI Journal*, June 2014, 159(3).

[15] Benest, 'British Atrocities', p. 86.

Brigadier Aitken was not allowed to cover 'command climate' in offending units as much as he would have liked.[16]

David Benest's longest paper is in *Civil Wars*, which contains another historical overview as well as a personal taxonomy of the causes of transgressions and alleged transgressions, all still linked to flawed or dysfunctional leadership. His list of given causes begins with simple lapses of judgement from 'senior British leaders who are under mental stress and conducting a difficult COIN [counterinsurgency] campaign', such as Kitchener destroying Boer farms and interning civilians in South Africa from 1900 to 1901. Following on from this is outright insanity, examples cited being Captain Bowen-Colthurst's rampage through Dublin in the wake of the Easter Rising in 1916, for which he was sent to Broadmoor, and Captain G. S. L Griffith's torture and murder of Mau-Mau suspects in Kenya in 1954. Then there is a misguided sense of duty or 'only obeying orders', as with Reginald Dyer at Amritsar in 1919. Finally, and perhaps most seriously, there is the explicit government policy of coercion via brutality such as the 'Air Policing' adopted across the Middle East from the 1920s to the 1950s.[17] In conclusion, David once again pointed an accusing finger at the attitude of officialdom, magnifying the impact of the criminal actions of small numbers, and makes his most explicit statement about the importance of leaders in preventing them: where senior commanders have imposed obedience to the law and proper conduct, the chance of transgressions has been 'diminished'; 'it is when individuals such as Percival, Harris, Hinde or Mitchell gain the ascendancy that trouble inevitably has followed'.[18] He closed with a statement unlikely to win friends in the British military:

> Yet, all went through the same officer 'factories' at Dartmouth, Woolwich, Sandhurst or Cranwell. These institutions appear not able to weed out individuals capable of such lasting damage, and that indicates just how challenging is the continuing task of ensuring the command excellence that prevents atrocities.[19]

In fairness to David, he moderated this opinion subsequently, acknowledging in 2014 that ethics were now included on the academic programme at the Royal Military Academy, Sandhurst, something he had advocated for years.[20]

So the overarching theme throughout David Benest's published work on the subject is that atrocities are a product of absent or toxic leadership, and the

---

[16] Ibid., p. 87.
[17] David Benest, 'A Liberal Democratic State and COIN: The Case of Britain, or Why Atrocities Can Still Happen', *Civil Wars*, 2012, 14(1), pp. 30–8.
[18] Ibid., pp. 45–6.
[19] Ibid., p. 46.
[20] Benest, Review of Aaron Edwards, *Mad Mitch's Tribal Law*, p. 101.

higher the level of command, the more the damage. This might be challenged on several levels. That he drew exclusively from the British experience in counter-insurgency situates his ideas historically and culturally and probably limits their applicability in other cases – the Russians in Ukraine, for instance, a non-Western regular army fighting a conventional war. His consistent emphasis on officers' responsibility removes any agency from soldiers and forgets the sway that non-commissioned officers (NCOs) can exert over units in the British and many other armies, as much part of 'command culture' as anything coming down from the CO – consider not just the Baha Mousa and Abu Ghraib cases in Iraq but also the role of *Dedovshchina* in brutalizing Russian recruits. Finally, a measure of David's passion about the issue is the very clear presumption of guilt running through all the cases he cites, including some still *sub judice* at the time of writing.

Nevertheless, David Benest's central point about transgression arising from 'command culture' and defective leadership is worth exploring further. If commanders and the culture they create do not cause such episodes, they must surely play some part in preventing them. David Fisher was also sure that the prevailing culture played its part in shaping behaviour: an issue interesting both Davids is how people decide upon what is a good action and what is a bad one. People do not come to moral problems completely fresh and inexperienced, nor do they make these decisions in a vacuum; they come with a past, with experiences and opinions shaped by what they have seen and done before, and they will often have to make those moral choices very quickly and under massive pressure, never more so than soldiers in combat. Moreover, they will work in an environment where peer and leader pressure play their part, particularly in an authoritarian and collective establishment like a military unit. It might, therefore, be a good thing if professionals of any kind underwent a degree of moral training before they were allowed to make such decisions; this is where the concept of 'virtues' comes in, David Fisher seeing this as a potential solution to soldiers going bad.

David Fisher on practical ethics

David Fisher followed the consequentialist school of moral philosophy, and its principles form the backbone of his book *Morality and War* published in 2012. To the consequentialist, the morality of an act is tied to its outcome – before we do something, we mentally weigh up the possible consequences of different causes of action and we choose which one we think will do less harm or, potentially, the greatest good. Thus it is the consequences of an action you should consider before taking it, especially the consequences to others.

The other side of the ethical argument is virtue ethics, which argues that your actions should be guided by strict moral laws – there are some human actions that are absolutely right and others which are absolutely wrong, and the real moral argument is what these things should be; consequently, we must consider the mental state of the person carrying out an act if we are to decide it is moral or not, based on whether or not their intentions are the 'right' ones. David Fisher synthesized this with consequentialism in true Hegelian fashion, producing the concept of 'virtuous consequentialism', that a truly moral act should have both good intentions and good consequences: we maximize the good and minimize the harm we do, and it is our intention to do this all along.[21] Our intentions are formed by our virtues.

What, then, is a virtue? This comes down from the Greek philosophers, particularly Aristotle, who defined it as 'a character trait that manifests itself in choice, lying in a mean that is relative to us, determined by a rational principle by which the man of practical wisdom would determine it'. A virtue, therefore, is an intrinsic part of your character, your personality, which affects your thought and behaviour; virtues are character traits that direct you towards behaviour which tends to benefit or protect yourself and others. A virtue can stem from many things – you might mysteriously be born with it, something going beyond what we are looking at here into theology or mysticism. But more commonly it is acquired, then evolves, through a combination of life experience, education or training, so that it becomes second nature. Virtuous acts, like acts of bravery on the battlefield or taking action to save comrades' lives, stem from virtuous patterns of thought, so both the act and the motivation are ethical. Moreover, for an act to be virtuous, most philosophers agree that there has to be an element of choice involved, otherwise they would be just habits or reflex responses in which the choice to do something good or not do something bad plays no part. Virtues are exercised when some kind of moral choice is necessary and will tend to lead you towards the path of action that benefits others the most or does them the least harm.

Having laid the foundations, we examine the military virtues, why they are so important to the military and why they might have the ones they have. David

---

[21] David Fisher, *Morality and War: Can War be Just in the Twenty-First Century?* (Oxford: Oxford University Press, 2011), pp. 134–48.

Fisher outlined four in *Morality and War* – justice, practical wisdom, courage and self-control. Although he did not list it explicitly, another virtue, loyalty, also threads through his discussion.

Justice translates very broadly as 'always seeking to do the right thing'. On one level, there is avoiding behaviour that is illegal under national or international law. For instance, the Geneva Conventions aim to protect the victims of armed conflict – the wounded and sick, the shipwrecked, prisoners of war and civilians, all classified as 'non-combatants' and not to be targeted with lethal force and also having a right to minimum standards of treatment. There is also the sense of 'just cause', that you are fighting for the right reasons as laid out most clearly by St Thomas Aquinas: your cause is just (you are fighting to defend yourselves or those who cannot defend themselves), you are sincere in your just cause, you are authorized to fight by a legal and competent authority, you are fighting as a last resort and you do not inflict any more death and destruction than is necessary to meet your just cause.[22] As David Fisher put it succinctly, justice is all about 'respecting and promoting the welfare of others' and we can infer already that it absolutely precludes the kind of behaviour described by David Benest.[23] However, to pursue justice in time of war, we need other virtues.

This is probably why David Fisher gave over much space to discussing practical wisdom, or what could otherwise be called 'common sense' or 'prudence'. According to him, this is the virtue that underpins all the others – we need practical wisdom in order to look at a situation, interpret it and decide which of our virtues or principles are being tested or which might apply. Practical wisdom tends to apply most forcefully to commanders, who quite literally have to make life-or-death decisions in which they have to weigh up the options available and decide which will fulfil the mission at least cost to lives, equipment and money. However, the growing prevalence of 'wars among the people' requires practical wisdom to be exercised by all ranks, particularly when operating in close proximity to the local population. For all in such situations, 'the exercise of practical wisdom needs to have become, *through long training and practice*, second nature, an ingrained habit of sound reasoning [my italics]' if such a war is to be fought justly in practice.[24]

Courage is the ability to overcome fear and do your duty despite possible bad consequences for you. It is not the absence of fear, but the confrontation with

[22] Ibid., pp. 64–84, 117–19.
[23] Ibid., p. 119.
[24] Ibid., pp. 120–1.

and overcoming of fear. As all text books state, there are two broad forms of courage. Physical courage is what we see most on the battlefield – the ability to overcome immediate fear of physical death or injury in order to carry on with what is required of you. Moral courage is the ability to behave in a moral way despite possible bad consequences for you, such as punishment, unpopularity or career damage. These are linked closely to self-control, 'the character trait that helps a man never lose his head, whether through anger or fear or lust for pleasure and so always to exercise a dispassionate judgement of what is the right thing to do', to allow him to retain a degree of rationality and restraint in the face of the death and destruction on the battlefield.[25]

Loyalty is linked closely to self-control. On one level, it is a sense of serving a country or cause and, combined with justice, it distinguishes a soldier from an armed thug. On another level, loyalty to the unit and to the people around you – your friends – and not wanting to let the side down builds cohesion and discipline and can keep somebody fighting. Yet, of all the virtues, loyalty is the most open to abuse, as David Fisher made clear in his discussion of the Baha Mousa case: drawing on the findings of the internal British Army report on the episode, he argued that the soldiers concerned showed a lack of justice and self-control while others lacked the moral courage to challenge what was happening; this was compounded by misplaced loyalty between the perpetrators, which betrayed loyalty to the country and to the army as a whole.[26]

He closes by arguing that it is essential to instil a moral code into soldiers for the profoundest of reasons:

> The virtues are needed in military life to ensure that soldiers are effective soldiers. But they are also needed to ensure that our service people are good people who deploy the lethal force with which society entrusts them only for the sake of a good end and in ways of which they and the society whom they serve can be justifiably proud.[27]

Moreover, and reflecting David Benest's concern with moral injury, an internalized moral code is essential for individual soldiers to see themselves not as 'pirates' or armed criminals, but as warriors serving their society and the general good.[28]

---

[25] Ibid., p. 121.
[26] Ibid., pp. 127–8.
[27] Ibid., p. 129.
[28] Ibid., p. 128.

Bringing it together

The Davids agreed that the kind of transgressions detailed earlier probably had deeper roots than the military experience of the perpetrators. David Benest stated that 'in the opinion of some', they originate in a 'broken society', that 'through a combination of family breakdown, the increasing abandonment of observed religion and a permissive sex, drugs, drink and violence culture among the young, British society had "lost its way"'. Perhaps the failure to create the right 'command culture' was due to a relaxation of officers' entry standards over several decades and the move towards a graduate officer corps exposed to the 'ethical or moral relativism that has dominated British university campuses'.[29] However, as he pointed out, the 'broken society' argument did not explain transgressions from earlier eras, or perhaps it does, albeit not in the context of the British Army. After all, some of the most terrible crimes against humanity – the Nazi Holocaust, Stalin's genocide of the Ukrainians and Crimean Tatars, the massacres in Yugoslavia and Rwanda of the 1990s – arose from malevolent leadership cultures toxifying entire societies.

David Fisher argued on similar lines, also wondering about the implications of pursuing an ethical military against the background of 'a society that is itself morally sceptical or indifferent'.[30] Under such circumstances, 'it would be difficult to establish what the military should be taught [about morality]' and that military would be (and perhaps is) operating in the context of a political class lacking the practical wisdom and sense of justice to make sound decisions about peace and war.[31]

Nevertheless, it is imperative to try, and David Fisher offered a solution to the problems that so vexed David Benest in the form of moral education and training for the military rooted in the virtues he outlined, especially justice and practical wisdom. This should extend to all ranks but particularly to leaders and would be taught ideally not just as a set of abstract principles, but 'Examples of virtuous behaviour need to be studied from both living and historical examples . . . [and] embedded in the daily practice and experience of the barracks and the battlefield'.[32] It is not enough that soldiers learn morality, they also need to behave in a moral way, and this might be achieved not just through educating them in just war principles and the laws of armed conflict, but also through

---

[29] https://www.militaryethics.org/British-Atrocities-in-Counter-Insurgency/10/.
[30] Fisher, *Morality and War*, p. 132.
[31] Ibid., pp. 28–42, 132.
[32] Ibid., p. 130.

integrating the virtues into training so that behaving in this way becomes an ingrained military trait, 'taking over' under fire just as other aspects of training do. To illustrate this, David Fisher cited the US Marine officer in Vietnam who stopped a traumatized young marine from murdering a Vietnamese woman by shouting 'Marines don't do that' in his direction: 'an appeal to the military virtues embodied in the marine's own code of honour worked.'[33] Therefore, a solution to the problems of 'command culture' at the centre of David Benest's arguments about atrocities might lie in a revival of the concept of *honour* – something requiring an extensive debate in itself.

As both Davids noted with satisfaction, the British Army has made some steps in this direction: post operations in Basra in southern Iraq, all soldiers and officers are trained in the Geneva and Hague Conventions not only as part of initial training but also annually and pre-deployment. This now includes prisoner handling and a set of 'values and standards' that it takes very seriously indeed, having been a first point of reference in a number of subsequent cases.[34] Continuing in this direction would be a good legacy for them both.

---

[33] Ibid., p. 128.
[34] It was moving in this direction from the early 1990s, although perhaps not quickly enough. The author qualified as an instructor in these matters when serving with the Territorial Army then.

3

Legal accountability at the tactical level and the Overseas Operations Act

Nicholas Mercer

Introduction

It was a great honour and privilege to be asked to write a chapter for the late David Benest. However, I must confess at the outset that I hardly knew David at all and never met him in person. I was in touch with him only for the last few months of his life as a result of a chance introduction in 2020 by the former *Guardian* journalist Ian Cobain.

Ian and I were in discussion about the Overseas Operations Bill, which had been recently introduced into the House of Commons. As many readers will know, this Bill came to Parliament as a result of a Conservative Party manifesto pledge to put an end to what had been termed 'vexatious' claims against British servicemen and women when fighting overseas.[1] Ian asked me whether I knew David Benest as he thought we might work well together. I had not heard of David but very soon made his acquaintance. We got on famously, forging an unlikely alliance between a former commanding officer of a teeth arms regiment and a military lawyer now turned clergyman.

Despite our very different backgrounds, both David and I were implacably opposed to the watering down of the laws of armed conflict (LOAC), which would be the inevitable outcome of the proposed legislation. David had served in the Falklands Conflict in 1982 and had seen, first-hand, how vital it was to have the highest standards of discipline on the battlefield. He maintained that war crimes had been committed during that conflict and saw any diminution of battlefield discipline as a deeply retrograde step. I belonged to a later military generation but had served as the Command Legal Adviser for the HQ 1st (UK)

---

[1] https://www.conservatives.com/our-plan/conservative-party-manifesto-2019.

Armoured Division during the Iraq War, 2003. I was similarly conscious as to how essential it was to have the strictest battlefield discipline and accountability. During my tenure in Iraq, I had to confront the wide-scale abuse of Iraqi prisoners of war. As a result of later revelations of 'black' sites in the Western desert, I was also suspicious that the state might have a vested interest in undermining the laws of war.[2]

David and I were introduced by email on 13 March 2020 and soon set to work. As a result of our initial discussions, we decided to fire the first shot in the battle against the proposed legislation by writing to the *Times*. We jointly drafted a letter, which was duly published just six days later on 19 March as follows:

War crimes statute

Sir, we wish to express our opposition
in the strongest terms to any statute
of limitations for war crimes (report 18 Mar)
on three grounds.
First, the Geneva Conventions and Protocols
do not have a time limit attached for the very
good reason that the battlefield requires the
strictest discipline and accountability for soldiers.
Second, the passing of a statute of limitations
would give the green light to rogue nations to follow
suit. It does not take much imagination to envisage
another nation citing its own statute of limitations
when being pressed about war crimes.
Third, to take this step would potentially undermine
the whole edifice of International Law on the battlefield.
The British Army is rightly regarded as one of the finest
Armies in the world. It does not need special laws to
"protect" it.
In our opinion, this is a deeply retrograde step
by the British Government.

Colonel David Benest, former Commanding Officer 2 Para,
South Armagh 1994–7

---

[2] https://www.middleeasteye.net/news/uk-and-us-forces-ran-secret-prisons-iraq-after-2003-invasion.

Lieutenant Colonel the Reverend Nicholas Mercer former
Senior military lawyer, HQ 1st (UK) Armoured Division,
2003 Iraq War

Thereafter, we began composing a letter to be sent to the Secretary of State for Defence setting out what we perceived to be the serious flaws in the Bill. However, we soon encountered the general reluctance of the military when it comes to taking a principled stand against the government. David was well connected militarily, but his attempts to galvanize opposition were to prove fruitless. There were many senior officers who did not want any part of such a campaign and we soon realized that we were going to have to put pressure on the government by other means. This did not dampen our enthusiasm however, and we pressed on regardless. Then, completely out of the blue, I received an email from his wife Genevieve telling me that David had died on 10 August 2020, just five months after I had 'met' him.

Her obituary for David in the *Guardian* in November 2020 described David as 'a humanist who believed that soldiers should be fully accountable for their actions'.[3] This is a noble epitaph, but David died knowing that this Bill had the potential to seriously undermine this accountability, which he deemed essential. However, the work in opposing the Bill was to continue in the hands of others until it was enacted in April 2021.[4] By that stage, however, the Bill had been substantially amended and our labours, started together in 2020, were not in vain.

However, given David's death at such an early stage of our collaboration, it feels appropriate to examine the Bill in its original form and the potential impact it could have had on accountability at the tactical level on the battlefield. Our objections give a deeper insight into David's deeply held principles borne out of his distinguished military career.

Overseas Operations Bill

The Conservative Manifesto in 2019 pledged to protect soldiers from 'vexatious legal claims that have recently undermined our Armed Forces and our ability to

---

[3] https://www.theguardian.com/uk-news/2020/nov/11/david-benest-obituary.
[4] The opposition to the Bill came from numerous other sources including members of the House of Lords (including the House of Bishops), International Committee of the Red Cross (ICRC), UN Rapporteur on torture, lawyers and various non-governmental organizations (NGOs).

fight wars.'[5] At first glance, such a manifesto pledge looks seductive and one that would no doubt attract support from a wide cross-section of the British public. After all, how could anyone not support such a proposal? There was just one snag for the government and that was the fact that the claim was not true.

'Vexatious legal claims'

As a young officer in The Parachute Regiment, David had realized the potential to distort reality with an alternative narrative. He admitted that he 'had swallowed the regimental line that our first Battalion had been under attack'[6] on Bloody Sunday on 30 January 1972 and was all too aware of the distortion of the truth when it came to defending the armed forces. The same syndrome persisted into the Iraq War, 2003. Although the populist press liked to portray cases against the armed forces coming out of Iraq and Afghanistan as 'vexatious', the reality was somewhat different.

This could not have been more clearly illustrated than when, during the Committee stage of the Overseas Operations Bill, the Right Honourable Johnny Mercer MP was asked to name a case that the courts had struck out as 'vexatious'. He was unable to name a single case. The Human Rights Committee of the House of Commons reported the exchange as follows:

> We asked the Minister [Johnny Mercer] to inform us of any cases where he believed the courts have failed or refused to use their powers to strike out unmeritorious claims. He was not able to do so.[7]

This populist myth about 'vexatious' claims against British forces, which, as Johnny Mercer knew only too well, plays so well with the voters on the doorstep, needs to be set alongside the preliminary findings of the International Criminal Court[8] into the United Kingdom's conduct in Iraq. The Report stated:

> On the basis of the information available, there is a reasonable basis to believe that, at a minimum, the following war crimes have been committed by members of UK armed forces [in Iraq]: wilful killing/murder under article 8(2)(a)(i)) or article 8(2)(c)(i)); torture and inhuman/cruel treatment under article 8(2)(a)(ii)

---

[5] Ibid., 1 above, see p. 52.

[6] https://www.theguardian.com/commentisfree/2019/may/22/northern-ireland-no-amnesty-veterans-amritsar-bloody-sunday.

[7] https://committees.parliament.uk/publications/3191/documents/39059/default/, dated 21 October 2020.

[8] https://www.icc-cpi.int/itemsDocuments/201209-otp-final-report-iraq-uk-eng.pdf, dated 9 December 2020.

or article 8(2)(c)(i)); outrages upon personal dignity under article 8(2)(b)(xxi) or article 8(2)(c)(ii)); rape and/or other forms of sexual violence under article 8(2)(b)(xxii) or article 8(2)(e)(vi)).[9]

The Report also addressed the issue of vexatious claims and stated:

> To characterize these various processes as arising from vexatious claims would appear to mischaracterize the events.[10]

This perhaps is the first illustration of why there is a need to ensure 'the strictest accountability on the battlefield', which David and I referred to in our letter to the *Times*. At the heart of this issue is a general reluctance by the public to believe allegations of misconduct by UK forces and therefore countenance legal action against them. There are numerous reasons for this, ranging from a misguided notion that 'war is war' to the oft-held view that members of the armed forces do not deserve such a level of scrutiny. In such a climate, it is hard enough to bring cases to trial at all, and a watering down of the legal framework would only make accountability more difficult. Despite our very different military backgrounds, both David and I knew the reality behind the public perception and contrived narratives. David told me he had first-hand knowledge of war crimes in the Falklands Conflict and the misperceptions about Northern Ireland. I too was an eye witness to prisoner abuse in Iraq. Those with first-hand experience of the conflict knew that the reality was somewhat different from the public narrative. It was from this false premise that the Bill was born and, not surprisingly, the rest of the Bill simply compounded the error.

'Endless investigations'

The Secretary of State for Defence stated in 2020:

> This Government made a promise to the nation to protect service personnel . . . from vexatious claims and endless investigations.[11]

Rather like the intention to end 'vexatious' claims, the idea that the Bill would also protect service personnel from 'endless investigations' was entirely disingenuous. Not only is the United Kingdom obliged to investigate alleged

---

[9] See ICC Final Report into the Situation in Iraq/UK, https://www.icc-cpi.int/sites/default/files/itemsDocuments/201209-otp-final-report-iraq-uk-eng.pdf, dated 9 December 2020.
[10] Ibid., 9 above.
[11] https://www.gov.uk/government/news/mod-delivers-robust-legal-protections-for-personnel-and-veterans.

war crimes under international law, but this obligation also cannot be curtailed in any circumstances. Like all other serious crimes, they have to be investigated and, to try and set a time limit on such investigations made no sense at all. It is self-evident that a war crime may not come to light for many years or even decades and may have to be re-investigated or re-opened when new evidence emerges. This happens all the time in the investigative process whether on the battlefield or elsewhere. As the former Judge Advocate General[12] pointed out, the Bill could not prevent investigations running their course and therefore would do nothing to protect service personnel from 'endless investigations' as claimed. Given our concern that there should be 'strict accountability' for battlefield crimes, this was something both David and I opposed in principle and was something that others were able to articulate during the passage of the Bill through Parliament.

Prosecutions

As well as seeking to curtail investigations, the government sought to curtail prosecutions of servicemen and women at the same time. This was the most egregious part of the Bill as far as David and I were concerned. The Bill contained what was called a 'triple lock' against prosecution. First of all, there was a statutory presumption against prosecution itself, which meant that those considering whether to bring a prosecution had to consider *not* bringing such a case in the first place. This was then compounded by a five-year statute of limitations from the date of the alleged offence itself. Although this could be waived in exceptional circumstances, there were elaborate hurdles that the Prosecutor had to leap in order to do so. Finally, if a case was recommended for trial, then the attorney general could bring an end to proceedings in any event. It made prosecution (except for sexual offences) almost impossible after five years had elapsed. Not only did this undermine accountability generally but the reality of both Northern Ireland and Iraq also illustrated the foolishness of this proposal. David was acutely aware of the Bloody Sunday Inquiry[13] and, as those who have followed the Inquiry will know, to this day there has been a wall of silence that has shielded the public and the families from the truth as to what happened on 30 January 1972.

---

[12] See comments of Judge Advocate Geoff Blackett: https://hansard.parliament.uk/commons/2020-10-08/debates/f7a00940-5c69-4b9d-9c03-dbc31feadc8d/OverseasOperations(ServicePersonnel And Veterans)Bill(Fourth Sitting).
[13] https://www.bloody-sunday-inquiry.org.uk/.

As the journalist Douglas Murray stated:

> As one soldier after another appeared before Lord Saville, it became clear that the soldiers of 1Para were intent on spurning the last effort to get to the truth of what happened. Almost without exception, they stonewalled.[14]

The same wall of silence was employed by the 1st Battalion of The Queens Lancashire Regiment over the death of Baha Mousa in Iraq in 2003.[15] To date, no one has been held to account and, as far as David and I were concerned, a five-year statute of limitations would make matters even worse. Soldiers would very soon realize that, to avoid accountability, they simple had to run down the clock.

'Undermining our armed forces'

Although the government claimed that recent litigation arising from Iraq and Afghanistan 'undermines our Armed Forces',[16] David and I saw the matter the other way around. Instead, to us, the proposed Bill threatened to undermine the very institution of the armed forces itself as it would potentially threaten the whole edifice of international law on the battlefield. In our view, the proposals in the Bill marked a very dangerous departure from 'rules based International order',[17] which the United Kingdom aspires to follow.

Geneva Conventions 1949

The Geneva Conventions 1949 and their protocols are the bedrock of battlefield discipline. They require the 'High Contracting Parties' to prosecute 'grave breaches' of the Convention and 'all acts contrary to its provision'. The International Committee of the Red Cross (ICRC) has stated emphatically that 'statutes of limitations may not apply to war crimes',[18] but the Bill ignored this direction. We both felt that the Bill would be unprecedented in introducing a statute of limitations to the Geneva Conventions.

---

[14] See article by Douglas Murray ('Bloody Liar') in the *Spectator*, 16 March 2019.
[15] https://www.theguardian.com/world/2009/sep/21/baha-mousa-inquiry-army-iraq.
[16] Ibid., 1 above.
[17] https://rusi.org/commentary/uks-overseas-operations-bill-good-questions-wrong-answers   by Professor Michael Clarke, dated October 2020.
[18] See written submissions of ICRC: https://publications.parliament.uk/pa/cm5801/cmpublic/OverseasOperations/memo/OOB04.htm.

UN Convention against Torture (UNCAT)

In our view, the most worrying example of the undermining of international law was the potential impact upon torture. The UNCAT specifically prohibits the imposition of a statute of limitations and the UN Committee on Torture stated during the passage of the Bill:

> By introducing a statutory presumption against prosecution and statutes of limitations, this bill undermines the absolute and non-derogable nature of the prohibition of torture and violates human rights law, as well as international criminal and humanitarian law.[19]

During the early passage of the Bill, Field Marshal the Lord Guthrie described it as the '*de facto* decriminalisation of torture'[20]potentially denying victims of torture an effective remedy at all.[21]

Other considerations

We also felt that there were other compelling reasons to oppose the Bill, such as the danger that lowering standards of accountability could result in lower standards being applied on the battlefield. Soldiers and commanders alike would know that the chances of prosecution had been lessened and therefore feel emboldened to break the law.

There was also the very real risk that crimes of torture and war crimes might go unpunished. No civilized society could sanction such a situation. The response of the responsible minister was singled out for criticism by the Joint Committee on Human Rights (JCHR) in the Committee stage who stated:

> We find it unacceptable that Johnny Mercer MP, the responsible Minister, would not confirm that he thought that members of the Armed Forces should be prosecuted in respect of war crimes.[22]

It almost goes without saying that such legislation could prove very attractive to those countries that have traditionally adopted lower standards than the United Kingdom. Russia, China, Central Asia and African nations could all

---

[19] https://www.ohchr.org/EN/NewsEvents/Pages/DisplayNews.aspx?NewsID=26342&LangID=E, dated 5 October.

[20] Letter to the *Times*, dated 20 June, 'Don't give wriggle room to torturers.'

[21] https://redress.org/wp-content/uploads/2021/01/Overseas-Operations-Bill-Briefing-January-2021 -2.pdf.

[22] Ibid., 7 above.

seek to emulate this legislation and the UK would then be unable to criticize them. Indeed, during the passage of the Bill, Sri Lanka, with a shocking record of war crimes and human rights violations, expressed an interest in following the 'example' of the United Kingdom.[23] The current situation in Ukraine further illustrates what a deeply retrograde step this Bill would have been if enacted as originally proposed.

Finally, there is a fundamental legal principle of equality before the law. This Bill created an inequality, not only between soldiers and civilians but also between the perpetrators and their victims. General Sir Nick Parker stated during the Committee hearings that UK armed forces should 'uphold the rule of law in the way that it is presented to everyone else'.[24] The Bill was, inadvertently perhaps, now delineating different classes of citizens before the law in the United Kingdom.

Brereton Report

The Brereton Report, published on 19 November 2020,[25] found credible allegations of unlawful killings of Afghan civilians by Australian special forces during the war in Afghanistan that are now being investigated by the police. In the course of the investigation, Australian special forces apparently remarked that 'the US and UK were far worse'. Needless to say, publication of the report was a timely reminder of how lack of accountability can undermine military operations overseas and just how dangerous the Bill could have been if enacted. At the time of writing, the British government is conducting a statutory independent judge-led inquiry[26] into the conduct of UK Special Forces in Afghanistan.

Conclusion

In May 2019, David wrote an article about a proposed amnesty for crimes committed in Northern Ireland during the so-called 'Troubles'.[27] While David

---

[23] https://mobile.twitter.com/rupertskilbeck/status/1368862363269685251.

[24] See Hansard: https://hansard.parliament.uk/Commons/2020-10-08/debates/0978324f-c831-4b3d-8f09-6f8302b7541d/OverseasOperations(ServicePersonnelAndVeterans)Bill(ThirdSitting)#contribution-18B7923E-67C2-40CA-A5A7-9B436B3C31A7.

[25] https://afghanistaninquiry.defence.gov.au/, dated 19 November 2020.

[26] https://www.theguardian.com/uk-news/2022/dec/15/inquiry-launched-into-claims-sas-soldiers-killed-afghan-civilians.

[27] https://www.theguardian.com/commentisfree/2019/may/22/northern-ireland-no-amnesty-veterans-amritsar-bloody-sunday.

was more than familiar with the pressure that soldiers were under on operations as a former army officer, he was nevertheless emphatic that 'all cases of serious crime needed to be investigated and prosecuted – without exception'. As he put it, 'only on that basis can high morale and good discipline be ensured.'

I too had written an article about the proposed amnesty arguing that the British Army must 'meet the highest standards under international and domestic law' and that such standards should not be 'watered down'.[28]

It was ironic that we had both written articles on the same subject unbeknown to each other and that our convictions had been born out of different first-hand military experience. These views pre-empted our fundamental objections to the Overseas Operations Bill the following year, which brought us together for the last few months of David's life.

It was an immense privilege to have known David for this brief moment in time but, as a parting word, I want to stress that this emphatic opposition to the legislation did not mean we were critical of the British Army. Indeed, it was quite the opposite. As we said in our joint letter quoted at the start of this chapter, 'The British Army is rightly regarded as one of the finest armies in the world. It does not need special laws to "protect" it.' In the profession of arms to which David dedicated his life and to which I dedicated part of mine, 'only the highest standards of International and domestic law will suffice'.

---

[28] https://www.theguardian.com/commentisfree/2019/may/19/penny-mordaunt-amnesty-incoherent-could-shield-governments-nefarious-actions.

Part Two

Legal and moral accountability

4

The Iraq war crimes allegations and the investigative conundrum

Andrew Williams

Introduction

There are very few veterans willing to explore the record of war crimes allegedly committed by the British Army in military actions since the end of the Second World War. David Benest was one of those retired officers who was willing to do so publicly. As discussed in the first two chapters of this volume, in 2011 and 2012, he published two articles on the 'atrocities' committed by UK forces in numerous counter-insurgency operations particularly in relation to treatment of detainees, at a time when investigations into the Army's activities in Iraq and Afghanistan were at their height. The evidence of crimes he outlined across seventy years of multiple 'small wars' made him question whether the 'ethos of the armed forces has ever properly addressed the issue of how to handle its opponents when they are no longer legitimate targets for lethal force'.[1]

Benest believed that the problem was a military command issue rather than a few 'rotten apples' and wrote:

> where leadership has been sound, the likelihood of misbehaviour by security forces appears to have been much diminished. It is when those lacking a 'moral compass' gained the ascendency that trouble inevitably followed.[2]

His article was instantly condemned as 'more akin to the work of a revisionist historian than a recently retired officer'.[3] But Benest's critique didn't end there. He argued that there was a systemic unwillingness for the British Army and

---

[1] David Benest, 'Atrocities in Britain's Counter-Insurgencies', *The RUSI Journal*, 2011, 156(3), pp. 80–7 at 85.

[2] Ibid.

[3] Major General D. P. Thomson (Rtd.), 'Letters', *The RUSI Journal*, 2012, 157(1), pp. 4–5.

successive governments ever to actively search for the truth of allegations. His concern shifted from the issue of 'ethical leadership' to 'the manner in which senior officials of the military, civil service and government thought it expedient to steadfastly refuse to face facts when atrocities took place'.[4] He complained that the system 'has long taken the view that while it knows these crimes have been (and are) committed, to admit to them – until forced by sheer weight of incontestable evidence' would 'give aid and comfort' to the enemy.[5] In other words, all institutions of state were complicit in ignoring allegations when they arose even if they believed they had good reason to do so.

Long before Benest, in the 1940s, George Orwell described the general willingness to believe that the enemy is always capable of atrocity whereas any suggestion that 'our troops' might be equally culpable is dismissed out of hand.[6] When military conflict occurs for whatever reason, it suits those in power, and perhaps the public too, to view one's side as essentially good and the enemy essentially bad. But Orwell noted that belief in one's own purity and in the wickedness of the opposition was possible only because of the lack of examination of any evidence. Such examination would not only help the enemy, it would also be a threat to morale and even a hindrance to the moral imperative to call out the enemy for *their* crimes of war.

Orwell saw this as essentially a matter of political and social psychology. And he wrote that attitudes were so fickle that 'at any moment the situation can suddenly reverse itself and yesterday's proved-to-the-hilt atrocity story can become a ridiculous lie, merely because the political landscape has changed'.[7] But he also recognized that 'the truth about atrocities is far worse than that they are lied about and made into propaganda. The truth is that they happen.' It's for that reason that since Nuremberg the international community has declared its resolve to pursue those responsible for crimes of war. The International Criminal Court (ICC) was created specifically for the purpose of conducting investigations into credible allegations and prosecuting those responsible when states have shown themselves unwilling or unable to do so themselves.[8]

---

[4] David Benest, 'A Liberal Democratic State and COIN: The Case of Britain, or Why Atrocities Can Still Happen', *Civil Wars*, 2012, 14(1), pp. 29–48 at 45.

[5] Ibid.

[6] George Orwell, 'Looking Back on the Spanish Civil War', 1942, made available by the Orwell Foundation at https://www.orwellfoundation.com/the-orwell-foundation/orwell/essays-and-other-works/looking-back-on-the-spanish-war/#:~:text=Everyone%20believes%20in%20the%20atrocities,bothering%20to%20examine%20the%20evidence.

[7] Ibid.

[8] Article 17 Rome statute of the International Criminal Court 1998.

Neither Benest nor Orwell would have been surprised that this is accepted wholeheartedly by the UK government, at least in so far as it relates to the crimes allegedly committed by other states. In the response to the current war in Ukraine, for instance, British ministers have been at the forefront of the call for war crimes investigations into the conduct of Russian forces. Following the direct targeting of civilians and non-military objects, the use of indiscriminate and prohibited weapons, crimes of sexual violence and general tactics of bombardment and siege, the United Kingdom has marshalled thirty-eight other countries to refer the situation to the Office of the Prosecutor (OTP) at the ICC in The Hague for investigation.[9] In June 2022, the attorney general also announced support for the Ukrainian Prosecutor General's Office and confirmed that she was

> determined that British expertise continues to be available to our friends in Ukraine in their search for justice. We will stand side by side as they uncover the truth and hold those responsible in Putin's regime to account for their actions.[10]

Police, legal and military experts have been provided to support these investigations.

The United Kingdom's staunch stand against war crimes committed in Ukraine, applying the principle that immediate and effective investigations of allegations lie at the heart of the ICC's commitment to end impunity for perpetrators, would undoubtedly have been approved by both Benest and Orwell. It reiterates contemporary international consensus that crimes of war are intolerable and those most responsible should be brought to account through some form of criminal justice process.

But how does this match the approach to those most recent and long-standing allegations in relation to British operations that Benest was at pains to reveal? Has the principle that credible evidence of war crimes should and will be pursued diligently at national and international level been fulfilled? Or is Orwell still right about political and public myopia when it comes to one's own crimes?

The ICC Chief Prosecutor's 2020 Final Report into alleged war crimes committed by British troops in Iraq between 2003 and 2009 might provide something of an answer.

---

[9] https://www.gov.uk/government/news/uk-leads-call-for-icc-to-investigate-russias-war-crimes.
[10] MoJ Press Release, 'UK Provides Lawyers and Police to Support ICC War Crimes Investigation', 6 June 2022, https://www.gov.uk/government/news/uk-provides-lawyers-and-police-to-support-icc-war-crimes-investigation.

The United Kingdom in Iraq, the ICC and the investigative conundrum

For some, the Prosecutor's Report brought an end to a long-standing scandal. After close to twenty years of accumulated accusations, state investigations, court proceedings and the OTP's own examination, the Chief Prosecutor, Fatou Bensouda, confirmed that claims of unlawful killing, rape, torture and ill-treatment in detention were credible and, in many cases, proven beyond reasonable doubt.

Numerous cases were referred to the ICC and of these the Chief Prosecutor's office found that there was 'a reasonable basis to believe that at least seven persons were the victims of unlawful killing constituting war crimes while in British custody between April and September 2003'.[11] It also found 'at least 54 victims of torture, inhuman and cruel treatment, outrages upon personal dignity and/or of rape and other forms of sexual violence were identified to the reasonable basis standard'.[12] But it only 'focussed on a sample pool of incidents which, while not reflecting the full scale of the alleged crimes relevant to the situation, were sufficiently well supported' to reach a conclusion on the facts.[13] Numerous out-of-court civil settlements, where compensation was paid in relation to credible claims of ill-treatment, also suggested there were many more breaches of the laws of war to be found. In the OTP's view, therefore, serious war crimes were committed by British personnel in the Iraq War and occupation. Notwithstanding the evidence, the Prosecutor acknowledged that all the UK investigations 'involving the examination of thousands of allegations, has resulted in not one single case being submitted for prosecution: a result that has deprived the victims of justice'.[14]

Despite these damning findings, the Chief Prosecutor felt unable to 'conclude that the UK authorities have been unwilling genuinely to carry out relevant investigative inquiries and/or prosecutions', or that it had shielded personnel from criminal responsibility.[15] After considering the history of investigative and prosecutorial processes adopted by the United Kingdom (prompted by numerous and lengthy judicial review proceedings that led to court rulings requiring human rights-compliant state investigations to be undertaken) and

[11] Office of the Prosecutor, International Criminal Court, 'Situation in Iraq/UK', 2020, para 2, https://www.icc-cpi.int/sites/default/files/itemsDocuments/201209-otp-final-report-iraq-uk-eng.pdf.
[12] Ibid., para 128.
[13] Ibid., para 129.
[14] Ibid., para 6.
[15] Ibid., para 502.

in a sequence of awkwardly phrased negative conclusions, she could not say that there had been 'unjustified delay in the proceedings' or that the United Kingdom's processes were not 'conducted independently or impartially' in a manner 'inconsistent with an intent to bring the person concerned to justice'.[16] On this basis there would be no further examination by the ICC.

That was the end of the matter.

But there is a serious problem here, one that Benest and Orwell would both have appreciated. Though the Prosecutor established that the 'initial response of the British Army in theatre at the time of the alleged offences was inadequate and vitiated by a lack of a genuine effort to carry out relevant investigations independently or impartially', this did not condemn the United Kingdom.[17] She accepted that the government's later attempts to rectify the investigative failings appeared genuine. Even though 'the dearth of forensic evidence and inconsistencies in witness testimony given the historical nature of the investigations, years after the events' seriously undermined these efforts, they were sufficient to forgive those failures.

Some have severely criticized the Prosecutor's decision for various political, legal and practical reasons.[18] Thomas Obel Hansen points out that the six years the Prosecutor took to decide that there should be no further examination in itself contributed to the delay in investigations into the truth of these allegations.[19] He identifies a central irony in the Prosecutor's complaint of the United Kingdom's delayed domestic proceedings while herself taking so long to reach her decision. Hansen argues that 'by setting the bar so high for what constitutes "unwillingness" [to investigate and prosecute international crimes], the Office effectively has created a blueprint for how resourceful states may avoid the opening of an ICC investigation'.[20] After first engaging in inadequate inquiries, simply construct a web of diverse and complex investigatory mechanisms, which will inevitably

---

[16] Ibid.

[17] Statement of the Prosecutor, Fatou Bensouda, on the conclusion of the preliminary examination of the situation in Iraq/United Kingdom para 4, https://www.icc-cpi.int/Pages/item.aspx?name=201209-otp-statement-iraq-uk.

[18] See, for instance, Kevin Jon Heller, 'The Nine Words that (Wrongly) Doomed the Iraq Investigation', *Opinio Juris*, December 2020, http://opiniojuris.org/2020/12/10/the-nine-words-that-wrongly-doomed-the-iraq-investigation/. This has led to a request by one of the parties to the 2012 referral to the ICC, the European Centre for Constitutional and Human Rights based in Berlin, for the Prosecutor to reconsider her findings. See European Centre for Constitutional and Human Rights July 2021, https://www.ecchr.eu/fileadmin/Juristische_Dokumente/20210701_ECCHR_Request_for_Review_ICC_Iraq-UK_Decision-FILED.pdf.

[19] Thomas Obel Hansen, 'The Multiple Aspects of "Time" Rendering Justice for War Crimes in Iraq', *International Criminal Law Review*, 2021, pp. 1–27.

[20] Ibid., p. 20.

delay action, and a state will be able to deflect international justice attention indefinitely, at least as far as the OTP is concerned.

It therefore looks as though the United Kingdom has succeeded in suppressing many serious allegations. And the Chief Prosecutor at the ICC is either unwilling, or prevented from, unpicking this institutional disregard for the commitment to 'uncover the truth' and hold those responsible to account. There would appear to be a tacit acceptance of Orwell's world-weary view.

Is this all that the law has to offer? Has the Iraq case shown the impotence of international criminal justice? And should we be surprised if so?

War crimes investigation and the failure of law

Cynically, we have come to expect that states will rarely examine their dirty secrets in public. Only the most naive will deny that national institutions, even in the most transparent of liberal democracies, have a psychological predilection towards secrecy that redoubles during times of military conflict. Governmental and military personnel worry about the consequences of uncovering the truth of scandals so that even if they don't actively cover up wrongdoing then they will tend to adopt strategies to ignore it, justify it or simply deflect attention away from it.

Stanley Cohen charted these familiar techniques some years ago.[21] He identified their different forms as including

> cognition (not acknowledging the facts); emotion (not feeling, not being disturbed); morality (not recognizing wrongness or responsibility) and action (not taking active steps in response to knowledge).[22]

All of these are recognizable in the UK government's approach to the Iraq allegations.[23] And all are essentially the product of epistemic failure. Without commitment to looking for the knowledge and understanding of what has happened in a situation (and making the findings public), any attempt to attribute responsibility to individuals or achieve some accountability for crimes of war will prove impossible. The primary response to war crimes then has to focus on the acquisition of that knowledge through proper investigation and analysis.

---

[21] Stan Cohen, *States of Denial: Knowing about Atrocities and Suffering* (Cambridge: Polity Press, 2001).
[22] Ibid., p. 9.
[23] See Andrew Williams, 'The Iraq Abuse Allegations and the Limits of UK Law', *Public Law*, July 2018, pp. 461–81.

International criminal law recognizes all this and has been at the forefront of trying to address it. The laws of war are premised on the notion that bad things happen in armed conflict but that the international community has an obligation to alleviate the inevitable human suffering and do something in response. Since Nuremberg, that has meant looking to establish individual responsibility for the most serious international crimes. In this respect, the laws of war are alive to the relationship between knowledge and doing criminal justice. Rule 158 of the International Committee of the Red Cross's (ICRC) rules of customary International Humanitarian Law (IHL) provides: 'States must investigate war crimes allegedly committed by their nationals or armed forces, or on their territory, and, if appropriate, prosecute the suspects.' Article 49 of Geneva Convention I imposes an obligation on states 'to search for persons alleged to have committed, or to have ordered to be committed, such grave breaches, and shall bring such persons, regardless of their nationality, before its own courts'.

The ICRC reinforces the importance of timely and effective investigation too. It has produced guidelines emphasizing the 'standards of independence and impartiality, thoroughness, promptness, and transparency that make up an effective investigation'.[24] Systemic as well as individual wrongs should be fully and properly examined as soon as reasonably practicable after they come to light. This is a state obligation, which should not be excused.

The UK government's approach to Ukraine and allegations of Russian war crimes reaffirms these commitments and for good reason. By ensuring that investigations are conducted immediately in theatre by experts, presuming rightly that Russian authorities will not carry out their own, the United Kingdom acknowledges the importance of the epistemic dimension to ending impunity through legal process. Without evidence properly obtained, linking crimes to individual perpetrators or systems of abuse, any later war crimes trial will be hard to pursue. And acquiring that evidence directly, using forensic technology, contemporaneous witness testimony and full and proper recording of all findings, is essential in that endeavour.

All of that is well and good. But the history of the Iraq allegations reveals failure to comply with these basic requirements without any effective response arising. The ICC Prosecutor found in her report that 'the initial measures taken by the British Army to investigate and prosecute alleged crimes in the midst and

---

[24] International Committee of the Red Cross, 'Guidelines on Investigating Violations of International Humanitarian Law: Law, Policy, and Good Practice', 2019, para 8, https://www.icrc.org/en/document /guidelines-investigating-violations-ihl-law-policy-and-good-practice.

immediate aftermath of the armed conflict fell short' of expected standards.[25] A similar conclusion was reached in various judicial review cases in the United Kingdom as well, starting with the case of Al Skeini.[26] But what is the sanction for failure to fulfil the investigatory obligations?

International criminal law offers some possibilities in theory. Based on the principles crafted to underpin the tribunals for crimes committed during the Second World War, courts have reiterated the concept of command responsibility and confirmed that this applies not only to the commission of offences but also to the failure to prosecute those responsible. Article 28 ICC Statute adopted the same requirement and applied it to military *and* civilian superiors. In both cases, failure to 'take all necessary and reasonable measures within his or her power to prevent or repress . . . the commission [of international crimes] or *to submit the matter to the competent authorities for investigation and prosecution*' [emphasis added] is an offence for which a commander can be prosecuted and punished through a criminal justice process.

The concept of command responsibility was introduced to capture those in positions of power who do not directly commit crimes of war but order or encourage others to do so (or tacitly approve of such crimes being committed after or before the event). In the case of Bagilishema before the International Criminal Tribunal for Rwanda in 2001, the court reaffirmed that the concept extended to a failure by superiors 'to prevent, suppress, or punish crimes committed by subordinates', which if proven would amount to a 'dereliction of duty that may invoke individual criminal responsibility'.[27]

Three elements of command responsibility have to be established for this to happen: effective control between the accused and the perpetrator of the crime; knowledge that the crime was 'about to be, was being, or had been committed'; and failure to 'take the necessary and reasonable measures to prevent or stop the crime, or to punish the perpetrator'.[28] But this offence is not a crime that relates to a whole military and political structure. It attaches to individuals only. There has to be a specific person identified who can be shown to have personally failed in their duty. And in order to establish that, you have to prove actual knowledge

[25] OTP n. 11 at para 494.
[26] Al-Skeini and Others v. the United Kingdom Application no. 55721/07 European Court of Human Rights Judgement, 7 July 2011.
[27] The Prosecutor v. Ignace Bagilishema (Trial Judgement), ICTR-95-1A-T, International Criminal Tribunal for Rwanda (ICTR), 7 June 2001, para 37, https://www.refworld.org/cases,ICTR,48abd5170 .html. Accessed: 4 August 2022.
[28] The Prosecutor v. Ignace Bagilishema (Trial Judgement), ICTR-95-1A-T, International Criminal Tribunal for Rwanda (ICTR), 7 June 2001, para 38, https://www.refworld.org/cases,ICTR,48abd5170 .html. Accessed: 4 August 2022.

of the crimes or that the individual had enough information to warrant further investigation. When it comes to the obligation to punish perpetrators, command responsibility applies if there is a personal 'failure to create or sustain among the persons under [that person's] control, an environment of discipline and respect for the law'.[29]

In the most egregious cases (as in Nazi Germany or under dictatorships), this may be fairly easy to prove. Lawlessness is already deemed a hallmark of the system and those operating within it already blameworthy simply by being willing members of that system. In otherwise functioning modern democracies, however, it becomes significantly harder, if not impossible, at least as regards those in government. In the matter of the Iraq allegations, any commander could legitimately rely upon the existence of established investigatory and prosecutorial systems as evidence that there was not an environment of indiscipline for which they could be held responsible. The fact that the system didn't operate effectively in certain cases is a reason to review the system, but it's hard to see how personal command responsibility for that failure could be established. Some individual military commanders close to the perpetration of any crimes might still be brought to account, but reaching any further up the command chain would be immensely difficult given the elements that would have to be proven beyond reasonable doubt.[30]

This is a central conundrum. If the investigatory systems are in place but not functioning as they should, how can you look for command responsibility for crimes committed when those systems do not even uncover the crimes in the first place? And even if the crimes eventually come to light, who will then investigate the failures of investigation? Those in positions of power might be condemned for failing to invest in creating efficient and effective investigatory structures, but that is not a crime in itself as things stand. Without a 'smoking gun' – some direct evidence of an order to cover up a known crime – the likelihood of proving culpability for overseeing a faulty investigatory body is non-existent in any liberal democracy.

All of this was recognized by the ICC Prosecutor's report on Iraq. Specifically, as regards systemic practices of ill-treatment of detainees (using long-banned techniques of hooding, stress positions, deprivation of sleep and physical and verbal abuse prior to interrogation), the report confirmed that 'several levels of

---

[29] Ibid., para 50.
[30] Lt Col Jorge Mendonca was prosecuted for neglect of duty but not command responsibility in relation to the killing of Baha Mousa, the most prominent victim of ill-treatment and unlawful killing in the Iraq conflict.

institutional civilian supervisory and military command failures contributed to the commission of crimes against detainees by UK soldiers in Iraq'.[31] It went on to confirm that 'the MoD and the UK Government appear to have failed to guard against the gradual erosion of doctrine and practice with respect to the treatment of detainees over the course of several decades' and that this 'collective failure is of extreme gravity in terms of its consequences for the treatment of civilians in conflict'.[32] But no one who was to blame could be identified. All the Prosecutor could do was recommend that these findings 'should continue to trigger deep institutional reflection'.[33] That will rarely satisfy those victims of the crimes committed or those intent on ending impunity for those responsible for atrocities.

The Prosecutor did spend time on reviewing the evidence of cover-up too. She examined the allegation that investigators employed to rectify the failures of the original investigations were prevented from carrying out their duties effectively. But she was not able 'to substantiate, with evidence that it could rely upon in court' that particular lines of inquiry were blocked 'or that viable cases with a realistic prospect of conviction were inappropriately abandoned'.[34] And, indeed, how could a concerted institutional belief that all allegations were false (after Orwell) and a general unwillingness to look for fault (after Benest) ever be pinned on any particular individual?

If anything, the ICC Prosecutor's examination established the basis for which any democratic state might avoid criminal responsibility for war crimes. It showed itself to be impotent when it came to those subtle means by which scrutiny of allegations can be deflected by disinterested domestic institutions. Looking to international criminal law and its institutions, like the ICC, therefore, seems futile except in the most obvious and egregious of cases. And these are unlikely to be found in modern democracies that generally support the idea of treating war crimes as intolerable.

So if the law offers no solution, then what can be done?

Resolving the conundrum?

Three possibilities present themselves. The first might be somewhat unrealistic: decouple the relationship between government and military so that the former

[31] OTP n. 11 at para 371.
[32] Ibid.
[33] Ibid.
[34] Ibid., para 409.

ensures full and proper scrutiny and democratic control of the armed forces. This would include establishing processes designed to respond specifically to allegations of war crimes as they arise without relying on the military to police itself.

Something analogous occurred with the police force in the United Kingdom, in so far as the need for an independent police complaints process was recognized and acted upon by government once high-profile cases of police misconduct became public. In essence, there was deep suspicion that the police would look into its own failings when infamous cases such as the Guildford Four, Hillsborough and Stephen Lawrence showed how public trust had begun to evaporate. But any similar efforts as regards the military would most likely go against all current political rhetoric in the United Kingdom. One of the certainties in political life at the moment is that any criticism of the military will provoke deep condemnation by the media. The Armed Forces Covenant has also gone some way to turn this rhetoric into a quasi-legal duty. Its terms state that the armed forces 'deserve our respect and support' whatever views we may have regarding the use of force in any situation or, indeed, whatever the military may do. 'Recognising those who have performed military duty', it continues, 'unites the country and demonstrates the value of their contribution.' The obligation applies to the 'whole of society' and has no caveat.[35] The presumption is that the military will at all times act properly. And if some armed forces personnel commit crimes, then the military can be expected to rectify the matter itself through the Royal Military Police despite questions over its independence. It is very hard to see any government changing this *status quo* so that suspicion enters the relationship rather than unqualified support.

A second more feasible option would be the establishment of a wholly new and independent investigatory body without attaching this to a new civil-military relationship. Much like the current Independent Office for Police Conduct, which can investigate complaints against police officers either by referral from particular police forces or on its own initiative, such a body could operate as an independent investigator when allegations of war crimes are made.[36] Although there exists a complex system of internal military complaints review bodies (from a Service Police Complaints Commissioner to the Service Complaints Ombudsman), these are designed to protect serving personnel from

---

[35] The Armed Forces Covenant, https://assets.publishing.service.gov.uk/government/uploads/system/uploads/attachment_data/file/578212/20161215-The-Armed-Forces-Covenant.pdf.
[36] The Policing and Crime Act 2017 reformed the whole edifice of police complaints.

ill-treatment of whatever kind, but particularly sexual and racial abuse, by their own side.[37]

Nonetheless, the principle of fully independent investigation could be extended to the clearly controversial issue of war crimes. Creating an independent, specialist and expert body to step in whenever crimes of war allegations are made could establish greater confidence that such matters would be taken seriously. At present, reliance is placed on the military to conduct such work without interference. But the Iraq allegations suggest that this system does not operate properly and has been subject to immense political interference. Fundamental reform to delink military command from investigations might overcome these failings in the future.[38] Again, however, the political climate that sees threat and danger in the world and maintaining security as the primary responsibility of government would not encourage the investment of time and public resources to create such a body. It seems unlikely to be a priority for government action of whatever political persuasion.

The third possibility is for the armed forces leadership themselves to assume responsibility for military conduct whatever the current political environment. This is where David Benest may well have been right. In the absence of established, independent and reliable institutions designed to address the issue of the crimes of war in a way that is effective and impartial, we are left with relying on the integrity of the officer corps to do the right thing. Many would argue that this is the most trusted first-line method for ensuring adherence to standards of conduct in warfare in any case. Undoubtedly, there is reason to presume that the general good sense and moral compass of British officers is a feature of the armed forces and that senior officers generally agree. There's reason to believe there is antipathy towards the commission of war crimes if only to distinguish 'us' from those who pay no regard to internationally accepted standards. But at an individual level, officers will always feel a conflict between protecting those under their command and enforcing legal and moral codes. Internal prosecution for war crimes reflects as much on the unit as the individual. That can make it difficult for a commander who has striven to establish a camaraderie that binds a group of troops into an effective fighting force. Should anyone commit an awful

---

[37] A good guide to how these all interlink, see Centre for Military Justice guide, https://centreformilita ryjustice.org.uk/guide/service-complaints/.

[38] I set out some of the possible requirements for such an institution elsewhere in Andrew Williams, 'War Crimes Allegations and the UK: Towards a Fairer Investigative Process', *Legal Studies*, 2020, 40, pp. 301–20.

crime, the whole unit might feel responsible, making its exposure significantly more complex.

Even if trust that those in military command will act properly and quickly when faced by allegations, Benest's worry was that the training and management of military personnel was failing to reinforce long-lauded attributes of a commanding officer at whatever level. Perhaps because of the nature of modern conflict, often asymmetrical and against irregular forces who rarely recognize international humanitarian law, the idea of fighting cleanly is tested to the limit. Royal Marine Alexander Blackman's killing of a wounded Taliban fighter accompanied by the words, 'it's nothing you wouldn't do to us' merely reflected the general experience of conflict in Afghanistan.[39] Equally in Iraq, a more casual acceptance of the abuse of detainees was identified by the Baha Mousa Inquiry (see Chapter 1), for instance. That Inquiry made recommendations for better training in the laws of war and there have been assertions that these have been implemented. However, Elizabeth Stubbins Bates's studies on these changes cast doubt that this is happening given the government's determination to close down all the inquiries into the Iraq allegations and pursue internal inquiries into recent allegations of past unlawful killing in Afghanistan.[40] She notes that the United Kingdom's practice of investigation into alleged war crimes in recent years has reinforced the narrative that scrutiny may not be required. By relying on a European Court of Human Rights ruling on the right to life that investigations may be avoided where they would 'impose an impossible or disproportionate burden on the authorities', the state has justified closing military police inquiries.[41] Stubbins Bates has demonstrated in great detail how this principle has been applied liberally by the British authorities in relation to Iraq War allegations.[42] '[N]arrowing the investigatory obligation in practice', as she puts it, not only erases the prospect of bringing those responsible for crimes of war to justice but also avoids deeper scrutiny as to any patterns and cultures of unlawful violence that might otherwise be detected.

The fact that the military had allowed training to become, or continue to be, deficient to such an extent that troops, including officers, were unaware of what was right and wrong suggests that the problem had permeated all levels

---

[39] The video of the incident was released to the media by the Ministry of Defence in 2017 and can be found at https://www.theguardian.com/uk-news/video/2017/feb/02/moment-marine-shoots-dead -wounded-taliban-fighter-video.

[40] Elizabeth Stubbins Bates, 'The British Army's Training in International Humanitarian Law', *Journal of Conflict & Security Law*, 2020, pp. 1–25.

[41] *Osman v United Kingdom* (1998) 29 E. H. R. R. 245 at [116].

[42] Elizabeth Stubbins Bates, '"Impossible or Disproportionate Burden": The UK's Approach to the Investigatory Obligation under Articles 2 and 3 ECHR', *E. H. R. L. R.*, 2020, 5, pp. 499–511.

of command. If that is right, then simply introducing new improved training courses will change little unless accompanied by a system that reinforces the commitment to meeting the norms of the laws of war through prosecution. There is real doubt, therefore, that the whole investigatory and prosecutorial system will allow any military command-led determination to apply a public zero-tolerance approach to allegations of war crimes to succeed. The political nature of the MOD, which oversees these functions, seems preconditioned to adopt one or other of Stanley Cohen's strategies of denial mentioned previously.

It is important to add also that none of the previous suggestions will address historic wrongs. David Benest's work showed how past crimes could not and should not be forgotten and still induced pain and suffering in the victims, if only because of the lack of acknowledgement of wrongdoing and the lack of institutional and personal accountability. Many conflicts fall into this category, as Benest noted, from Kenya to Northern Ireland and Iraq to Afghanistan. Changes in the training regime and commitment to investigation and prosecution may help for future allegations, but they will not resolve these persisting claims. Ethical leadership has not shown itself when considering past crimes. We will therefore have to wait for a change in political and public understanding before the truth of these enduring allegations can be uncovered. Until then, investigative journalism may reveal significant concerns (witness the latest BBC revelations about SAS killings in Afghanistan), but it is unlikely to provoke meaningful accountability.[43]

We can hope that it does not take so long for justice to be done in relation to the conduct of Russian forces in Ukraine.

---

[43] See BBC Panorama investigation into repeated killings by an SAS unit in Afghanistan, https://www.bbc.co.uk/news/uk-62083196.

5

From forgetting to institutional failure

The army as a non-learning organization

Matthew Ford

Since the end of the Cold War, Britain's armed forces have gone from victory against the IRA (Irish Republican Army) to defeat in Iraq and Afghanistan. Over that time, the British Army undertook activities that governments had outlawed but neglected to implement tactics, techniques and procedures that might save soldiers' lives. As David Benest observes, for example, in 1972 the then prime minister Sir Edward Heath banned the armed forces from using the five torture techniques. By 2003, however, the army was employing these techniques on Baha Mousa, an Iraqi citizen.[1] Even as reprehensible interrogation methods were being employed in Basra, 'the collective experience of the army of dealing with the Improvised Explosive Device (IED) threat had wasted out during the long period of ceasefire in Northern Ireland'.[2] On the face of it, the army appeared able to remember what it had been told to unlearn but had forgotten how to defend itself from Iraqi insurgent bombmakers. By themselves these anecdotes do not explain the institutional failings of 'the best little army in the world'.[3] Nevertheless, they do invite us to reconsider what it is for a military organization to remember and forget in the context of war and defeat.

One way to explain how an army reproduces understanding and circulates important knowledge is by studying how it trains, institutionalizes the identification and dissemination of lessons and writes this learning into doctrine. One of the most prominent exponents of this approach to organizational

---

[1] David Benest, 'A Liberal Democratic State and COIN: The Case of Britain, or Why Atrocities Can Still Happen', *Civil Wars*, 2012, 14(1), pp. 29–48.
[2] Official report of the Iraq inquiry. Evidence given on 14 December 2009. Official website of the Iraq Inquiry: http://www.iraqinquiry.org.uk/media/236689/2009-12-14-transcript-riley-wall-s2.pdf.
[3] Simon Akam, *The Changing of the Guard – the British Army since 9/11* (London: Scribe Publications, 2021), p. 19.

learning is retired Lieutenant Colonel Dr John Nagl. Instrumental in helping the US Army rewrite its counter-insurgency doctrine during the Iraq War, for Nagl the learning cycle is based on the work of Richard Downie and has six key steps.[4] The initial phases of this process involve some kind of data collection from the battlefield and a recognition that something has not worked out as well as it might. After this, the process moves towards the identification of a performance gap, then recognizes the need for and agrees on an alternative solution and then finally disseminates a solution through doctrine and changed behaviour within the military.[5]

Developing historical arguments along lines that Nagl would recognize, a number of scholars have argued that armed forces that incorporate what they have learnt and adapt more quickly than their enemies stand a chance of winning in war.[6] However, whereas Nagl explores learning as an explicit process, a number of historical studies have shown how this works informally outside the official channels that an army might put in place to share best practice.[7] More recently, researchers have sought to explain institutional memory within NATO as an exercise that depends on interpersonal communication, private documentation and crisis simulations.[8]

Much of the informal process of sharing tacit knowledge depends on maintaining personal networks. In these contexts, people within the military institution are prepared to reveal 'what really happened' to those colleagues they have grown to trust. They do this knowing that individuals are not exposed to explaining themselves in ways that are detrimental to career advancement. The implications of this are threefold. First, there is a shadow process of sharing knowledge that is not subject to organizational oversight. Second, this sets the conditions for establishing informal patronage networks that shape how military officers are promoted. Finally, the capacity to implement lessons over the long haul depends on sustaining these personal networks for considerable time and in a context where individual memory is reproduced in subjective ways.

---

[4] Richard Downie, *Learning from Conflict: The US Military in Vietnam, El Salvador and the Drug War* (Westport: Praeger, 1998).

[5] John Nagl, *Learning to Eat Soup with a Knife: Counterinsurgency Lessons from Malaya to Vietnam* (Chicago: The University of Chicago Press, 2005).

[6] Gary Sheffield, *Forgotten Victory: The First World War: Myths and Realities* (London: Headline, 2001); Jonathan Boff, *Haig's Enemy: Crown Prince Ruprecht and Germany's War on the Western Front* (Oxford: Oxford University Press, 2018).

[7] Aimee Fox, *Learning to Fight: Military Innovation and Change in the British Army, 1914–1918* (Cambridge: Cambridge University Press, 2019).

[8] H. Hardt, 'How NATO Remembers: Explaining Institutional Memory in NATO Crisis Management', *European Security*, 2017, 26(1), pp. 120–48.

In this respect, individual memory is never settled but always in a constant state of being remade. As such it is active: a site of consciousness that 'is an imaginative reconstruction, or construction, built out of the relation of our attitude towards a whole active mass of organised past reactions or experience'.[9] Remembering is dynamic, imaginative and, counter-intuitively, an essential aspect of what it means to live in the present. As such, memory is always new and continually emergent, shaped by what is going on around us.

Bearing this in mind, memories are constantly in flux and changing according to context and need. Memory isn't truth and memory decay has real institutional outcomes. Indeed, during the Iraq War Inquiry, Adjutant General Lieutenant General Sir Alistair Irwin observed that

> in respect of an institution, the only lessons that are learned and put into effect are the ones that are put into effect immediately, because the nature of an institution, with the individuals in it passing in and out and changing jobs and so on, is that unless the lesson is applied immediately, it will never be remembered. That's one of the real difficulties about lessons learned.[10]

From a military point of view, the point at which memory as tacit knowledge becomes explicit institutional practice needs clear articulation if armed forces are to sustain their learning in ways that translate into battlefield advantage. Yet, the one variable that regularly appears to be left out of this equation is that which locates individual memory in its proper organizational context. Specifically, this is where institutional archive practices, branch politics and personal advancement shape what stories can be recalled and what becomes taboo.

In this short chapter, I intend to recentre the politics of memory into the story of institutional learning. I will do this, first, by examining the structural constraints on developing an appreciation of a military campaign both in terms of collating materials and in contextualizing it in the light of defeat or controversy. I will then relate the structural challenges associated with writing formal lessons learnt to Paul Connerton's seminal paper, 'Seven types of forgetting'.[11] This draws on the defeats in Iraq and Afghanistan and their implications for the army as it has come to terms with its role in British society over the past decade.

---

[9] F. C. Bartlett, *Remembering: A Study in Experimental and Social Psychology* (Cambridge: Cambridge University Press, 1932). See also S. Brown and A. Hoskins, 'Terrorism in the New Memory Ecology: Mediating and Remembering the 2005 London Bombings', *Behavioral Sciences of Terrorism and Political Aggression*, 2010, 2(2), pp. 87–107.

[10] Official report of the Iraq Inquiry. Evidence given on 21 July 2010, https://webarchive.nationalarchives.gov.uk/ukgwa/20170831105243/http://www.iraqinquiry.org.uk/media/95382/2010-07-21-Transcript-Irwin-Palmer-S3.pdf?d=2010-07-21.

[11] Paul Connerton, 'Seven Types of Forgetting', *Memory Studies*, (2008) 1/1, pp. 59–71.

The politics of institutional memory

The learning or failing to learn military lessons in an institutionally sanctioned form is made visible through the publication of official history (OH), the principal function of which is to provide a sober, well-researched text that lays out the official version of events and acts as the point of departure for academic discussion going forward. Any interpretation and critique of events must be based upon high-quality evidence and be balanced and objective. Securing that objectivity is difficult but important because it constitutes an opportunity for a government department or a sub-branch of the armed forces to come to a formally agreed position on its role in a particular set of events and to set a baseline for change at an institutional level. Consequently, OH demands a greater deal of scrutiny, objectivity and balance than might be found in those modes of organizational learning that demand faster cycle times and are typically associated with military adaptation.[12]

Institutional learning at this level was partly made possible by the way that archives were released to the public. In Britain, these used to be subject to the thirty-year and now the twenty-year rule. Effectively, the length of time before historians had a chance to examine official records gave more opportunity for public officials to reconcile themselves to events. In the twentieth century, this put a premium on the relationship between the paper archive and recorded media. Successive waves of digitalization, however, have disrupted the capacity of government – indeed, as Michael Weatherburn shows, in fact everyone with a digital presence – to keep proper digital records. According to Weatherburn, this constitutes 'memory decay'.[13] As a result, settled narratives based on older archival practices have created a sedimented historical perspective. This unhelpfully frames contemporary archival practices where vast quantities of data are lost, misplaced or destroyed when people leave an organization.

Within the contemporary military, where everything is digitized and officers are changing jobs every two years, institutional memory is in constant flux, not just as a result of the fragile nature of memory but also because of the structural challenges posed by the organization itself. Information technology (IT) systems

---

[12] Good examples of the literature on military adaptation include Theo Farrell, 'Improving in War: Military Adaptation and the British in Helmand Province, Afghanistan, 2006-2009', *Journal of Strategic Studies*, 2010, 33(4), pp. 567–94; Sergio Catignani, '"Getting COIN" at the Tactical Level in Afghanistan: Reassessing Counter-insurgency Adaptation in the British Army', *Journal of Strategic Studies*, 2012, 35(4), pp. 513–39.

[13] See Dr Michael Weatherburn, *Project Hindsight*. For more, see https://projecthindsight.co.uk/current-projects/.

must be set up to reflect the demands of static headquarters at home and the ever-changing requirements of those units in the field. During operations, data has to be captured by archivists before a hard drive is repurposed. At the same time, the rotation of personnel as part of a career cycle designed to create resilience undermines institutional memory. This is evidenced in the £5.5 billion investment by the British Army in the replacement for the Warrior Armoured Fighting Vehicle. The fact that the MOD (Ministry of Defence) is in dispute with General Dynamics over vehicle requirements implies that somewhere during the long procurement process, there has been system failure connected to memory decay.[14]

Even without the contemporary challenge created by officer rotation and maintaining a digital archive, OH as a process of learning takes a considerable amount of effort to produce. This is because it must be both balanced and designed to help drive change within and across a department of state or a military sub-branch. One particular hurdle relates to the relationship between the author of the OH and those who are being observed. Typically, OH authors have 'had access to classified official documents and to a variety of authoritative persons, have had financial or other support, and that in many cases they have written from within an official office'.[15] At the same time, however, the proximity to the source material and its sponsors opens up the possibility that they lack sufficient independence to be capable of composing a publication that has the meaningful capacity to produce change.

As Higham notes, this reflects deeper challenges for these authors and reflects the paradox of OH, which he argues is 'in itself a contradiction in terms'.[16] From the military's standpoint, OHs are not intended as independent or objective but as offering a perspective weighted towards the specific records set being used and the privileged access being afforded to them. This is further limited by the military's willingness to sanction an official account that could damage its work or its reputation. In this context, OH represents a negotiation between the ambition to write a balanced history based on an expert and objective use of sources and the immediate demands of the organization to protect itself from unhelpful scrutiny.

---

[14] Tom Cotterill, 'Is the "Disastrous" £5.5billion British Army Ajax Tank Now Set for the Scrap-Head?', *The Daily Mail Online*, 17 October 2022, https://www.dailymail.co.uk/news/article-11323383/Is -British-Armys-disastrous-5-5bn-Ajax-tank-destined-scrapyard-coming-service.html.

[15] Higham R. D. S., ed., *Official Histories: Essays and Bibliographies from Around the World*, Kansas State University Library Bibliography Series (Manhattan: Kansas State University Library, 1970), p. 1.

[16] Ibid., p. 1.

To this end, one common, if informal, strategy for attaining greater objectivity involves sharing key draft passages for comment with participants in the events being documented, thereby facilitating a more negotiated account, although this may not be evident in the final product. In this respect, there is precedent. For example, Brigadier General C. F. Aspinall-Oglander's *History of the Great War: Military Operations Gallipoli (Vol.II) May 1915 to the Evacuation* published in 1932 was 'based on official documents by direction of the Historical Section Committee of Imperial Defence'.[17] A letter from Major General Sir John Duncan (also serving in the British Army in Gallipoli) to General Aspinall-Oglander dated 15 February 1931 (recently discovered by HB (A)) comments on a full draft of this manuscript, recommending a series of changes to the text (including some based on his own memories of events of the day). In this instance, General Duncan writes: 'In discussing the operations you have naturally found it necessary to criticise individuals. I agree with most of your remarks, but it is to me questionable whether it is wise to be quite as frank as you have been.' He continues: 'I think I would omit such a sweeping statement as "there can be little doubt that the situation was aggravated by a total absence of higher leadership". There is sufficient in the remainder of the para to indicate this without stating it so brutally and frankly.' This sentence (along with numerous others identified by General Duncan) did not make their way into the published official history. However, it clearly points to the way in which the military themselves seek to moderate OH and demonstrates the limitations of this form of publication.

Self-censorship is not new in the context of career advancement and reputation management. Tracking its trajectory is rendered more complex, however, in an environment framed by digital memory decay. Thus, as John Spencer observes:

> for those wars with no living veterans – whether the American Revolution or World War I – we can remember. We can access digital archives of battlefield maps. We can examine lists online of personnel who fought in each battle. We can read orders from commanders, or personal diaries, journals and letters sent by soldiers to their loved ones. Unfortunately, our recent conflicts will be difficult to remember in this way.[18]

In these circumstances, the politics of institutional memory has to be understood in relation to how armed forces manage their information infrastructure and

---

[17] C. F. Aspinall-Oglander, *History of the Great War: Military Operations Gallipoli (Vol.II) May 1915 to the Evacuation* (London: William Heinemann, 1932), p. 127.
[18] John Spencer, 'How the Military is Making it Hard to Remember Our Wars', *The Washington Post*, 10 November 2017.

maintain and sustain archives in circumstances where online and accidental archives are being built everyday by the public as they keep track of what the armed forces are actually doing.

The politics of institutional forgetting

If trying to remember has a politics, then so does trying to forget. From an institutional perspective, remembering is expressed in OH and the commemoration of the war dead. Remembering and forgetting, by contrast, have a wider social function for society as it come to terms with the violent rupture that is war. Defining this process as a 'memory boom', Jay Winter notes how different generations relate to this process in different ways at different moments in time.[19] In the hyperconnected environments of the twenty-first century, this has framed how the wars in Iraq and Afghanistan have been commemorated in real time even as they are being fought. Commemoration in this respect has escaped the top-down direction by the state and instead has taken on a more organic social direction. These churning campaign narratives in turn shape the politics of institutional forgetting.

Connerton's typography of forgetting[20] can help us to contextualize the process of institutional memory as it relates to the armed forces in times of war and defeat. For Connerton, 'repressive erasure' can be deployed to deny the fact of a historical rupture and to make a clean break with the past. 'Prescriptive forgetting', by contrast, recognizes that it is in the interests of all parties to collectively forget. In 'forgetting that is constitutive in the formation of a new identity', the goal is to forget in an effort to create newly shared memories from which renewal and collective change generate new community. 'Structural amnesia' is built around forgetting those aspects of the past that are otherwise considered socially unimportant. What is agreed to be important is remembered and the rest is quietly forgotten. 'Forgetting as annulment' emerges from a 'surfeit of information'.[21] 'Forgetting as planned obsolescence' emerges as a result of the process of economic change and mass consumption. One product replaces another and the memory of the old is lost. Finally, 'humiliated silence'

---

[19] Jay Winter, *War Beyond Words: Languages of Remembrance from the Great War to the Present* (Cambridge: Cambridge University Press, 2017).
[20] Connerton, 'Seven Types of Forgetting', pp. 59–71.
[21] Ibid., p. 64.

is 'covert, unmarked and unacknowledged' but is, nonetheless, and somewhat paradoxically, well known because the humiliation is so difficult to forget.[22]

Several of these types of forgetting have direct application to the way armed forces make sense of their experience of war and are particularly salient in relation to defeat. In this respect, two recent books on the wars in Iraq and Afghanistan serve to illustrate the utility of Connerton's ideas. While Britain's soldiers could demonstrate their capacity to adapt under difficult conditions, they still could not deliver campaign success. In *The Changing of the Guard* by Simon Akam and *Blood, Metal and Dust* by Ben Barry we have two alternative explanations for these failures.[23] One accuses the army of indolence, arrogance and unjustified overconfidence, the second of systemic failings in strategy-making, political direction and the challenge of working within an alliance structure. Both offer excoriating analyses of a defeated army muddling through.

They are interesting for different reasons. Akam is a journalist and one-time British Army Short Service (Limited) Commission who looks at the Army as a 'total institution'.[24] By contrast, Ben Barry is a retired brigadier responsible for writing a critical internal review of British land operations in Iraq in 2010 in a document that stood as a testament to the army's 'willingness to learn hard lessons'.[25] Barry's ambition was to help the army drive change and deliver future success. Akam was concerned with exploring the soldier's experience of war in Iraq and Afghanistan. The implication in Barry's analysis is that the military could have prevailed if British politicians had thought strategically and used their influence to shape American policy and decisions. For Akam, the army struggled because the Chief of the General Staff had decided to recommend that the United Kingdom break its central defence planning assumption and get involved in two wars at the same time.[26] Boiled down, Barry argues that the military did everything it could but the politicians failed. For Akam, the generals were overly focused on institutional self-preservation and were prepared to put options to politicians that defied military logic.

Published in 2021, both these books came out before the official record set was released to The National Archive (TNA). Without immediate access to the archive, Akam and Barry have relied on material made available as a result of the

---

[22] Ibid., p. 67.

[23] Akam, *The Changing of the Guard*; Ben Barry, *Blood, Metal and Dust – How Victory Turned into Defeat in Afghanistan and Iraq* (Oxford: Osprey Publishing, 2021).

[24] Akam, *The Changing of the Guard*, p. 46.

[25] Letter from Army Secretariat to Brigadier Ben Barry, 8 September 2016. Released under a Freedom of Information Request, FOI2016/07003/77396.

[26] Akam, *The Changing of the Guard*, p. 245.

Iraq War Enquiry – an enquiry into Britain's decision to go to war in Iraq – and interviews with officers and men. Barry had the advantage of being a former insider who worked on the lessons of the invasion of Iraq and could talk to senior officers involved in decision-making. Akam drew on 260 interviews with officers and men of various ranks. Both had to rely on a limited record set and on the vagaries of individual memory. There is nothing especially new about their methodology, but what makes both books especially interesting is that, while they agree that the army was defeated in Iraq and Afghanistan, they have radically different interpretations as to why this occurred.

Akam and Barry's respective conclusions clearly reflect the evidence set available to them. Equally, the politics of their analyses is latent but, nonetheless, demands further exploration. This is especially the case as their views will shape future interpretations of the wars in Iraq and Afghanistan and ought, therefore, to be recontextualized in light of Connerton's seven types of forgetting. For example, the different patterns of what is considered relevant and thus remembered reflects the different standings of Akam and Barry. Akam held a low-ranking commission for a short period of time. Barry rose to brigadier. For Connerton, the patterns of what might be remembered reflect what he describes as structural amnesia where a person remembers only 'those links in his or her pedigree that are socially important'.[27] By contrast, where individuals have underperformed, or an aspect of the campaign might be contentious or loaded with ambiguous outcomes with implications for unit conduct, then another form of forgetting might explain away the memory hole.

The British government's post-Iraq War effort to restrict the chance for public interest lawyers like Phil Shiner to prosecute the MOD for breaking international laws of armed conflict is an example of how future memory might be controlled.[28] Equally, the public campaign to exonerate Sergeant Blackman from committing a war crime is both about justice for Blackman and designed to prevent the besmirching of the armed forces more widely. Connerton might describe this political move as repressive erasure where the ambition is to deny the recovery of facts that implied British soldiers were engaged in illegal activity. In this respect, this closing down of discussion is prescriptive in nature. It is in the social interests of both soldiers and government to limit the possibility of remembering historically awkward activity even as there are aggrieved social groups who must recover these narratives if justice is ever to be carried out. In

---

[27] Connerton, 'Seven Types of Forgetting', p. 64.
[28] Akam, *The Changing of the Guard*, p. 508.

this context, then, it becomes easier to see why Akam's book received such a hostile reaction from those who viewed it as 'unjust and untruthful', preferring instead to try and control the narrative about how the army was represented.[29]

By contrast, Ben Barry's analysis of the wars in Iraq and Afghanistan has a particular political goal: to improve the effectiveness of the army. Inevitably, then, *Blood, Metal and Dust* is also part of an effort to help the army 'move on' and forge a new post-war identity. In this new institution, the lessons have been identified and are already being learnt. This is Connerton's 'forgetting that is constitutive in the formation of a new identity'. Barry's diagnoses of the reasons for campaign failure are designed to cast a shadow on aspects of decision-making that the army itself could not control and on politicians or parts of the MOD that he believes to be sclerotic. For Barry, in its failure to increase armoured protection in the face of sustained attack by IEDs, the bureaucracy 'seemed to demonstrate a lack of commitment to the war in Iraq'.[30] The core processes, values and outlook of the army are sound whereas those around it need to embrace change. This process of apportioning blame brings renewal and an opportunity to overlook an inconvenient alternative framing of events.

That these arguments over memory and forgetting produce serious and real-life outcomes is evidenced in the way that the army had forgotten how to manage IED threats even as it had remembered how to engage in torture. To blame professional military education for this shortcoming, as Barry proceeds to do in *Blood, Metal and Dust*, nonetheless ignores the political challenges facing the Army in decades past.[31] In the 1990s the key issues facing the British Army related to maintaining international peace and security in the face of civil war in Somalia and genocide in Yugoslavia and Rwanda. As Barry notes, the Army had produced two soldier scholars specializing in counter-insurgency in the form of Sir Robert Thompson and Sir Frank Kitson and was well steeped in low-intensity warfare. Nevertheless, if the staff colleges had been teaching Kitson or Thompson, they would have been confronted with a curriculum very much skewed towards a particular narrative that emphasized 'minimum force' and 'hearts and minds' over an 'iron fist'. Only since 2001 have authors such

---

[29] Jamie Doward, 'In No Man's Land: Anger as Publisher Puts Book Criticizing Army on Hold', *The Observer*, 18 August 2019, https://www.theguardian.com/books/2019/aug/18/writer-aghast-publisher-halts-history-of-british-army-book. A follow up story appeared after *The Changing of the Guard was* published. See Sian Cain, '"A Terrifying Precedent": Author Describes Struggle to Publish British Army History', *The Guardian*, 23 July 2021, https://www.theguardian.com/books/2021/jul/23/author-describes-struggle-to-publish-army-history-simon-akam-the-changing-of-the-guard. Accessed: 1 December 2022.

[30] Barry, *Blood, Metal and Dust*, p. 445.

[31] Ibid., p. 404.

as Caroline Elkins, David Anderson, Matthew Hughes, Karl Hack and Huw Bennett started to paint a picture that also acknowledges the place of atrocity, torture and illegal killing in post-war British military actions in Kenya, Palestine and Malaya.[32] That these inconvenient truths had been left out of the story of British low-intensity operations has a political connotation and is itself an indication that the armed forces often prefer to stay silent and avoid confronting such taboos.

Conclusion

That a military institution might prefer to leave out difficult aspects of its past from its history might not be a surprise. Yet, confronting the pain that comes from humiliation, defeat and social taboo makes it easier to challenge behaviour and attitudes that otherwise prevent an organization from embracing change. Relating Connerton's seven types of forgetting to the history of Britain's armed forces is not to excuse any institutional failings. Rather, it is to explain why organizations sometimes say they have moved on when in reality they have simply and quietly forgotten those aspects of their past that might prove to be unhelpful through institutionalizing corporate memory, both formally and informally. The politics of forgetting smudge out the difficult for want of sustaining personal reputation and limiting the damage to the social standing of the armed forces. In my experience, David Benest was willing to confront such awkward silences and ask the questions that needed to be asked. This is one of many reasons why I was very grateful to have known him.

---

[32] Caroline Elkins, *Britain's Gulag – The Brutal End of Empire in Kenya* (London: Pimlico, 2005); David Anderson, *Histories of the Hanged: The Dirty War in Kenya and the End of Empire* (New York: W.W. Norton, 2005); Matthew Hughes, *Britain's Pacification of Palestine: The British Army, the Colonial State, and the Arab Revolt, 1936–1939* (Cambridge: Cambridge University Press, 2019); Huw Bennett, *Fighting the Mau Mau: The British Army and Counter-Insurgency in the Kenya Emergency* (Cambridge: Cambridge University Press, 2012); Karl Hack, *Defense and Decolonization in Southeast Asia: Britain, Malaya and Singapore, 1941–68* (Richmond: Curzon, 2001).

6

Accountability, responsibility and culpability

Are British senior officers truly 'professional'?

Frank Ledwidge

Introduction

For many years, the British armed forces have claimed, and rightfully, the status of a 'profession'. There is an extensive literature on what this constitutes, both in the context of a military force and more widely. I do not propose to critique or add to it here. Most commentators are content to see the idea of a 'profession' as possessing variations of the following characteristics: a body of expert knowledge upon the basis of which the public accords certain privileges on the understanding that they self-regulate and operate for the common good.[1] American General Jack Dempsey glosses on this as follows:

> Our profession is distinguished from others in society because of our justified expertise in the justified application of lethal military force and the willingness of those who serve to die for their nation. Our profession is defined by our values, ethics, standards, code of conduct, skills and attributes. As volunteers, our sworn duty is to the Constitution. Our status as professionals is granted by those whom we are accountable to, our civilian authority and the American people.

The British Army, along with the other services has always been strong on those 'values, ethics, standards, code of conduct, skills and attributes'. For example, its values are said to be courage, discipline, respect for others, integrity, loyalty and selfless commitment. Its standards are declared as 'lawful, acceptable behaviour and professional'.[2] The British Army 'Values and Standards' guide states that 'a

---

[1] Pauline Shanks-Kaurin, 'Questioning Military Professionalism', in *Redefining the Modern Military*, ed. Finney and Mayfield (Annapolis: Naval Institute Press, 2018), p. 11.
[2] Ibid.

defining characteristic of a profession is the requirement to set clear standards for the conduct of its members. The Army is no different.'[3] For the army then, what is it to be professional? There is an answer:

> To be a professional British Army soldier means abiding by the Army's policies and regulations on, among other issues, the handling of official information; alcohol and substance misuse; control of public and non-public funds and management of personal affairs.

The Army Leadership Code requires soldiers to be 'totally professional' but refrains from further explanation. The purpose for being 'totally professional' is said to be to 'protect and promote the Army's reputation.'[4]

Further, there are explicit requirements to comply with the laws and customs of war. The idea of these may seem somewhat archaic, but they still sit at the heart of the military profession today. David Benest would point out that not only are they an ethical imperative, but they also comprise the direct orders of the Sovereign. The King's Commission states that officers are 'to observe and follow such orders and directions as from time to time you shall receive from us, according to the Rules and Discipline of law'. Warrants for warrant officers contain the same text. This point is made in the British Army's 'Values and Standards' document.[5]

There can be no question that these are explicitly woven into the fabric of the culture and implicitly demonstrated in the behaviour of the vast majority of British servicemen and women. David Benest was a living embodiment of those ideals. They are also expressed at the tactical command level by Oliver Lee in Chapter 7 of this book.

However 'professionalism' is defined, and in whatever context, a key and common element is that those who claim the term owe a responsibility *internally* to the other members of the profession, by means of values, standards and a common ethical code, and also *externally* to society as a whole. The function of the military profession is the management of violence and (violent capability) in the service of the state. Military professionals owe a profound duty of accountability to the state and its people for the privileges they are accorded in this and other respects. The central argument of this chapter is that some of the

---

[3] 'Values and Standards of the British Army', 2016, https://www.army.mod.uk/media/5219/20180910 -values_standards_2018_final.pdf.

[4] 'The Army Leadership Code: An Introductory Guide', 2016, p. 10, https://www.army.mod.uk/media /2698/ac72021_the_army_leadership_code_an_introductory_guide.pdf.

[5] 'Values and Standards of the British Army', https://www.army.mod.uk/media/5219/20180910-values _standards_2018_final.pdf TICLE.

senior ranks of the British armed forces have failed and are failing to discharge those professional duties and responsibilities and are failing to assume the accountability that is an essential companion to responsibility.

Accountability for strategic failure

General George Patton had this to say about military leaders and responsibility:

> A General officer who will invariably assume responsibility for failure, whether he deserves it or not, and invariably give credit for success to others whether they deserve it or not, will achieve outstanding success.[6]

The last twenty years have seen a series of strategic and operational failures on the part of British strategic commanders that is unprecedented in our military history. Some of the responsibility for these disasters can be redirected towards 'politicians' who placed our armed forces in impossible circumstances. It is worth recounting briefly the essence of what happened, as the significance of these catastrophes is often lost in time and, of course, through the considerable efforts of the Ministry of Defence (MOD) to avoid processes designed to produce lessons that might be decidedly uncomfortable.

No amount of 'sloping shoulders', as the military term goes for the evasion of responsibility, can account for the Basra debacle in Iraq. Here, the United States was forced to bail out a British force which had essentially capitulated to local militias. The British were 'defeated, pure and simple'.[7] The debacle in Helmand in Afghanistan was, if anything, even worse. The British campaign began (at scale) in 2006 with the scattering of small groups of infantry troops to indefensible settlements around a province the size of Northern Ireland wherein the British had no awareness of the conflict dynamics. They never recovered from the ensuing mayhem. A four-year cycle of 'Sisysphean'[8] six-monthly operations of varying degrees of relevance to the overall campaign followed. All were united by their strategic and operational irrelevance and failure. In 2010, the bulk of the US 'Surge' was sent to Helmand to rescue the mission.

---

[6] Peter Tsouras, ed., *Greenhill Dictionary of Military Quotations* (London: Stackpole Books, 2002), p. 418 quoting George Patton in 'War as I Knew it' (1946).

[7] British general, speaking off the record, in Paul Wood, 'Uncertainty follows Basra exit', *BBC News Online*, 15 December 2007, available at: http://news.bbc.co.uk/1/hi/world/ middle_east/7145597. stm.

[8] Rajiv Chandrasekaran, *Little America* (London: Bloomsbury, 2012), p. 206.

The overall mission in Afghanistan was a total strategic failure. This became obvious, even to the most obdurate enthusiasts, in 2021 with the expulsion of the international troops, and along with it the government they had installed, both in their entirety. Despite tactical success throughout the war, no operational objectives were achieved. At the grand strategic level, for the United Kingdom, the effect was radical. There can be little question that the UK's role as the US ally of first resort – desperately desired by the military establishment – has been compromised. As one US special forces officer put it in Helmand: 'the British wrote cheques they couldn't cash', leaving the Americans with the bill. This was true in both Iraq and Afghanistan and it was not the politicians who sighed these 'cheques' describing, as it were, the levels and scale of commitment, but British military leadership.

Yet, no senior officer, of the dozens who served in the mishandled Iraq and Afghan campaigns, went without decoration. In an environment where responsibility is difficult or impossible to pin down, that is perhaps not surprising. As Aaron Edwards points out in Chapter 1, David Benest regularly raised this issue, specifically but by no means exclusively with respect to Bloody Sunday in Northern Ireland on 30 January 1972 where, again, no officer has been nor ever will be held legally liable.

The question must be asked as to whether the aversion to identifying and learning honest lessons is a deeply rooted cultural problem. It is worth raising what happened after both World Wars. It took four years for the British Army to attain a level of war-winning excellence in 1918. The German Army, too, made serious and repeated mistakes. Yet, General Hans Von Seekt, the commander of the remaining German Army just after the First World War, ordered a huge study of their performance, composed of over fifty different committees to examine lessons.[9] No similar review of lessons to be identified from the First World War troubled the inter-war British Army, with entirely predictable results in the Second. Similarly, the British Army awaits a comprehensive formal review of its performance in either the Iraq or the Afghan wars.

It does not have to be like this, and nor should it be. As we will see in what follows, there are very real consequences for the defence of the nation in failing to account for or learn from failure, whether that failure is occasioned by incompetence, negligence, mistakes, hubris or any combination of these or other defects.

---

[9] Williamson Murray, 'The Culture of the British Army 194-945', in *The Culture of Military Organisations*, ed. Murray and Mansour (Cambridge: Cambridge University Press, 2019), pp. 196–7.

One way through a mess similar in nature and for the scale of the country concerned was the way Israel dealt with its, probably unnecessary, Lebanon War in 2006, which was considered to be badly mishandled. Defence is a matter of vital concern in Israel. Each Jewish citizen is a soldier and few, indeed, have any illusions about senior officers or much respect for notions of immunity of the institution from criticism; nor would such immunity be tolerated. An inquiry was convened composed of a senior judge and two retired officers. The initial report appeared after six months. The assessment was that there was 'flawed performance by the army, deficient preparedness' and 'because of the conduct of the high command, it failed to provide an effective military response'.[10] As a result, the chief of staff was dismissed, other senior officers removed and the prime minister was forced to resign. The report appeared two years after the end of the war. Many observers in Israel thought that this was far too long.

Accountability for operational failure

The strategic lessons and mistakes of senior British military command in recent years remain formally unidentified. At the operational level, the approach might be summarized by repeating the observation that every brigade and divisional commander throughout the recent Iraq and Afghan wars was decorated.

The approach of British senior officers to individual disasters was epitomized by what happened after the famous 'Camp Bastion raid' in September 2012. Fourteen Taliban commandos entered the vast UK–US–Afghan base in the Helmand desert, destroyed six US Marine Corps Harrier jets and a C130 transport aircraft and killed two US servicemen, one of whom was the marine squadron commander. Perimeter security on the base was the responsibility of British forces. A rather damning US investigation identified one of the deficiencies contributing to the disaster being that, on the night in question, twelve of the twenty-four watchtowers on the camp perimeter were unmanned. It is important to state that this was largely due to resource constraints. That said, someone within the British chain of command – probably at a fairly high level – made the decision to hold the security of the camp at risk by assenting to the undermanning of the towers.

The two most senior American generals in southern Afghanistan were not simply dismissed from their posts but also made to retire. In dismissing his

---

[10] Winograd Report (2008) summary of findings paragraph 20, http://www.mfa.gov.il/mfa/mfa
-archive/2008/pages/winograd%20committee%20submits%20final%20report%2030-jan-2008
.aspx.

colleagues, the US Marine Corps Commandant General – a personal friend to both generals – stated: 'My duty requires me to remain true to the timeless axioms relating to command responsibility and accountability . . . commandership is sacred responsibility and the standard for general officers is necessarily high.'[11]

While the two marine generals, Sturdevant and Gurganus, were held responsible, and *accountable*, it is a stretch to consider them culpable. It is not the job, generally or indeed in this case, of general officers to oversee guard arrangements. Those matters are rightly delegated to other responsible officers who, on this occasion, were British. Neither was disciplined in any way. Indeed, both were in due course promoted. This did not go unnoticed in the United States, nor in the UK Parliament during its own inquiry into this rather embarrassing incident[12]. One can only speculate on this failure to hold responsible officers accountable. It may well be that neither was considered at fault, but this is in no way adequate. Thus the case of the 2011 'Bastion Raid', while involving no crime, was almost poetically illustrative of the cultural gap that exists between ideals and action. The ideal posits that, regardless of culpability or fault, the responsible officer is accountable. The reality, for British officers, appears to be somewhat different.

To quote another senior US Marine officer, General Charles Krulak, 'the fusing of accountability and responsibility is what makes Marines effective leaders and followers'.[13] Indeed, one might go further, and ask whether without such accountability, exactly for what reason are such officers so well paid and accorded any deference at all?

Culpability, command responsibility and accountability in operations

There are clear and obvious distinctions between the concepts of culpability, responsibility and accountability. Culpability, by definition and etymology, implies fault. Within a military context, responsibility often attaches to an office or role. Accountability rests with the office holder, whether they are culpable or

---

[11] Chris Carol, 'Two Marines Fired in Wake of Brazen Taliban Attack on Camp Bastion', *Stars and Stripes*, 30 September 2013, https://www.stripes.com/theaters/middle_east/two-marine-generals -fired-in-wake-of-brazen-taliban-attack-on-camp-bastion-1.244316#:~:text=Two%20Marine %20generals%20fired%20in%20wake%20of%20brazen%20Taliban%20attack%20on%20Camp %20Bastion,-By&text=WASHINGTON%20%E2%80%94%20Citing%20a%20failure%20to,of %20the%20Marine%20Corps%20Gen.
[12] See in general https://committees.parliament.uk/work/2225/afghanistan-camp-bastion-attack/.
[13] General Charles C. Krulak, 'Responsibility, Accountability and the Zero-Defects Mentality', *Marine Corps Gazette*, May 1997.

not. For example, in the Camp Bastion case described earlier, for the US Marines, the two generals had their careers ruined due to the apparent culpability of British military planners or security officers. These either held or, more likely, were forced by circumstances to hold, at risk the security of the camp by undermanning towers. Nonetheless, the two US Marine officers were responsible *and were held accountable.* Perimeter security is not something with which a general concerns himself or should concern himself; the generals were not culpable.

It is worth stating here that for centuries the Royal Navy has drawn these lines clearly and they are written into the law. If any mishap befalls a ship – a collision, perhaps, or a running aground – the commanding officer is held almost automatically accountable, whether or not he is actually to blame. A recent example of this was the removal of the commanding officer of the submarine HMS *Astute* after it (rather publicly) ran aground off the island of Skye in October 2010. Similarly, the commanding officer of HMS *Cornwall* was removed some months after the kidnapping, in extraordinary circumstances, of thirteen members of his crew by Iranian forces in 2007. These were, of course, relatively junior officers.

Nonetheless, this traditional practice collocates the two different notions of responsibility and fault or culpability. It does so for good, human reasons that, until recently, did not need elucidating – a commanding officer will take care to ensure that those under his command are competent and well trained if he knows that he will have to carry the can for any mistakes they make. The idea of holding commanders responsible for events for which they are not to blame was carried to its extreme with the execution of Admiral Byng for 'failing to do his utmost' to prevent the loss of Minorca to the French in 1757. His ships were in disrepair, and his forces were far too few to defend the island. Nonetheless, he was executed *'pour encourager les autres'* as Voltaire said of the incident. Some naval historians,[14] incidentally ascribe to this incident – at least partly – two centuries of uncompromising aggression on the part of the Royal Navy.

Accountability: Essential to mission command

Does it matter if there is an apparent culture of evasion of responsibility and accountability in the higher reaches of the British armed forces? If those beneath them are highly capable, well trained and imbued with the aggression, tactical

---

[14] For example, N. A. M. Rodger, *Command of the Ocean; a Naval History of Britain 1649–1815* (London: Penguin, 2006), p. 272.

competence and courage for which British soldiers, sailors and aviators are justly famous worldwide, need it be of concern if their leadership is effectively immune to accountability for operational and strategic failure? Central to all British military doctrine is 'mission command'. This idea is usually ascribed to German 'Auftragstaktik', practised by the Royal Navy long before the Germans arrived at it. Its essence is that if a junior leader understands his commander's intent, he or she should be given the discretion and, vitally, the authority to achieve that objective in the best way he or she sees fit. The rationale is that the junior leader is closer to the realities, opportunities and constraints applicable on the ground.

In simple terms, the junior leader is deemed to carry the authority of the senior officer who has set the objectives. Clearly, this implies in turn that a great deal of trust is reposed in the junior leader. However, for this idea to work properly, there must be an understanding that if matters go wrong, the junior leader understands that his commander, while not culpable, is responsible and accountable for the operation. Trust flows both ways. The soldier, sailor, marine or aviator at the front end needs to know, as it were, that his commander 'has his back'. In the words of Major General Sir Julian Thompson, who commanded 3 Commando Brigade to victory in the 1982 Falklands War, and is therefore the most successful living British general, a 'golden umbrella' must be extended over a trusted subordinate's actions.[15] It is this that, in practical terms, will allow for the subordinate to take appropriate risk – to understand that trust flows and must flow both ways.

Command responsibility and accountability: The criminal element

Under international humanitarian law, the situation is limpidly clear. Rule 153 of Customary International Humanitarian Law[16] states that commanders (at all levels) are responsible for the actions of their subordinates if they knew, *or had reason to know* [my italics] that unlawful acts were being committed by their personnel, and did not take reasonable measures to prevent and punish them. It remains lamentably open to question – to put it mildly – whether this rule has always been applied within the British armed forces.

---

[15] Interview with Sir Julian Thompson, August 2016.
[16] 'Customary International Humanitarian Law'; Volume 1; Rules (ICRC 2005–regularly updated) Rule 153, https://ihl-databases.icrc.org/customary-ihl/eng/docs/home?opendocument.

Applying the international customary law rule, the British Army Leadership Code 'requires commanders to take responsibility for the actions of others and set an appropriate example'.[17] Yet, in all the cases of disgraceful, unethical and criminal behaviour by members of the British armed forces, not a single officer – let alone a senior officer – has been indicted or tried for any crime or even a service offence arising out of war crimes allegations. In those rare cases where allegations have been investigated and prosecuted, the reflex would seem to be to find the lowest-ranking person directly culpable for a crime and prosecute them, leaving the commissioned ranks entirely untouched. Simon Akam, in a review of Langley Sharp's book *The Habit of Excellence* about the army as an exemplar in the field of leadership, summarizes this aspect well: 'almost everyone uniformed who ran these wars, even those on whose watch large scale failure took place, got promoted and showered with decorations, while junior individuals faced hounding by a novel series of accountability probes, some of which, though not all, were certainly nefarious'.[18] This despite the fact that the crime or crimes concerned may well have been, and indeed invariably were, committed in environments where, to put it mildly, the nature of leadership was – or should have been – a major concern.

US Army Col John Yingling has famously observed: 'As matters stand now, a private who loses a rifle suffers greater consequences than a General who loses a war'.[19] What kind of command climate allows a junior non-commissioned officer (NCO) who shoots a detainee to go to prison, while the commanding officer who tolerated or encouraged a culture of disregard for the laws and customs of war, within which that soldier operated, is promoted? No recently serving soldier, sailor, marine or aviator will regard such a situation as in any way surprising. On the contrary, were such a senior officer to be prosecuted on an indictment of, for example, gross dereliction of duty or even something so simple as failure to report a serious offence, such as murder of a non-combatant, now that *would* be a shock.

The consequences of such a lack of criminal accountability is clearest in the case of special forces, and UK special forces in particular. Due to the opacity surrounding their activities, about which more later, no official information is available as to where they are deployed. Over the last few years we can be

---

[17] 'The Army Leadership Code: An Introductory Guide', p. 10.
[18] Simon Akam; 'Surfeit of Rank', *London Review of Books*, 44, no. 5, available at https://www.lrb.co.uk /the-paper/v44/n05/simon-akam/a-surfeit-of-rank.
[19] John Yingling, 'A Failure in Generalship', *Armed Forces Journal*, 1 May 2007, http://armedforcesjournal .com/a-failure-in-generalship/.

reasonably confident that they have been engaged in Syria,[20] Libya, Kenya, Somalia and Yemen.[21] Clearly, these are very capable combat soldiers. However, almost uniquely in the West,[22] and indeed uniquely among the United Kingdom's security and intelligence services, including MI5, MI6 and GCHQ, there is an almost total lack, not only of transparency as to deployment, but of any form of democratic oversight. This accountability gap would be troubling enough in itself. However, taken together with a series of credible allegations of abuse (specifically serial murder)[23] – some of them raised by Afghan partner forces – there is reason to believe that the accountability gap has become extremely dangerous not only to the United Kingdom's reputation but also, more importantly, to the welfare of civilians within their areas of operations. It may well be that the Inquiry being chaired by Lord Justice Haddon-Cave (ongoing at the time of writing)[24] on these matters may produce some formal elucidation of these issues, much as the Australian Brereton 'Afghanistan Inquiry'[25] into similar matters did for Australia.

Exceptional people?

The British Army makes the curious claim, without explicitly explaining why, that its 'values and standards set us apart from other occupations'.[26] This is almost by definition 'exceptionalism'. It also displays a certain naivety and adds

---

[20] Two special forces soldiers were injured in January 2019 and another killed in March 2018. Neither deaths were followed by a review. See Liam Walpole, 'The US Congress Understands the Importance of Special Forces Oversight – Why Doesn't the UK Parliament?', 23 March 2019, https://blogs.lse .ac.uk/usappblog/2019/03/23/the-us-congress-understands-the-importance-of-special-forces -oversight-why-doesnt-the-uk-parliament/.

[21] Several injuries to UK special forces have been sustained in Yemen, reported widely by the press. For example, see Marc Nicol, 'Our Secret Dirty War, Five British Troops are Wounded in Yemen', *Daily Mail*, 23 March 2019, https://www.dailymail.co.uk/news/article-6843469/Five-British-Special -Forces-troops-wounded-Yemen-advising-Saudi-Arabia-campaign.html.

[22] See Britain's Shadow Army, *Policy Options for External Oversight of Britain's Special Forces* (ORG, 2018), pp. 19–26, https://www.saferworld.org.uk/resources/publications/1278-britainas-shadow -army-policy-options-for-external-oversight-of-uk-special-forces, looking at the oversight models of France, Denmark, Norway and the United States.

[23] Dan Sabbagh, 'MOD Asked Why it Withheld Evidence on 33 Suspected Afghan Civilian Executions by SAS Soldiers', *Guardian*, 2 August 2020, https://www.theguardian.com/uk-news/2020/aug/02/ mod-asked-why-it-withheld-evidence-on-33-suspected-afghan-civilian-executions-sas-soldiers. Further credible allegations were detailed in BBC Panorama, 'SAS Death Squads Exposed; A British War Crime', *BBC*, 2022, https://www.bbc.co.uk/programmes/m0019707.

[24] Inquiry investigating matters arising from the deployment of British Armed Forces into Afghanistan from 2010. Website of the Inquiry is available at https://www.iia.independent-inquiry.uk/.

[25] See https://www.defence.gov.au/about/reviews-inquiries/afghanistan-inquiry for details and report.

[26] British Army, 'Values and Standards', p. 3, https://www.army.mod.uk/media/5219/20180910-values _standards_2018_final.pdf.

credence to the idea that the military still believe themselves to be different and somehow perhaps better than the rest of us. This attitude is perhaps best expressed polemically by Colonel Nathan R. Jessup played with feeling by Jack Nicholson in *A Few Good Men*:

> Son, we live in a world that has walls, and those walls have to be guarded by men with guns. Who's gonna do it? You? You, Lt. Weinberg? I have a greater responsibility than you could possibly fathom. . . . You don't want the truth because deep down in places you don't talk about at parties, you want me on that wall. You need me on that wall. We use words like honor, code, loyalty. We use these words as the backbone of a life spent defending something. You use them as a punchline. I have neither the time nor the inclination to explain myself to a man who rises and sleeps under the blanket of the very freedom that I provide, and then questions the manner in which I provide it! I would rather you just said 'thank you' and went on your way, Otherwise, I suggest you pick up a weapon and stand a post. Either way, I don't give a *damn* what you think you are entitled to![27]

A variation on this, as we see in Chris Green's Chapter 8 of this book, was expressed by Andrew Roberts in the *Sunday Times* in August 2020 that, in Afghanistan, 'the SAS has done much violence on our behalf' and 'deserve protection from scrutiny, as their enemies almost never play by the rules'.[28] Such scrutiny, he argues, diminishes 'our ability to win'. As Green points out, it was the activities of the SAS, rather than any scrutiny that diminished 'our ability to win'. That aside, the article represented a slightly more polished version of Jessup's speech.

The Jessup/Roberts line is predicated upon the somewhat utilitarian assumption that the activities of the deviant members of the US Marines in *A Few Good Men* or the SAS should not be subject to the scrutiny of the courts or, indeed, anyone else. To do so, the suggestion goes, is that the efficacy of our brave but tough defenders is thereby diminished. There is also the strong insinuation that 'unless you can walk in my boots, you have no right to tell me how to behave under extreme stress'. Colonel Jessup is made to state explicitly that he has neither the time nor the inclination to explain himself to the likes of lawyers, judges or juries.

It must be said that few officers or senior ranks really believe this. Colonel Jessup was a caricature. His job, in the fictional film, was to secure Guantanamo

---

[27] Speech from *A Few Good Men* (Columbia Pictures, 1992).
[28] Andrew Roberts, 'With its Hands Tied, the SAS Loses', *The Sunday Times*, 9 August 2020.

Bay, at no time since the 1960s under serious threat of military attack. Milder versions of such ideas certainly exist and one does not have to go far in a discussion with military personnel, especially perhaps certain sectors of the veteran population, to hear them.

Doctors, nurses or other professionals including, in fact, lawyers, might offer similar excuses for criminal behaviour to those offered by Jessup and Roberts. They might argue that ordinary people cannot fathom the experiences and knowledge they have gained, nor understand the immense day-to-day pressures under which they work. Sometimes decisions that might be ethically questionable have to be made that should not, in those circumstances, be subject to scrutiny or accountability. While such professions cannot, like the armed forces, lay claim to 'unlimited liability' *vis-à-vis* themselves, they may certainly do so by proxy on behalf of their patients' lives or, indeed, in the case of lawyers, their clients' freedom. It is unlikely that they would receive much sympathy. Nonetheless, such arguments were – in former decades – made to warrant highly unsatisfactory systems of self-regulation of the medical and legal professions. Dr Shipman's murderous activities put an end to this argument for doctors. It took a little longer for lawyers to be subject to forms of external oversight. Yet, it might be said, the military profession has had no Shipman, at least as far as we know.

The strategic cost

So much for the basic operational advantages of appropriate accountability. What is the strategic cost for senior officers failing to take accountability for their actions? Above all, there is the still unresolved failure to discharge the basic duty of success in armed conflict in a series of disastrous campaigns characterized by 'careerism, excessively rotating command appointments and upwards pointing leadership that was unwilling to present military truth to political power'.[29] This has not gone unnoticed in the wider army. An infantry officer commented in an article on the influential British military comment website 'Wavell Room' that 'the General Staff of the British Army are more likely to be held accountable for inappropriate relationships, dishonourable conduct or the dubious interpretation of education allowances than they are for failure

---

[29] Akam, *The Changing of the Guard.*

in their actual jobs – that of leading the British Army at home and abroad today and preparing for tomorrow.'[30]

Further, there seems to be no responsibility taken for the outrageous wastage and mismanagement of billions of pounds of public money by senior officers entirely unequipped, trained or capable to deal with the vast projects with which they were charged. This has left the British Army with an equipment programme that, according to the House of Commons Defence Select Committee, constitutes 'a woeful story of bureaucratic procrastination, military indecision, financial ineptitude and general ineptitude'.[31] Our soldiers would 'be forced to go into battle in a combination of obsolescent or even obsolete armoured vehicles, most of them at least 30 years old or more, with poor mechanical reliability, very heavily outgunned by more modern missile and artillery systems and chronically lacking in adequate air defence'.[32] Another report by the same committee asserts that the Royal Navy is 'increasingly reliant on allies for many capabilities, with a limited scope for sovereign action'.[33]

At the end of the careers of very many senior officers, instead of public inquiries and shame, there is the appearance of, at the very least, financial and moral compromise in the so-called revolving door that directs them to well-upholstered sinecures in the boardrooms of major arms companies. One might be given to ask whether these companies value their financial or managerial acumen rather less than their contacts and retained influence. The degree to which these cosy arrangements have adversely affected the capability of armed forces evidently ill-equipped for what is a very challenging combat environment has yet to be assessed.

Surely no other 'profession' could have survived without a root and branch review and reform of its entire structure. Yet, the UK armed forces march, fly and sail on unmolested by meaningful internal accountability, let alone external oversight.

David Benest was the epitome of professionalism. Throughout his service he insisted on weaving an ethical approach into all he did. Fearless in expressing his reasoned views, he lived and breathed ethics as a core competency. Towards

---

[30] James Burton, 'Culture: Addressing Apathy and Dishonesty within the British Army', 4 April 2021, https://wavellroom.com/2021/04/13/addressing-culture-apathy-dishonesty-british-army-part-2/.

[31] See the Report of the House of Commons Defence Committee, 'Obsolescent and Outgunned: The British Army's Armoured Vehicle capability', March 2021, https://committees.parliament.uk/publications/5081/documents/50325/default/or.

[32] Ibid., p. 6.

[33] See Report of the House of Commons Defence Committee, 'We're Going to Need a Bigger Navy', 2022, https://committees.parliament.uk/work/1209/the-navy-purpose-and-procurement/news/159793/were-going-to-need-a-bigger-navy/.

the end of his life, he paid a considerable price for advocating accountability for those, particularly senior officers, who failed to meet the exacting standards required of a professional. All too often, for reasons outside the remit of this chapter, it is the conformists and careerists who float to the top, characteristics not, perhaps, conducive to assuming accountability when the chips are down.

The question must therefore be asked: Do we have a high command that is capable of changing as matters stand? The answer must be no. There are simply no incentives to do so, together with a lack of imagination and an almost wilful failure to apply a healthy degree of objectivity to what has been a series of tragedies and disasters for all of us involved in them. This is a cultural problem and it is chronic. Accountability is essential for well-functioning organizations. It enables and allows reflection, understanding and improvement and incentivizes positive action. Without it, an organization is simply a hierarchy.

During the nineteenth century, command of large, important or high-profile missions was a matter of very great prestige – as it is now. Responsibility and accountability for the success or failure of operations lay squarely with clearly identified individuals. Failure (or perceived failure) resulted in quick dismissal and equally quick despatch into the world of gardening leave. Matters are rather different now. No fewer than thirty-six officers of major general rank equivalent or above gave evidence to the Chilcott Inquiry. In no case did any officer take responsibility for failure. Were there to be an inquiry into Afghanistan, the numbers of general officers involved would run easily into three figures. To coin an adage, many were in charge, but no one, it seems, was responsible.

We are far, indeed, from the approach taken by the founder of the US nuclear submarine force Admiral Rickover's famous principles, expressed best in a pithy quotation: 'If responsibility is rightfully yours, no evasion, or ignorance or passing the blame can shift the burden to someone else. Unless you can point your finger at the man who is responsible when something goes wrong, then you have never had anyone really responsible.'[34] One might add to that the rider that accountability is one of the prices paid for the privileges, ever more lavish the higher up the chain, received for the title 'professional'.

---

[34] Radiation Safety and Regulation: Hearings before the J. Comm. on Atomic Energy, 87th Cong., p. 366 (1961) (statement of Vice Adm. H. G. Rickover, Chief, Naval Reactors Branch)

Part Three

Combat realities

7

The operational design for Nad-e-Ali South, Afghanistan, 2011

Oliver Lee

Introduction

The early years of my military career brought plentiful opportunity, privilege and learning, and I found them to be immensely satisfying and thought-provoking. Among other experiences during this time, I served operationally in Bosnia, Northern Ireland, Iraq and Afghanistan; commanded at troop and company level; led the instruction of new entry Royal Marine recruits; worked personally for an exemplary chief of Defence Staff, Admiral Sir Michael Boyce as he was then, to include the 9/11 period; spent two years in the private offices of defence ministers; and undertook almost two years of junior and then advanced command and staff training. All of these technicolour experiences were immensely instructive to me though not all were positive, particularly the tragic helicopter crash in Iraq in 2003 when I was the operations officer of 42 Commando, but various others too.

These first thirteen years caused me to read, research and think with real care about the profession of arms and the surrounding morals and ethics on which it seemed inescapably that it must be based. It struck me that equipping human beings with superhuman power concomitantly required them to possess almost superhuman judgement, compassion and morality. However, such a culture would not emerge by magic; rather, it had to be led and followed. I concluded that leadership shadow and the preparedness of the follower to embrace that shadow lay at the heart of achieving this alchemy. Consequently, ethics and battlefield atrocity, and their relationship with leadership, lay at the heart of the dissertation I wrote on my advanced staff course.

These experiences and the thinking that they had stimulated culminated in my greatest privilege: command of 45 Commando Group, which I assumed in summer 2009. This wonderful job had countless highlights, the biggest of which was our tour to Afghanistan in 2011. We were bound for the district of Nad-e-Ali South in Helmand Province. Setting the conditions to succeed on this tour took a great deal of thought and time.

Design

Having been involved in Afghanistan by now for a number of years, I had become deeply interested in it. I had studied it on courses, read about it extensively, lectured about it, provided advice on it in the Ministry of Defence (MOD) and, more widely, visited it on a number of occasions since 2002, and served there myself in 2006 and 2007. I viewed it and still do as the litmus test of leadership at all levels. I also grasped the immense and multifaceted cost of the campaign and I had thought carefully about this, not least from the funerals I had attended, the friends I had lost and the wounded and bereaved I regularly saw around 45 Commando.

By the time I assumed command I had drawn the conclusion that the campaign was not being managed to best effect. There were the clear strategic flaws but I had no control over these. What I could influence was 45 Commando's approach, and this dominated my thinking. As our tour drew closer, I saw the efforts of our predecessors 1 Royal Irish, who had a highly distinguished and thoughtful tour; I was convinced that we were going to be bequeathed a golden opportunity to make real progress and I was determined we would not squander it.

I disagreed with much of the military activity that had taken place in Afghanistan. I felt that the concepts of risk and rigour, fundamental to the traditional analysis of the demands associated with a military endeavour, were unhelpful in an Afghan context. Afghanistan was not a war, but a counter-insurgency; the Afghan people and not body bag numbers would be the prize. The campaign needed consistency of approach and the recognition that it was a game of inches where often no news was the best news. I disapproved of the six-month command tour cycle where the allure of the career-defining operational sunshine could incentivize behaviours that created the news. Foreign forces needed to lead surreptitiously and quietly from behind, enabling Afghans to set the obvious agenda and be the news.

Put simply and as a gross generalization, Western forces contributing to the intervention in Afghanistan had participated in altogether too much violence.

Perversely, this had come at great sacrifice, founded on untold courage, but while reducing the chances of mission success. Afghanistan is a warrior nation where picking a fight could not be easier; the problem is that such fights are then difficult to extract from and many of them lay counter to the mission we were pursuing. The exception to this was the forensic and calculated targeting of the most malign and irreconcilable actors, and doing so while minimising collateral damage and civilian casualties as a foremost consideration. But the majority of fighting was overall favourable to the insurgency and thereby counter to the efforts to defeat that insurgency by establishing the proper writ of Afghan governance.

For numerous reasons, the insurgency relied on violence to survive and make its point. In a society where literacy levels are low, deed matters and people watch with their eyes skinned. The violence therefore became the insurgent's metaphoric television screen or newspaper column; it propagated his narrative. In the process, it undermined Afghan legitimacy by demonstrating its inability to fulfil its principal task: keeping its people safe. In turn, this cycle of violence kept those people, the trump card in any counter-insurgency, cowed and silent. Rather than asserting their will in defining their sovereign future – the one thing the insurgent could not cope with – bitter experience incentivized them to do nothing. The logical mantra of the people was to survive through anonymity. This was entirely pragmatic in the face of such violence and uncertainty driving the pendulum of ascendancy hither and thither. The sensible thing was not to side with anybody if you weren't to pay the price for doing so when they were knocked off their perch.

Fighting of course leads to death and this played further to the insurgency. First, the mores of Afghan culture meant it bred other insurgents bent on revenge. And those reinforcements with a sense of grievance were in plentiful supply both in Afghanistan and from beyond its almost entirely porous borders. Related to this, life is sadly cheap in Afghanistan, but much less so in the Western nations involved there. So death was a recruiting sergeant for the insurgency, while in the United Kingdom and elsewhere it served to erode public and political support for the campaign. The violence also prevented progress on the reconstruction of Afghanistan, its infrastructure and its governance; in essence, fighting slowed everything else down. This suited an insurgent whose time was unlimited and who would quite happily hand the baton of infidel resistance to future generations. Conversely, its impact was entirely debilitating for the political masters of foreign forces who were impatient for progress, set timelines and clear exit strategies.

What Afghanistan truly needed was for its people to become the counter-insurgents, and 80,000 such people were available in Nad-e-Ali. This game-changing force needed to be unshackled from its fear, imbued with confidence, and brought decisively to bear. The only way to do this was to break the cycle of violence, blunting, marginalizing and rendering the insurgency irrelevant. Every unnecessary bullet or bomb would be counterproductive and had to be resisted. What was needed was to resist the temptation of playing the insurgency on the attritional field of play and, instead, to silence him by playing him off the field.

While I felt sure of these concepts, I had little idea how to turn them into a plan. Faced with this, I made one decision that on reflection was a very good call; thereafter, it was the unit that succeeded, not me. I decided to delegate the production of the plan throughout all the constituent parts of the Commando. The plan could not come from my ivory tower and me. It had to be a team plan or it would not hold water and would leak at the first sign of stress. This changed the game, transforming the Commando's individual and collective mindset and delivering a plan that all had contributed to and thus felt a personal responsibility to protect at every turn. Various things sat at the heart of this work, which was undertaken for the full year before the tour started.

I delegated the production of the plan but I did so within clear parameters. I opened the process with a presentation to the entire Commando in order to get the thinking going inside a sensible framework. I insisted that the unit read a minimum of three related books covering historic operations in Vietnam and Malaya and a contemporary, cultural description of Afghanistan. Everyone had to understand the environment within which we would be operating. Each of these books and what could be drawn from it was discussed in facilitated groups. The Commando came together every fortnight to discuss the different parts of the plan that were being developed across it. These included culture, ethics and the risk of atrocities, the people, the fabric of Nad-e-Ali, Pashtun language, the insurgency, the Afghan security forces, Afghan history, how we might innovate, the impact on operations of the summer heat and so on. These sessions enabled me to keep abreast of the thinking and to tweak it as appropriate.

I put in place one further check or balance on myself. I was fearful of my status as commanding officer separating me from the reality of the unit's thinking. I knew that the men had their views, anxieties, worries, thoughts and ideas regarding the Afghanistan tour that lay ahead. But was I truly alive to those views and in tune with them or did I hold my own inaccurate version of them? Did people really tell me the truth or did they tell me the version of this that they thought I wanted to hear? If it were the latter, this would be a critical flaw. I redoubled my efforts really to know the Commando and I ranged routinely across it in its base in Arbroath and on our various deployments, particularly to Norway in winter 2010.

The house I lived in was in the centre of the Commando and some of my best instruction came at the weekends or in the evenings. It was always fun to sit in the garden and listen to the happy parties playing out in the men's accommodation and messes. On occasion, in shorts, T-shirt and flip-flops and carrying a pack of beer, I would head for one of these gatherings. I would knock and politely ask if they minded if I joined them. I had no intention of cramping their style and so I rarely stayed long, but I spent enough time to have a proper chat. Beer, no uniform and informal surroundings where I was the visitor fuelled the honesty of the conversation. These thermometer checks allowed me to provide reassurance and explanation but also meant I could weave the perspectives I received into our preparations. Concurrently, they reassured me that I was not separated from reality in the parallel universe of the leader and I feel sure they made me more persuasive to follow. There were those who felt this sort of personal engagement without an entourage by my side was risky. For my part, I did not view it as such. It was enjoyable, important and helped me prepare the Commando for what lay ahead.

These parameters and controls were certainly not intended in a Machiavellian way for me to design the plan while others felt that they were doing so. The whole Commando contributed to it, there was no monopoly over or control on ideas, and as ever much of the best thinking came from the most unexpected places, to include the most junior. However, this activity did take place with some control measures surrounding it, and this felt right and proper given my ultimate accountability for it all.

We linked the immense sacrifices that had already been made in Afghanistan, including those by 45 Commando, to the outcomes we sought. We collectively agreed on a commitment to enabling tangible progress in 2011 so as to ensure that sacrifice had not been in vain. This galvanized the Commando with a collective purpose on behalf of the giants on whose shoulders it stood. We unlocked the Commando's individual and group humanity and appetite to make a difference for the better by always doing the right thing.

The last thing that enabled this to happen was the Regimental Sergeant Major, Steph Moran, who by now had taken the reins from the equally superb Shep Shepherd. A charismatic and unyielding Glaswegian, Steph had spent the majority of his immensely distinguished career in 45 Commando. As operationally proven as anyone in the Royal Marines, tales abounded of his bravery and his generous heart. He was justifiably revered and idolized by the

Commando, which viewed him as its talisman. At such moments, rank and position has its limitations and I could never have carried this sort of equity with the men. Consequently, Steph had to buy into the approach I was seeking. He did so in full and, therefore, so did the rest of the Commando.

The document that follows is the outcome of that year's work. While I wrote it, it was easy to do so as it was nothing more than a codification of all the collective planning and ideas. It was the overarching design for our tour beneath which occurred the numerous specific plans we undertook in Afghanistan. It proved its worth time and again and delivered an unprecedented set of outcomes; the collective endeavour and endless toil of formulating this plan was priceless.

15 March 2011

OPERATIONAL DESIGN FOR COMBINED FORCE NAD-E-ALI SOUTH

INTRODUCTION

1. The opaque challenges of operating in Afghanistan oblige our operational design to be clear and coherent from the outset. This document is the conceptual framework for our tour. It is not a tactical directive, which will follow in due course, but it provides the intellectual basis for our tactical activity. It is generic – the detail will come in baseline orders – and neither didactic nor doctrinaire. It aims to provide a common baseline upon which ingenuity and initiative can flourish and obstacles can be overcome. It should be read in concert with my recce report, your recce experiences and the various milestones as our thinking has developed over the last year. I am issuing it early deliberately to give you time to consider it carefully.

2. The challenge ahead of us is enormous; the associated burden of responsibility likewise. We will carry the responsibility lightly but recognize it absolutely. Our task is about Afghans. We will resist our own paradigms and, in concert with Afghan people, the Afghan forces and civilian partners, deliver security that meets Afghan needs. In order to do so, we will understand and counter the drivers of instability. We will recognize the inherent Afghan pride, particularly derived through the Pashtunwali code, and always treat Afghans with respect, empathy and dignity. Our every action will protect the mission, moving the campaign forward and making a difference for the better. The single moral and logical justification for any damage we suffer is that we sustained it while making progress.

3. It is a command responsibility that the tenets of this design are understood throughout the combined force. Its concepts must be reflected in every action on the ground where we must practice what we preach; to do otherwise will cede the initiative to the enemy and damage the campaign. The temptation under pressure will be to revert to the conventional; we will resist this and remain sympathetic to the environment and mindful of the campaign.

THE PEOPLE

4. The Afghan people come first. This is about them more than the insurgent, our partners and us. One characterization of this is that we protect the people to harm the enemy rather than harm the enemy to protect the people. The level of violence on our tour will not define its success; the appetite of the people to reject the insurgency and accept the writ of the Afghan government will. We must convince the people that this government is the best long-term solution.

5. The intricacies of the people are more complex than anything with which we are familiar and we must seek fully to decipher this. We must understand the dynamics by constantly working at our relationships with the people. We will understand who is who, who needs what, what allegiances exist and what actions create what response. Achieving this requires us to act in a way that earns the trust of the people. We must truly respect their culture and custom, empathize with them, interact closely with them and always show them respect. It will often be difficult to distinguish friend from foe, as, among the people, it is easy to mistake one for the other. We must have the self-discipline not to act on the basis of mistaken identity: to do otherwise will lose us the trust of the people, help the enemy and damage the campaign. We will prevail by appealing to the will of the mass, thereby generating a schism between it and the insurgent. This is the real opportunity and challenge.

6. The people will determine the outcome. Winning the popularity contest – for that is what this is – for the people will take consistency, measure, even-handedness, respect, nerve, sympathy and more. We must remember that the popularity contest is not ours to win; our role is enabling the Afghan government to win it. We must tread softly, recognizing how easily our footfall can compromise the government's chances of securing that victory.

THE INSURGENT

7. The enemy is complex and covers a myriad of relative evils. We must be quicker than him and, given his greater knowledge of the operating environment, this will not be easy. To achieve it we must draw maximum assistance from our Afghan partners and exploit our technological superiority. Most insurgents are not ideological and we will exploit this opportunity by attacking their strategy rather than forces piecemeal. We will give all but the irreconcilable a way out

that spares blushes; thus we will reduce the number of fighters and fights. The elders will be central to this. Some 'enemy' elements will respond to information or influence; others may need persuasion or coercion. We will find the various groups, differentiate between them and act accordingly.

8. Low-level tactical engagements favour the enemy because they demonstrate instability and insecurity. Therefore, they undermine the credibility of the Afghan government. They further the claims of the insurgent's perverse brand of security and deter the activities of agencies crucial to Afghanistan's future. And however justifiable our kinetic actions, they result in Afghan funerals, which generate brothers and cousins bent on revenge. Thus the cycle of violence continues. The enemy also invites such engagements, as he understands that the western value placed on the lives of international soldiers outweighs that he places on his own. Every unnecessary bullet or bomb is therefore counterproductive and we must not resort to violence unless we are certain both that the target is legitimate and that prosecuting it lies in the interests of the campaign.

9. While we will avoid the many playground fights on offer, we will target the real bullies; when we do so, the terms, times and places will be of our choosing. We will be unpredictable and ingenious. Afghans respect power, cast their lot with the owner of the biggest stick and must see their government defeating the insurgent. We must ensure that the irreconcilable insurgent rejects our overtures in fear of his life. We will hunt him ruthlessly and relentlessly and, once sure of the legitimacy – legally and to the campaign – of the target set, we will bring force to bear upon it. This application of force in certainty will defeat the enemy without enhancing his cause or increasing his following. Thus we will remove the vehicle against which he chooses to express himself and steal from him the people's sympathy, which he cannot afford to lose. When we do use violence, we will magnify its impact on the insurgent by protecting the people above all.

AFGHANISTAN

10. Patience and realism are vital in Afghanistan. In the interests of the campaign, we must accept frustration and forsake our appetite for tempo and quick solutions. This is about Afghans and we will respect Afghan timelines and capability limits. The shura process [the Afghan way of conducting meetings in order to make decisions] is crucial but lacks agility and responsiveness. This is the Afghan way. Equally, beware a promise undelivered: Afghans 'hear with their

ears and their eyes' – the deed matters. We must enable truly Afghan solutions to germinate and develop at a sustainable Afghan pace. Forcing artificially fast progress and activity will be counterproductive. We will pick our moments to inject energy with care or our capital will devalue fast. We must avoid being seduced by the military bravado that flows from our western outlook. If we succeed in this calibration we will expedite the time when Afghans can take the baton from us; push too hard and we will delay that moment.

AFGHAN FORCES

11. We must develop the Afghan forces and set the security conditions to transfer our activities to them. We have our part to play and we will do so in full. We will be neither arrogant nor complacent and we will really partner with our Afghan counterparts at all levels. The Afghan adage 'if you sweat for it you protect it' applies; we will help the Afghan forces to sweat for it, sweating alongside them when appropriate but resisting the temptation to do it all ourselves. We will live separately (but very closely) from them but plan everything together and operate cheek by jowl. We must always be culturally sensitive, building trust and understanding. Inter alia, play cricket, recognize special dates, be patient and always treat the Afghan forces with respect and dignity. As described above, we will resist the seductive appeal of an operational tempo that is unachievable and unsustainable by those who will secure Afghanistan long after we have gone. Being true to this will take courage and expectation management of our men.

12. Various areas are achieving local transfer in all but name; these places find us close to being in district over watch, providing reassurance and preventing failure. Placing Afghan forces at the front, we will prevent regression and spread this progress. Equally, transfer will be carefully controlled and unheralded: to do otherwise risks providing the insurgent with a *cause célèbre* against which to express himself and also might arouse Afghan sensitivities surrounding their readiness to stand alone and, by extension, the steadfastness of our commitment to them.

SOLDIERING

13. The quality of our soldiering will define our tour. Done well, it will win the popularity contest for the people and provide the irreconcilable insurgent with a nightmare. We will soldier in a way that is more appealing to the people

and more unpalatable to the insurgent than either has experienced before. The quality of our soldiering will also keep us alive. The biggest single ingredient to achieving this level of soldiering is discipline. Every member of the force must soldier peerlessly, relentlessly pursuing and rehearsing an unachievable perfection. We must never set patterns. Offensive spirit is vital and, inter alia, we will use this to turn the night to our advantage, intimidating the intimidators and dislocating the insurgent by where he finds us in the morning. We will maintain our discipline always and in every eventuality; there is no place, for example, for feral soldiering because of austere conditions. High standards will win.

14. We must lead peerlessly. We must be comfortable with change and uncertainty, resisting preciousness or myopia over our role and recognizing the wider context. Things will change and we must lead the force to remain agile and responsive to fleeting opportunities. We must inspire, sharing risk and hardship but weighing carefully our command location. We must judge the balance between maintaining situational awareness and inspiring our men on the ground by example. In General Toolan's words, 'lead your men to be hard to kill and never grow tired of doing so'. We must lead our men to calibrate their use of force appropriately, always operating legally and according to our ten principles and this design. But we will also delegate through mission command and trust our people because they are superb and we cannot be everywhere; we will encourage them to innovate and be unorthodox. Their ideas will often be the best. Embracing risk is fundamental to success; reckless gambling is not. We will consider, manage and offset risk and escalate its ownership where appropriate. If you have thought about it and the end justifies the means, I am unlikely to gainsay you but I may wish to carry the risk myself. We must also consider the combined impact of the risks we are taking, which may exceed the sum of the parts.

15. To soldier effectively in a protracted counter-insurgency, we must campaign. We must be humble towards and ready to learn much and quickly from our predecessors who have done a superb job. The handover must be forward-led with us laying down as per the existing template and resisting the temptation for sharp tweaks on the tiller. We will find and feel first, semaphoring minimal change to the people and the insurgent.

CONCLUSION

16. We are well prepared and entirely ready. Please be absolutely confident in yourself and your people. Consider this operational design carefully and then go and drive your piece of the campaign to success. Unless something outrageous

happens, I will always support the commander or man on the ground who makes difficult decisions in good faith.

17. Good luck.
{*Oliver Lee – original signed*}

The words in the design laid out needed to be understood by every single person involved in the deployment, and they were. However, they had to be boiled down into something pithy and able to be remembered verbatim, something that would guide people in the moment, including in the face of the inevitable fear, confusion, shock, anger, uncertainty and fatigue. We came up with the ten principles in what follows for this purpose. Every man carried these on his person on a small credit card and every one of our thirty-four bases had them plastered up on the walls. Essentially, these were the values through which we collectively agreed we would approach our time in Afghanistan. We identified and highlighted number eight as the pre-eminent of the ten.

45 Commando's Key Principles for HERRICK 14

1. It is an Afghan counter insurgency and we must keep Afghan needs at its centre.
2. The average Afghan wants his interests to be looked after and his security to be ensured.
3. The campaign will be won by satisfying Afghan hopes.
4. Kill the enemy when necessary but remember body count will not always indicate success.
5. Have the courage to use the absolute minimum force.
6. Always think clearly even when angry or afraid.
7. Military operations will not occur in isolation.
8. Always treat Afghan people with dignity.
9. Promise low and deliver high.
10. Minimise cultural mistakes.

Ahead of deploying to Afghanistan, the final training serial I led was an eleven-mile speed march to the iconic Lunan Bay. I spoke to the entire Commando once we were complete on the beach. I used this as another opportunity to reinforce the fundamentals of the plan and the following is what I said:

'45 Commando: the chaplain has just blessed the most awesome and arresting sight. It is a sight that I adore – a band of brothers, the most special club. We will give those who seek to oppose us an honourable way to become part of the legitimacy of Afghanistan. But if they refuse that and become irreconcilable, we will fight them hard and ruthlessly as 45 Commando always does. And we must look after the people who have known nothing other than war and oppression in their lives to date. It is about Afghans before it is about anything else, ourselves included. We must and we will – I know deep in my heart – get this right. I wish you good luck, God's speed and I will stand at your shoulder throughout.'

I distilled the plan in one other way. Most Royal Marines are interested in football and those who aren't know the rules of the sport. I said that we needed to win 4:0. 4:1 would not be good enough as the insurgent would have scored and the people would remain hidden. 3:0 would not be good enough as the insurgent needed to be defeated in a way that gave him no opportunity to seek a replay. I repeated this aim over and over again during the tour as the score began to move in our favour.

Outcome

The plan worked. The graph that follows shows an 86 per cent reduction in violence in Nad-e-Ali South during our 2011 tour versus the previous year. It is unchanged and the title refers to significant acts, which in simple terms equates to the level of violence. The dotted lines entitled 'poly' simply smooth the spikes into a trend curve.

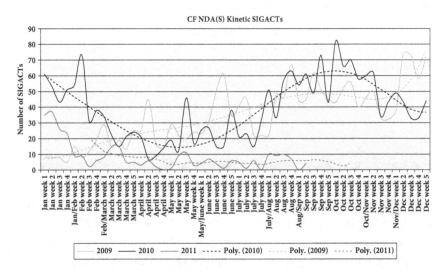

The summer fighting season in 2011 never materialized. This delivered an irrelevant and discredited insurgency, which repeatedly sought to reconstitute its leadership, received stiffening orders from afar but, in spite of concerted efforts, simply could find no opportunity to re-enter the fray. In its stead emerged confident, wilful people eager for a stake in their destiny and prepared decisively to defend the *status quo* by standing against the insurgent. They did so and this led the area to transition early to Afghan security lead, the litmus of mission success.

I did not achieve this success; indeed, any role I had in it was very modest, indeed. Afghans achieved it. Our predecessors in the area who bequeathed us the opportunity to make real progress achieved it. An excellent plan that held water, and to which all had contributed and therefore wanted to protect, achieved it. Most of all, the humanity and insatiable desire of 1,250 people to make a difference achieved it. Those 1,250 people were many and various and far from only Royal Marines. I wrote afterwards to our Gurkha contingent (B Company of the 2nd Battalion) and said I would not have swapped them for Royal Marines. This was the highest praise I could give and I meant every word – the Gurkha empathy for Afghan culture outstripped our own and was an immense force multiplier.

The plan delivered another unprecedented and priceless outcome: every person who deployed returned home alive. In the myriad dangers of Helmand and having conducted 7,600 patrols, not a single member of the force was killed, and no civilian casualties or collateral damage were inflicted. I had not thought these achievements possible, but our people proved me wrong. In doing so, they delivered the mission in the face of immense twenty-first-century complexity. I shall forever be beyond proud both of these peerless men and women and of the Afghans whom they so selflessly served.

Conclusion

Many people have asked me since whether I think it was worth it, doubly so in the context of where Afghanistan is today. This is an immensely difficult question to answer. In simple terms, I am glad that ordinary, delightful Afghan people had a period of respite from lives otherwise so indelibly benighted by violence and fear. I am pleased that they saw a different world in which hope existed. To me, that was and remains deeply worthwhile. However, what has happened since casts a very dark shadow over years of effort and sacrifice by so many Afghans, Afghan National Security Forces, and civilian and military members of the international coalition. I shall never understand the rationale behind building such a vastly expensive house and then refusing to pay its infinitesimally smaller annual repairs and upkeep, and I think our ill-considered and mismanaged withdrawal was precisely this.

8

Killing over winning

How fluid ethics turned success into failure for Britain's special forces

Chris Green

Introduction

In 1992, the year I served as a young captain with 2nd Battalion The Light Infantry (2LI) in South Armagh, Northern Ireland, eighty-nine people lost their lives as a result of the 'Troubles'. In a terrible war of sectarian attrition, loyalist and republican paramilitaries used what we would now call 'targeted killing' to murder government officials and adversary leaders in their homes or workplaces, often while their families were present. As prime minister, Margaret Thatcher expressed the views of many in condemning these attacks as 'cowardly, wicked and evil'.[1] Only the British government, it seemed, concerned itself with legitimacy and the Law of Armed Conflict.

Some twenty years later, serving as an elderly captain with 1st Battalion Grenadier Guards (1GG) in Helmand Province, Afghanistan, it became apparent that British special forces, subsumed into an American-led Special Operations Command, had enthusiastically adopted near identical tactics to target alleged insurgents in their homes under cover of darkness. According to some estimates, these so-called 'night raids' became so routine that they were being conducted at a rate of up to 1,000 per month.[2] As with the Irish paramilitaries, collateral damage was a persistent feature of these tactics. According to the testimony

---

[1] Remarks condemning the IRA attack on Sir Peter Terry, 19 September 1990: 'I was utterly appalled and deeply grieved. The IRA now seem to be going for people who are defenceless at the time when they are attacked. It is thoroughly cowardly and we shall have to consider how we can strengthen even further our defences against them. It is a wicked, evil thing to do'. Margaret Thatcher Foundation.

[2] 'The Cost of Kill/Capture: Impact of the Night Raid Surge on Afghan Civilians', *Open Society Foundations and The Liaison Office*, 19 September 2011.

of Afghan eyewitnesses, those targeted were often unarmed and usually surrounded by their families. In the face of bitter complaint by Afghan-elected officials and repeated calls from President Hamid Karzai for them to be stopped, successive NATO commanders insisted the raids were both necessary and highly successful at disrupting insurgent networks.[3] This claim seems less certain when viewed through the prism of a resurgent Taliban and the miserable failure of the ISAF (International Security Assistance Force) mission in Afghanistan. What happened in the intervening twenty years to turn right-minded revulsion and condemnation at terror tactics into adoption and enthusiastic support for an 'industrial scale counter-terrorism killing machine'[4] that not only prioritized killing over winning the hearts and minds of the Afghan population but which also, seemingly, resulted in catastrophic moral and strategic failure?

That night raids violated Afghan cultural norms and diminished the ethical and moral legitimacy of the ISAF mission does not warrant intelligent debate or dispute. To any reasonable person who has ever conducted a compound clearance, put their boot to a door and looked into the eyes of a terror-stricken homeowner over the barrel of an assault rifle, it is immediately obvious: such tactics should be used sparingly, particularly in a counter-insurgency context. The reaction to armed men bursting into private homes under cover of darkness, forcibly separating women and children from men of fighting age and then incarcerating or killing them is universal and will elicit precisely the same visceral and enduring response in Kenilworth as in Kandahar. Such tactics are more commonly associated with totalitarian regimes, such as the 'disappearances' in Chile during the Pinochet-era, than with liberal democracies purporting to emancipate a downtrodden people from a tyrannical regime. Setting aside the need to debate the revulsion and anger that night raids induced in the local population, were they even legal?

Targeted killings

According to the United Nations Human Rights Council, a targeted killing is defined as 'the intentional, premeditated and deliberate use of lethal force,

---

[3] Joshua Partlow, 'Karzai wants U.S. to Reduce Military Operations in Afghanistan', *Washington Post Foreign Service*, Sunday, 14 November 2010.

[4] Lieutenant Colonel (retired) John Nagl, FRONTLINE documentary Kill/Capture directed by Dan Edge: 'We're getting so good at various electronic means of identifying, tracking, locating members of the insurgency that we're able to employ this extraordinary machine, an almost industrial-scale counterterrorism killing machine that has been able to pick out and take off the battlefield not just the top level al Qaeda-level insurgents, but also increasingly is being used to target mid-level insurgents.'

by States or their agents acting under colour of law, or by an organized armed group in armed conflict, against a specific individual who is not in the physical custody of the perpetrator.[5] However, unlike other terms with which it is often interchangeably used, such as 'extrajudicial killing', 'summary execution' and 'assassination', all of which are illegal, 'targeted killing' is not a term defined under international law.

In recent years, a number of countries, notably the United States, have exploited this lack of agreed definition to permit targeted killing as a legitimate response to terrorism and asymmetric warfare.[6] The United Kingdom is not one of them. UK Defence Doctrine is unequivocal: 'Military operations must comply with the underpinning principles of the law of armed conflict.'[7]

In the counter-insurgency context, targeted killing by British forces may be lawful when the target is a combatant or fighter but only for such time as the person 'directly participates in hostilities'.[8] This specifically excludes those who provide financial support, political or ideological advocacy and food or shelter. Given these very stringent limitations, even at a conceptual level, it is difficult to fathom how targeting individuals while asleep in their homes and, therefore, not directly participating in hostilities received official sanction. While other contributing nations to the ISAF mission may have felt able to exploit a legal grey area to conduct night raids, no such legal ambiguity existed for members of the British Army.

The components of 'Fighting Power'

If night raids ran counter to the strategic aims of the ISAF mission and failed to meet the legal threshold for British participation, were they so desirable to military commanders that these limitations could be overlooked? There is a school of thought espoused by historian and author Andrew Roberts, writing for

---

[5] Philip Alston, 'Report of the Special Rapporteur on Extrajudicial, Summary or Arbitrary Executions. Addendum: Study on Targeted Killings', United Nations Human Rights Council, 28 May 2010.

[6] *Definition of Asymmetric Warfare* [online]. Oxford University Press, 2021, https://www.lexico.com. Accessed: 29 July 2022: 'Warfare between forces unequal in size, composition, or means; specifically warfare in which a smaller or ostensibly inferior force uses unexpected, unconventional tactics to its advantage in combating a larger or apparently superior adversary.'

[7] Army Doctrine Publication: Land Operations (updated 31 March 2017).

[8] Geneva Conventions Common Article 3, AP I, art. 52(1) and (2); AP I, art. 50(1); International Humanitarian Law Research Initiative, HPCR Manual and Commentary on International Law Applicable to Air and Missile Warfare, Harvard University Program on Humanitarian Policy and Conflict Research, 15 May 2009, http://www.ihlresearch.org/amw/manual (HPCR Commentary), section C.12.(a).

the *Sunday Times*, that 'events have taken place in war that are best ignored and forgotten'. He further argues that, in Afghanistan 'the SAS [Special Air Service] has done much violence on our behalf' and 'deserve protection from scrutiny, as their enemies almost never play by the rules'. Such scrutiny, he argues, diminishes our ability to win.[9]

Roberts's thesis rehashes a populist viewpoint that was widely condemned by *Times* readers, most notably those within the military community. To anyone with even a basic understanding of UK Defence Doctrine and the principles of 'Fighting Power', this should not have come as a surprise.

Enshrined in the unassumingly titled JDP 0-01, Defence Doctrine outlines the broad philosophy and principles underpinning how UK Defence is employed and is the capstone from which all other subordinate national doctrine is derived. It advances the principle of 'Fighting Power', which defines operational effectiveness – the ability to fight and to win. Fighting Power is made up of three components: Conceptual; Moral; and Physical.

The conceptual component is the force's knowledge, understanding and application of doctrine – the ideas behind how to operate and fight – kept relevant by its ability to learn and adapt. The moral component is the force's morale, leadership and ethical conduct: the ability to get people to operate and fight and to do so appropriately. The physical component consists of manpower, equipment, sustainability and resources: the means to operate and fight. As JDP 0-01 makes clear, 'none can claim precedence and each mutually supports and informs the other'.

With regard to the moral component, subordinate doctrine further elucidates that 'to be effective, a force's actions must reflect a sound and appropriate ethical, moral and legal foundation, and be perceived as such by the audience. If they are not, campaign authority will be undermined, reducing, if not removing, the opportunity to translate tactical military success into desired political outcomes.'[10]

Tellingly, US Army doctrine does not use or recognize the Fighting Power model whereas for British military commanders at all levels it is fundamental. Consequently, it is hard to imagine British commanders enthusiastically overlooking the obvious moral shortcomings of night raids, not least because they so obviously undermined campaign authority and demonstrably failed to translate into desired political outcomes, on an almost daily basis.

[9] Andrew Roberts, 'With its Hands Tied, the SAS Loses', *Sunday Times*, 9 August 2020.
[10] Army Doctrine Publication: Land Operations (updated 31 March 2017).

Perhaps General Erwin Rommel was right when he famously stated that 'the British write some of the best doctrine in the world; it is fortunate that their officers do not read it'. It may be convenient to think so, but the increasing professionalization of military studies and a highly competitive career landscape in a diminishing army make it unlikely. As incomprehensible as it may seem, it is more probable that commanders simply did not know and, if they did, were powerless to intervene and prevent it.

The SAS are Britain's tier-one special forces and, as such, are national strategic assets that bypass the normal military chain of command. Not only are their activities shrouded in secrecy – the MOD steadfastly refuses to comment on SAS operations and activities – but they also receive their orders directly from defence chiefs or defence ministers. In some instances, missions can be so sensitive that the final go/no go decision rests with the prime minister.

Command and lack of control

In an anonymous interview with journalist David Collins for the *Sunday Times*, one former Task Force Helmand commander admitted he had no idea what the SAS were doing. 'I suspect I would have been able to find out, if I had really pushed,' he said.[11] His seeming lack of curiosity is regrettable, but this freedom to operate beyond the scrutiny of the military leadership on the ground is unlikely to have been popular with field commanders – indeed, it is a lesson from history we seem to have overlooked.

Field Marshal Sir William Slim, one of Britain's foremost wartime military leaders, who led Imperial British forces in Burma from defeat in 1942 to overwhelming victory in 1945, expressed deep reservations about the command and control of special forces in his theatre of operations.

> The question of control of these clandestine bodies is not without its pitfalls. In the last war among the allies, cloak-and-dagger organisations multiplied until, to commanders in the field, they became an embarrassment. The trouble was that each was controlled from some distant headquarters of its own, and such was the secrecy and mutual suspicion in which they operated that they sometimes acted in close proximity to our troops without the knowledge of any commander

---

[11]   David Collins, 'The SAS Put Soldiers in Grave Danger', *Sunday Times*, 17 July 2022.

in the field, with a complete lack of coordination among themselves, and in dangerous ignorance of local tactical developments.[12]

Slim's analysis of the command pitfalls in 1940s Burma rings true seventy years later in Afghanistan where another anonymous British officer observed, 'special forces operated under different rules of engagement. They would go in, do whatever they were doing and f*** off again. Next morning there would be villagers banging on the door of the regular army's forward operating base saying, "What was going on last night? You just murdered a whole family."'[13] Such concerns are not confined to anonymous sources.[14]

It is not especially difficult to understand why the UK government might so readily accept subordinating the SAS to a US command in Afghanistan. The relatively small numbers of personnel and resources committed was far outweighed by the strategic capital gained by such close cooperation with our most important military ally. For the soldiers and officers directly involved, it offered a tantalizing opportunity to significantly enhance the physical component of their fighting power with access to the deeper pockets of the US Department of Defense (DoD) – and with it better resources and equipment. For those drawing up this arrangement, it must have seemed a 'win-win', but it had profound, possibly unanticipated, consequences.

In the first instance, US military doctrine does not embrace the concept of Fighting Power and the mutually supportive balance that must be maintained between the conceptual, physical and moral components as a necessary condition for success. Consequently, undoubted physical enhancements came at the expense of a loss of capability in the conceptual and moral domains.

These most obviously manifested themselves as a diminution in legal and ethical foundations compounded by an absence of appropriate leadership. Unlike their UK allies, US experts concluded that targeted killings, in keeping with enhanced interrogation techniques, were legally sound and embarked on an ambitious programme of kill/capture missions. If British operatives under a US command were to have utility, they had little option but to embrace tactics that would not meet British legal or ethical thresholds. The removal of field command over British troops was the final nail in the coffin and prevented

---

[12] Defeat into Victory, *Field Marshal Sir William Slim*, 1956 extract sourced from Daniel N. White, 'Why America is Losing its Wars', *The Contrary Perspective*, 15 January 2014.

[13] Collins, 'The SAS Put Soldiers in Grave Danger'.

[14] Frank Ledwidge, *Losing Small Wars: British Military Failure in Iraq and Afghanistan* (London: Yale University Press, October 2011); Mike Martin, *An Intimate War: An Oral History of the Helmand Conflict 1978-2012* (London: C. Hurst & Co. Publishers Ltd, July 2014); Chris Green, *Spin Zhira: Old Man in Helmand* (London: OMiH Ltd, May 2016).

effective oversight, even when 'alarm bells were ringing' in the mind of the senior British Army officer in Afghanistan at the time.[15]

Understanding how elements of the British Army came to be operating outside of mandated UK Defence Doctrine, beyond the legal threshold imposed upon UK forces and without the control of British field command, is instructive and troubling enough but, regrettably, it is not the complete picture.

Credible evidence

Rumours and allegations of 'a lack of respect for human life and dignity, "death squads", war crimes, cover-ups and botched investigations'[16] have been a persistent feature of ISAF special forces operations in Afghanistan. Contributing nations to the ISAF mission have initially responded to these allegations by remaining either tight-lipped or issuing denials. In some cases, those who stand accused have received operational awards, promotions and even an executive grant of clemency.

However, a dogged persistence by some service members to uphold international humanitarian law and the observance of military values and standards has exposed a pattern of behaviour and abuse that appears to have become organizationally routine within ISAF special forces – and even exceeds the different boundaries and constraints of US military doctrine and legal codes. The Inspector General of the Australian Defence Force (ADF) Afghanistan Inquiry Report,[17] commonly known as the Brereton Report, has revealed serious failings in the leadership and culture of the Special Air Service Regiment (SASR) resulting in killings and cover-ups in Afghanistan that have taken years to expose.

Insiders speak of 'a collapse in basic morality'[18] and believe prosecutions for war crimes and sweeping reforms of the secretive unit must follow if it is not to be rendered 'strategically irrelevant'.[18] Australian prime minister Scott Morrison acknowledged that 'It is a very, very serious issue and the government will be taking it very seriously'.[19]

---

[15] Collins, 'The SAS Put Soldiers in Grave Danger'.

[16] Dr Samantha Crompvoets, 'Special Operations Command (SOCOMD) Culture and Interactions: Perceptions, Reputation and Risk', February 2016.

[17] Australian Government Department of Defence.

[18] Statement attributed to Major General (retd.) Jeff Sengelman, DSC, AM, CSC, Australian Army with further detail of a letter signed by Sengelman in April 2016, '"Collapse in Morality" behind SAS War Crimes', *The Sydney Morning Herald*, 26 September 2020.

[19] 'The Prime Minister Says Report on Australian Defence Force is "Highly Sensitive"', *The Australian*, 7 November 2020.

In the United States, President Trump controversially intervened in the military justice system to pardon, acquit and even promote US special forces soldiers implicated in war crimes.[20] These acts of clemency were not universally welcomed either by Congress or by the military chain of command. In July 2019, following numerous allegations of misconduct appearing in the US media, Rear Admiral Collin Green, the head of Naval Special Warfare Command, stated in a letter to all United States Navy Sea, Air, and Land (SEAL) formations: 'I don't know yet if we have a culture problem, I do know that we have a good order and discipline problem that must be addressed immediately.'[21] In March 2020, a sweeping USSOCOM (US Special Operations Command) review mandated by Congress concluded: 'Army Green Berets and Navy SEALs, have developed a problematic culture that overemphasises combat "to the detriment of leadership, discipline and accountability."'[22]

Within days of President Trump vacating the White House, the DoD Inspector General's office announced a review to 'determine the extent to which US Central Command (USCENTCOM) and USSOCOM developed and implemented programs . . . to reduce potential law of war violations when conducting operations.'[23] The timing hardly seems to be coincidental.

The actions of special forces soldiers belonging to other ISAF contributing nations, including the British and New Zealand SAS, have also been subject to media scrutiny. These include investigations by the *Sunday Times* Insight Team[24] and BBC *Panorama*[25] into claims by Afghan nationals of extrajudicial killings perpetrated by so-called 'rogue troopers'. In New Zealand, investigative journalists Nicky Hagar and Jon Stephenson[26] published claims of war crimes and cover-ups by New Zealand special forces following a raid in Baghlan Province in 2010. Both the British and New Zealand investigations lean heavily on service personnel to corroborate eyewitness accounts.

[20] Bryan Bender and Wesley Morgan, 'Trump Pardons Soldiers Implicated in War Crimes', *Politico*, 15 November 2019.
[21] Gina Harkins, 'Head of Navy SEALs Says "We Have a Problem" Following High-Profile Scandals', *Military.com*, 1 August 2019.
[22] 'Elite U.S. Forces Critique Themselves: Overused, Underled, Raid-Obsessed', *The New York Times*, 29 January 2020.
[23] Michael J. Roark, 'Evaluation of U.S. Central Command and U.S. Special Operations Command Implementation of the DoD's Law of War Program (Project No. D2021-DEV0PD-0045.000)', Deputy Inspector General for Evaluations, 25 January 2021.
[24] 'Rogue SAS Unit accused of Executing Civilians in Afghanistan', *Sunday Times*, 2 July 2017.
[25] 'War Crimes Scandal Exposed', *BBC Panorama*, 18 November 2019; 'SAS Death Squads Exposed: A British War Crime?', *BBC Panorama*, 18 July 2022.
[26] Nicky Hagar and Jon Stephenson, 'Hit & Run: The New Zealand SAS in Afghanistan and the Meaning of Honour', 1 January 2017.

Unfortunately, these allegations have not led to the same level of debate as with their US and Australian allies. In the case of UK special forces, valid concerns have either been ignored or covered up. Despite the findings of the Brereton Report, United Nations condemnation of the use of Presidential Pardon[27] and the ongoing DoD evaluation, the UK MOD continues to maintain that an independent inquiry is unnecessary, (incorrectly) noting that 'the Australian report did not implicate British personnel'.[28]

While the report is confined to examining the actions of the Australian Defence Force, an informant to the 2016 Inquiry that sparked the investigation is recorded as saying, 'Whatever we do, though, I can tell you the Brits and the US are far, far worse.'[29] The report's author, military sociologist Dr Samantha Crompvoets, is in no doubt that 'it wasn't just confined to Australian troops'.[30] What appears to have happened inside ISAF special forces that enabled its soldiers to behave like 'self righteous [*sic*] entitled prick[s] who believed the rules of the regular army didn't apply to them'?[31]

'Warrior culture'

Why do good people do bad things? History teaches us that perpetrators of war crimes very often sincerely believe that what they are doing is right.[32] It is significant that many of those interviewed by the Brereton Inquiry were found to be 'in denial' with regards to wrongdoing. There is plenty of research within the field of human psychology to explain what may have gone wrong in the Special Operations Task Group in Afghanistan. What processes occurred that allowed commanders and their subordinates to disengage their moral reasoning and principles in order to justify their bad behaviour?

Psychologists refer to this as a 'deactivation of moral standards',[33] which occurs in a variety of ways. First, we begin to focus on desired outcomes and

---

[27] 'US Pardons for Accused War Criminals Contrary to International Law: UN Rights Office', *UN News*, 19 November 2019.

[28] 'Call for Inquiry into Afghan "War Crimes"', *Lucy Fisher, Times*, 21 November 2020.

[29] 'Special Operations Command (SOCOMD) Culture and Interactions: Insights and Reflections', *Dr Samantha Crompvoets*, January 2016.

[30] 'The Expert Whose Work Sparked the Afghan War Crimes Report Says the Alleged Conduct is "Unbelievable"', *SBS News Australia*, 19 November 2020.

[31] Statement attributed to ADF Special Operations Commander, Major General Adam Findlay. Nick McKenzie and Chris Masters, 'Special Forces Chief Acknowledges War Crimes, Blames "Poor Moral Leadership"', *The Age*, 28 June 2020.

[32] Matthew Talbert and Jessica Wolfendale, 'War Crimes: Causes, Excuses and Blame', November 2018.

[33] Craig E. Johnson, 'Meeting the Ethical Challenges of Leadership: Casting Light or Shadow', PhD.

rationalize the means by which to achieve them. This overriding belief that the end justifies the means is endemic in American culture. It has been normalized in countless Hollywood movies and popular TV shows from *Rambo* to *A Few Good Men, 24* and Netflix's *Punisher*. It was used to legitimize extraordinary rendition, waterboarding and other crimes in the minds of the perpetrators and those that sanctioned them at the highest levels of the US government.

This 'problematic culture' appears to have leached into US special forces' *modus operandi* in Iraq and Afghanistan and was subsequently adopted by other ISAF special forces' national components who all operated under a US command based at Bagram Airbase. Without identifying the assimilation of US military culture as the source, the Brereton Report notes: 'A substantial indirect responsibility falls upon those in [the]Special Air Service Regiment who embraced or fostered the "warrior culture" and the clique of non-commissioned officers who propagated it.'

Revelations in February 2019 that one UK SAS squadron adopted the *Punisher* skull emblem[34] as part of its uniform in recognition of its service alongside US Navy SEALs, evidenced not only the closeness of those ties but also the extent of cultural diffusion within UK special forces. *Punisher* is the name of a Marvel series made for Netflix, which follows fictional marine veteran Frank Castle who becomes a vigilante after the murder of his family. He routinely employs murder, kidnapping, extortion, coercion, threats of violence and torture in his campaign against crime and is unequivocally a poor role model for the professional soldier.

Not only did coalition special forces adopt questionable US culture, tactics and emblems but they even used the same 'the dog ate my homework' falsifications in their after-action reports. Brereton noted: 'This became so routine that operational reporting had a "boilerplate" flavour, and was routinely embellished, and sometimes outright fabricated.' In the United Kingdom, some of these 'cut and paste' reports have been released to solicitors Leigh Day as part of a High Court ruling[35] and barely stand up to even the most basic scrutiny. Leaked emails reveal that they were met with incredulity even within the UK special forces community.[36] It is reasonable to assume that far more effort and energy would have been invested if so-called 'rogue troopers' had felt the need to convincingly cover their tracks. They had been culturally conditioned to believe the end

---

[34] Bryony Jewell, 'Army Bosses Order SAS Troops to Stop Wearing Skull Badges', *Mail Online*, 5 February 2019.
[35] 'Did UK Special Forces Execute Unarmed Civilians?', *BBC News*, 1 August 2020.
[36] '"Rogue SAS Afghanistan Execution Squad" Exposed by Email Trail', *Times*, 1 August 2020.

justifies the means, or as the Brereton Report observes: 'An understanding of how to describe an engagement to satisfy reporting expectations, combined to contribute to the creation of a sense of impunity among operators.'

Another recognized method by which people defend their bad behaviour is what psychologists refer to as 'diffusion of responsibility'.[37] In other words, everybody was doing it.

Counterproductive 'counter-insurgency'

The Joint Special Operations Command (JSOC) based at Bagram had principal responsibility for delivering 'Joint Prioritised Effects', a military euphemism for kill or capture. To be placed on the Joint Prioritised Effects List (J-PEL) all too often amounted to the former rather than the latter in the form of a special operation night raid, so much so that the J-PEL was unofficially known as the 'kill-list'.[38]

The stated aim of night raids was to immobilize insurgents by removing their commanders, to 'cut the head off the snake'. However, by April 2011 according to some estimates, night raids in Afghanistan were being conducted at a rate of 1,000 per month.[39] Everybody was doing it.

The total number of ISAF night raids conducted may never be publicly revealed, but there is no doubt from statistics provided to the international media in early 2011 that they numbered in thousands.[40] That they killed a large number of Taliban commanders and fighters as ISAF repeatedly claimed is not disputed. It is harder to establish the total number of non-combatants killed or incarcerated, but analysis of officially released figures in a ten-month period in 2010–11 indicates they were substantial.[41]

Little, if any, consideration was given to the wider strategic impact in the battle for the hearts and minds of the Afghan people. Some experts believe this failure to discriminate between combatants, persons who are *hors de combat*,

---

[37] Udochi Emeghara, 'Bystander Effect and Diffusion of Responsibility', *Simply Psychology*, 24 September 2020.

[38] Nick Davies, 'Afghanistan War Logs: Task Force 373 – Special Forces Hunting Top Taliban', *Guardian*, 25 July 2010.

[39] 'The Cost of Kill/Capture: Impact of the Night Raid Surge on Afghan Civilians', *Open Society Foundations and The Liaison Office*, 19 September 2011.

[40] Emma Graham-Harrison, 'Factbox: Night-time Raids in Afghanistan', *Reuters*, 26 February 2011.

[41] Gareth Porter, 'ISAF Data: Night Raids Killed Over 1,500 Afghan Civilians', *Inter Press Service News Agency*, 3 November 2011.

non-combatant sympathizers and innocent civilians terminally undermined the counter-insurgency narrative and materially contributed to NATO's defeat.[42]

It is also the conclusion of the ADF report: 'Fundamental principles of counter-insurgency warfare were disregarded; in particular, local nationals were presumed to be hostile; and the winning of the hearts and minds of local nationals was not given priority'. This view is mirrored at the Royal Danish Defence College.[43] As one Danish officer summarized, 'ISAF won all the battles but NATO lost the war.'

Moral disengagement and exceptionalism

Other ways by which people justify unacceptable behaviour is to employ 'euphemistic labelling' to downplay injurious or harmful behaviours and reduce responsibility for it from the individual.[44] Whether it be doctrinal jargon or squaddie slang, euphemism is commonplace in military language. Authorized terminology such as 'kinetic' and 'collateral damage' rub shoulders with widely adopted language such as 'jackpot' and 'flat pack' as well as other vocabulary that does not receive official sanction. While this is certainly not unique to special forces, it plays a contributory role in normalizing immoral behaviours and activities. It also plays a role in dehumanizing victims who become simply 'bravos'. Thousands on the J-PEL were reduced to randomly assigned 'objective' names.

Advantageous or exonerating comparison is another form of moral disengagement identified by Albert Bandura[45] whereby individuals contrast their conduct with those of others. The Brereton Report observes that, even in the face of fabricated 'boilerplate' reports 'there was a presumption, not founded in evidence, to discount local national complaints as insurgent propaganda or motivated by a desire for compensation'. More extreme versions of advantageous comparison have been reported in the British press to justify the actions of UK special forces operators during the same period.[46] These include the claim by

[42] Ledwidge, *Losing Small Wars*; Martin, *An Intimate War*; Christina Lamb, *Farewell Kabul: From Afghanistan To A More Dangerous World* (London: William Collins, April 2015); Theo Farrell, *Unwinnable: Britain's War in Afghanistan, 2001-2014* (London: Bodley Head, September 2018).

[43] Afghanistan: Lessons Identified, 2001-2014. The Royal Danish Defence College.

[44] Albert Bandura, 'Moral Disengagement in the Perpetration of Inhumanities', *Personality and Social Psychology Review*, August 1999, 3, pp. 193–209.

[45] Ibid.

[46] Mark Nicol, 'The Truth About SAS Shoot to Kill Night Raids', *Mail on Sunday*, 9 July 2017.

an anonymous former SAS soldier that 'We went in hard and I admit that the tactics do sound gruesome, but these were bad men. So for me, the end justified the means.' Regrettably, it is probable that many of those killed in night raids were not, in fact 'bad men' but included Afghans holding non-combat functions in the Taliban network as well as victims of misidentification or a malicious intelligence tip.[47] Even General Petreus, an advocate for night raids, is reported to have acknowledged that 'There's just a limit to how many precise targets you have at any one time'.[48]

Leadership, organizational structure and history are also key to the science of why good people do bad things. The British SAS, formed during the Second World War, is widely credited as the first modern special forces unit and the model for most other Western units of its kind. Founded on a classless (rather than rankless) organizational structure, its origins lie in the contrary characteristics of David Stirling and Jock Lewes, its first commanders. It typifies a leadership style, recently coined 'ambidextrous leadership'[49] that has been identified in high-performing organizations. Successful ambidextrous leaders must balance the competing demands of innovation, risk taking and experimentation (termed 'exploration', i.e. Stirling) with efficiency, implementation and execution (termed 'exploitation', i.e. Lewes). However, studies show that where ambidextrous leaders employ both authoritarian and benevolent behaviours to achieve goals, they, wittingly or unwittingly, increase the likelihood for moral disengagement within an organization.[50]

This model characterized ISAF special forces command in Afghanistan. A very high operational tempo was demanded of special forces soldiers but normal military standards, such as observance of rank and dress codes, were relaxed or dropped entirely. The Brereton Report identifies that alcohol consumption and relaxed levels of personal hygiene contributed to an erosion of standards over time and a 'logic of exceptionalism warranting the application of different rules and behaviours to those that applied to other ADF members'. On a visit to meet British special forces, a former commander of the United Kingdom's Task Force

---

[47] Gareth Porter and Shah Noori, 'UN Reported Only a Fraction of Civilian Deaths from U.S. Raids', *Inter Press Service News Agency*, 17 March 2011.

[48] Statement attributed to US Army General (retd.) David H. Petreus, 'Obama's Wars', Bob Woodward, May 2011.

[49] Kathryn Rosing, Michael Frese, and Andreus Bausch, 'Explaining the Heterogeneity of the Leadership-Innovation Relationship: Ambidextrous Leadership', *The Leadership Quarterly*, 11 August 2011.

[50] Kang Hwa Shaw, Na Tang, and Hung-Ye Liao, 'Authoritarian-Benevolent Leadership, Moral Disengagement, and Follower Unethical Pro-organizational Behavior: An Investigation of the Effects of Ambidextrous Leadership', *Frontiers in Psychology*, 21 April 2020.

Helmand recalls, 'I remember thinking their uniforms were pretty sloppy, and they all had these enormous beards. There was a casualness about it all that rang alarm bells for me.'[51] The Australian investigators also observed that many of the leadership failures identified 'are founded in attitudes which are, in themselves, commendable: loyalty to the organisation, trust in subordinates, protection of subordinates and maintenance of operational security'.

As their report highlights, it can be a toxic combination that not only accounted for the atrocities themselves but also the wall of silence that followed: 'given the arduous selection process and how hard it is to get there in the first place, it is to an extent understandable that some might not be prepared to risk that position at the time to try to stop what was seen as an organisationally routine practice.'

History has a role to play in normalizing immoral behaviours. Like all regiments, the SAS takes great pride in the manner of its formation and celebrates the 'maverick' nature of its founders, none more so than Paddy Mayne who won four DSOs. Mayne, undoubtedly fearless, was also callous, so much so that SAS founder, David Stirling, expressed concerns of 'executions in cold blood'. Despite Stirling's grave misgivings, Paddy Mayne is today revered by serving SAS soldiers even more than Stirling himself. Despite his many wartime achievements and successes, Mayne is a deeply questionable role model, especially so when others from the regimental annals, such as Major John Tonkin,[52] serve as exemplars of the values and standards to which the modern SAS might more usefully aspire.

It is also revealing that, in 2016, author Ben Macintyre was given exclusive access by regimental headquarters to SAS archives for his book, *Rogue Heroes*. Alongside tales of great heroism, extraordinary daring and courageous restraint, it also reveals some of the regiment's darker wartime secrets. In their unprecedented support for his book, the SAS leadership exposed a tolerant, some might say lax, attitude towards what most would consider to be war crimes.

A seemingly permissive organizational structure can also exacerbate wrongdoing by appearing to give it legitimacy. Brereton observes an 'excessive willingness of so many people to take things at face value' and a reluctance from those behind the wire to challenge the boots on the ground. This absence of curiosity was compounded by commanders and legal officers 'embellishing operational reporting to demonstrate the legitimacy of engagements' which in turn enabled 'those who were "on the ground" to act in the knowledge

---

[51] Collins, 'The SAS Put Soldiers in Grave Danger'.
[52] Ben Macintyre, 'SAS Bravery Cannot be Counted in Kills', *Times*, 21 November 2020. https://www .thetimes.co.uk/article/sas-bravery-cannot-be-counted-in-kills-mc2wq066q.

that their immediate superiors would be reluctant to call into question their professionalism and propriety, and unable to contradict their accounts.'

The culture of secrecy and self-regulation, so heavily criticized by 1st Viscount Slim in the Burma campaign, was a hallmark of ISAF special forces in Afghanistan. Brereton identifies the absence of 'national command' and 'separation from the conventional army' as significant contributory factors in wrongdoing and notes: 'This phenomenon is not limited to Australia; the Inquiry encountered it among coalition partners also.'

Lack of accountability

As we know from the parliamentary expenses[53] and media phone hacking[54] scandals, self-regulatory mechanisms are seldom effective and easily abused. Given the UK government's long-standing policy never to comment on UK special forces operations, it seems improbable that the British SAS were any more immune to this abuse than their Australian counterparts. The available evidence appears to point in the opposite direction.

Revealingly, in the same year the Inspector General of the Australian Defence Force commissioned the Brereton investigation, concerns with regard to a lack of transparency and accountability within UK special forces were raised by the Oxford Research Group.[55] Later the same year, in a written question to the MOD, Labour MP Yasmin Qureshi asked whether the government would 'assess the potential merits of appointing a committee of parliamentarians to oversee the operations and budget of special forces'. Sir Michael Fallon, then Secretary of State for Defence, replied bluntly: 'No'.[56] This blanket refusal at the very top of the UK government to discuss special forces operations, even within Parliament, makes it almost impossible for whistle-blowers to come forward to report abuses. It also removes important protections for special forces soldiers and damages the reputation and legitimacy of the unit to which they proudly belong.

The findings of the Brereton Report, the impending DoD evaluation, the allegations of UK complicity and the shared psychology under which wrongdoing was perpetrated should all be cause for concern. The MOD's

---

[53] Wikipedia, 'United Kingdom Parliamentary Expenses Scandal', *The Free Encyclopedia*.
[54] Wikipedia, 'News International Phone Hacking Scandal', *The Free Encyclopedia*.
[55] Paul Rogers, 'UK Special Forces: Accountability in Shadow War', *Oxford Research Group*, 2 May 2016.
[56] Special Forces: Finance. Question for Ministry of Defence. UIN41980, tabled on 5 July 2016.

confidence that British personnel are not implicated seems at best misplaced and at worst complicit in the denial. It is not shared by General Lord Richards, head of UK Armed Forces from 2010 to 2013, when many of the alleged extrajudicial killings took place.[57] It is deeply troubling that even the Chief of the Defence Staff appears not to have had oversight of SAS operations in Afghanistan during this period and himself publicly called for an enquiry based on the 'compelling nature' of the evidence presented to him. These include claims that senior special forces officers, including General Sir Mark Carleton-Smith, did not report alleged murders and failed to disclose evidence to the military police.[58]

Major General Justice Brereton concludes his report with a quote from Dr Crompvoets testifying to the very many 'exceptional soldiers and officers' who contributed to the inquiry and who 'upheld Army values and whose character was unquestionably of high standing'. He also provides a postscript of his own: 'The [ADF] SF community is . . . an organisation that recognises that something has gone very badly wrong and is determined to put it right.'

It would appear that UK special forces, equally populated with exceptional soldiers and officers, have not yet reached that point of self-realization. However, there is cause to believe the tide may be turning. Having repeatedly insisted for over a decade that there was 'insufficient evidence'[59] to warrant an independent investigation into allegations of war crimes, on 15 December 2022, the MOD announced a dramatic U-turn to formally establish an independent, judge-led inquiry. Chaired by the Rt Hon Lord Justice Charles Haddon-Cave, its terms of reference are to investigate 'certain matters arising from the deployment of British armed forces to Afghanistan between mid-2010 and mid-2013.'[60] In July 2023, the then Secretary of State for Defence, Ben Wallace, confirmed that the inquiry would focus on the conduct of UK special forces and allegations of extra-judicial killings.[61] Haddon-Cave stated, 'the public, and all those who serve in the military, are entitled to expect a fair, fearless and thorough examination of the facts and clear answers to the questions raised . . . within a reasonable timescale.'

Following the successful SAS operation to end the 1980 Iranian Embassy siege, Margaret Thatcher, then prime minister, insisted on a personal meeting with the troopers involved. 'Gentlemen,' she said, 'there is nothing sweeter

[57] Hannah O'Grady and Joel Gunter, 'SAS Killings: Former Head of UK Armed Forces Says he Would Order Investigation', *BBC News*, 12 July 2022.

[58] 'SAS Death Squads Exposed: A British War Crime?', *BBC Panorama*, 18 July 2022.

[59] Dan Sabbagh, 'MoD Asked Why it Withheld Evidence on 33 Suspected Afghan Civilian Executions', *The Guardian*, 2 August 2020.

[60] www.iia.independent-inquiry.uk.

[61] Defence Secretary Ben Wallace Says, 'Afghanistan War Crimes Inquiry Focused on Conduct of UK's Special Forces', *Sky News*, 5 July 2023.

than success, and you boys have got it.'[62] Given her instinctive revulsion at the cowardly, wicked and evil tactics of night raids, the allegations of war crimes that resulted and their catastrophic impact on the bitter failure of the Afghan campaign, have the boys still got it? It now falls upon Haddon-Cave to elicit the truth and provide the answer.

'The darkly hidden truth seeps from the margins and laps against the shore.'
Anon

---

[62] Comment to the SAS group gathered at Regents Park Barracks, at 21.45 pm following Operation Nimrod, 5 May 1980.

9

Must liberal democracies compromise their values in order to defeat insurgencies?

Louise Jones

Introduction

When I deployed to Kabul in the autumn of 2017, my role often required me to travel through the city in an armoured car, wearing body armour, and with my loaded rifle close to hand. As we inched through the interminable city traffic, I would look at the beautiful roses in Wazir Akbar Khan Park and wish that I could get out and walk among them. I knew even then that the fact that it was too dangerous for me to take a stroll in the main park of the capital city of Afghanistan after fifteen years of Western security efforts was probably not a good sign. And so it was that I, like many other veterans of that conflict, were hardly surprised when in August 2021, reality finally broke through and the Taliban resumed their place as head of Afghanistan's government.

As I write, a year on from those chaotic few days, the debate about our role and performance in the Afghan campaign has gently sunk out of public sight, helped on its way by a mixture of fatalism, apathy and, of course, the explosion in 2022 of the war in Ukraine sharply refocusing attentions. Narratives that enforcing security processes in a country known as the 'Graveyard of Empires' was futile, or that Western forces did an admirable job and were let down only by penny-pinching governments and unreliable allies in the Afghan security forces, meant that many in positions of responsibility were only too content to extol the virtues of 'moving on'.

This would be even easier to do now that President Putin has decided to invade Ukraine. The loudest contemporary military debate is once again centred on tank divisions and rolling artillery barrages in Eastern Europe and not on how to deal with tribal power structures and complex IEDs (Improvised

Explosive Devices) in the desert. But, if anything, the conflict in Ukraine has made understanding Afghanistan even more urgent: if the failures there were caused by political naivety, military under-resourcing and a failure to adapt to the situation on the ground, then those same failures are going to take their toll on a confrontation with the Russians much as they did with the Taliban. Except this time, the Russians are on the edge of NATO's territory and the stakes are the survival of the modern European system.

As a veteran, I can see that the failure of twenty years of Western interventionism in Afghanistan should therefore surely have us asking the big questions as to why. And one of those big questions relates not to the physical prosecution of that war: the tactics, the weapons, the soldiers. Rather, it is to the narrative that lies at the heart of the refusal to consider these elements: that peace cannot be brought to Afghanistan, and if it can, certainly not by Western liberal democracies.

Liberal democracies at war

It is this theme I want to take further in this chapter. Was the fatal weakness for Western intervention caused by the very nature of those countries, that is, to ask: What is it about liberal democracies that makes them incapable of defeating seemingly militarily inferior enemies as seems to have been shown in Afghanistan and Iraq? Why is it, as Afghanistan falls under the baleful influence of the Taliban that, just over its eastern border, China seems to have achieved the opposite in Xinjiang? I will therefore look at what it means to be a liberal democracy at war, and to see if it is this that really led to the strategic weaknesses in the campaign in Afghanistan. Is our desire to do and act good in this world merely leading to failed strategy and the cause of more harm?

To answer this, we must understand what it means when a liberal democracy conducts warfare in line with its own values. In theory, we are all familiar with the principles that underpin liberalism: individual rights, liberty and equality before the law. Democracy is closely related to this in that in theory there could be an illiberal democracy, such as tyranny of the majority, but that it usually is based on the values of consent of the governed, freedom of assembly and freedom of speech – all liberal values applied to a political system. Here in theory, then, we have some yardsticks by which to measure countries who at least claim to be liberal democracies.

So taking these political values, how do you apply them to the conduct of warfare? Surely this is an oxymoron. War after all aims to force a particular outcome on an actor, which is neither a liberal nor a democratic thing to do. Were war to be characterized as always being a choice for a liberal democracy, then perhaps this is true. However, war is often not a choice, but a last resort. Democratic means must have a framework to be carried out: if there is no forum for cooperation recognized by both sides, then violence is often the only way to compel a resolution. A non-liberal actor will have no compunction in forcing their views on a liberal one, who must then use force to repel them. War therefore is vanishingly rare between liberal democracies, who are good at creating organizations and mechanisms to sort out differences, and yet liberal democracies often find themselves at war, and, most often, fighting an insurgency.

If war is taken to be sometimes necessary, then what does it mean to conduct it in a way consistent with a liberal democracy? Usually this means adherence to the Law of Armed Conflict (LOAC), a body of international law including the Geneva Conventions and UN protocols, that has roots in the liberal-democratic tradition. Liberal values of accountability, just punishment and individual rights, which arguably could rule out violence of any kind, instead are interpreted in this context to lead to rules allowing violence, so long as it is necessary and proportionate. Harm to civilians, critical infrastructure and national heritage sites must be avoided. Weapons deemed to be needlessly barbaric, indiscriminate or that can linger long after the conflict has ended are banned. There are clear rules for managing prisoners of war (POWs) and anyone caught in the conflict who is not a combatant. The aims here are to so contain war that its disastrous effects are limited to soldiers and battlefields.

These international treaties and protocols are usually signed by the majority of state actors, including most, but not all, liberal democracies as well as countries governed under other systems. However, they are never signed officially by non-state armed groups, meaning that if the other side has no obligation or intent to adhere to LOAC, then the pressure for the counter-insurgents to drop such a 'constraint' can be high. It also makes it harder to follow LOAC even when the state retains the intent to do so. Insurgents are not easily distinguishable from civilians in that there is often no formal enlistment, uniform and identification, or de-enlistment procedures, so who really is a non-combatant? There is also a tension over which law to obey, that is, between prosecuting insurgents with the civil law of that territory, which demands things like proof of a crime for detention, or via LOAC where POWs can be held until the end of the conflict without conviction of a crime.

So does adhering to LOAC hinder counter-insurgency efforts? As we are considering this at the campaign level, let us compare NATO efforts to bring security to a mountainous Central Asian region with a long history of decentralized power and autonomy with that of Afghanistan's neighbour, the mountainous Central Asian region with a long history of decentralized power and autonomy: the Chinese Autonomous Region of Xinjiang.

China's approach

The Government of the People's Republic of China is not a liberal democracy. The power of the government is unchecked at the highest levels of the court system. There are no legal means to fight unlawful imprisonment, and the Chinese government can order its citizens as it wishes, with little formal mechanism to stop it becoming despotic. In practice this actually results in a lot less authoritarianism in most of the country than many in the West assume; overreaching local officials often suffer consequences after local outcry, presuming the outcry remains well behaved and limited. However, this system rapidly reveals its ugly side in Xinjiang.

Xinjiang, until recently, was not as well known a case in the West as Tibet, which would have served equally well as a case study here. Both regions underwent a period of relative independence in the early twentieth century before re-exertion of control by the Chinese Communist Party (CCP) in the late 1940s and 1950s. After suffering the Great Leap Forward and Cultural Revolution, China's interest in Xinjiang grew more important as her great rival the Soviet Union invaded neighbouring Afghanistan. Fearing encirclement by yet more pro-Soviet Communist countries, China chose to arm the Afghan Mujahideen. Anti-CCP sentiment flared up and in 1990 a mass protest by Uyghurs, allegedly armed by Afghans, in Barin Township was severely put down.

Violence flared up again in the twenty-first century, most notably in 2009 in Xinjiang, which saw multiple protests morph into riots as well as sporadic knife and IED attacks. I should make clear at this point that this violence cannot be classed as an 'insurgency' – it is not organized, not always clearly aligned with political motives and usually does not involve weaponry more complex than knives or crude bombs. The main political movements for independence in Xinjiang also do not support such violence and disown it when it occurs. In short, there is little to distinguish it from sporadic violence found in any poor and remote area of the world. However, its relevance here is that China has most certainly adopted a 'counterinsurgency' policy, that is, a military and police-led approach to enforcing order on an area. This securitization is now heavily supported by the latest in surveillance technology, allowing Beijing to maintain a control on citizens in the region as never before. There is little talk here of winning 'hearts and minds', rather President Xi's philosophy of 'round up those who should be rounded up'.[1]

But the CCP's totalitarian response goes far beyond just the security response. The CCP views the anger against its rule not as a questioning of its legitimacy or ability to provide economic success but, rather, a rejection of 'Chinese civilization'. The aim, then, is not to persuade or compel the population to appreciate the benefits of Beijing rule but to remove the cultural impediments, that is, to quell cultural differences and to 'sinicize' the population. Here, both Western 'hearts and minds' counter-insurgency doctrine and Beijing's security policy identify the wider civilian population as key to defeating the small number opposing them. However, whereas the West views population as 'key terrain' to be won over, Beijing still seems to agree with Mao's old dictum that insurgents 'move through a population as fish move through water'. The water must be drained to catch the fish.

Beijing is attempting to achieve this in two ways: first, by changing the ethnic make-up of the population by encouraging mass Han Chinese immigration as well as mass sterilization of Uyghurs; and second, by repressing expressions of traditional Uyghur culture and 're-educating' the population away from their traditional practices. Beijing is gambling that as opposition to its rule stems from a sense of ethnic identity, then removing the latter should remove the former.

Analysis of government documents has revealed many illiberal measures such as mass sterilization of Uyghur women, reports seemingly borne out by the 50 per cent drop in birth rates between 2017 and 2019.[2] Eighty per cent of IUDs (intrauterine devices) implanted in 2019 in China were reported to have been in Xinjiang. Significant numbers of Uyghur children have been removed from their parents to state-run orphanages, where they learn nothing of their traditional culture.[3]

A leak of classified government documents in 2019 has also revealed the extent of other efforts by Beijing to suppress Uyghur identity. The 'Xinjiang

[1] Dr David Tobin, *The 'Xinjiang Papers': How Xi Jinping Commands Policy in the People's Republic of China* (University of Sheffield, 2022), p. 32, https://www.sheffield.ac.uk/seas/news/xinjiang-papers-how-xi-jinping-commands-policy-peoples-republic-china.
[2] Dr James Leibold and Nathan Ruser, *Family De-planning: The Coercive Campaign to Drive Down Indigenous Birth-rates in Xinjiang* (Australian Strategic Policy Institute, 2021).
[3] Tobin, *The 'Xinjiang Papers'*, p. 80.

Papers' have shown that over a million Uyghur men and women have been extrajudicially detained in 're-education camps', allegedly to instil loyalty to the CCP over their Islamic faith although many of these facilities appear now to be little more than forced labour camps.[4]

These papers also detail the crackdown on expressions of Islamic faith including bans on veils and certain beard types, the use of Muslim names and Muslim marriage ceremonies. Fasting has been discouraged and some Uyghurs have allegedly been forced to eat pork, Han China's staple meat, and drink alcohol. Sixteen thousand mosques have been destroyed since 2017 alone. Those still standing are not allowed to show any signs of 'non-traditional Chinese culture', such as Arabic writing or minarets, and must display both the Chinese flag and copies of the Chinese Constitution.[5]

It is clear then that Beijing's approach to securing Xinjiang is the antithesis of liberal-democratic ways. There is no recognition of the right to freedom of religion, to a family life or to not be imprisoned indefinitely without a trial. Uyghurs do not even have rights to their own bodily autonomy and reproductive choices. There is no aspect to China's strategy that is not horrifying to read about. The government defends its policies through a series of misdirections as to the truth of what is occurring there, which we know to be false, and then finally that such actions are necessary to bring security and economic prosperity to the region. Herein lies the difficult question: Are China's actions in Xinjiang, nonetheless, succeeding where the liberal democracies in Afghanistan failed?

Has China succeeded?

It is, indeed, true that the situation in Xinjiang has not developed to the same extent as Iraq in 2014, or Afghanistan in 2021, with widespread organized militias conducting complex attacks on official forces. But it is difficult to look at the current situation, even dispassionately, and see it as a success. The Roman historian Tacitus once wrote of that empire's military operations that they 'make a desert and call it peace'. This seems particularly fitting with regard to Xinjiang. An insurgency has not overthrown the government, but the impact on the population has been just as devastating. Any civilian casualties prevented as a result of Beijing minimizing terrorist or insurgent activity must surely be

---

[4] Ibid., p. 22.
[5] Ibid., p. 12.

dwarfed by those now suffered as a result of the CCP's policies. When the cure is worse than the disease, it is hardly a cure.

There are also signs that the policies are not actually achieving lasting peace in the region or preventing violence from escalating. Periods of unrest in the 1990s in Xinjiang were in direct opposition to the mass Han immigration that was even then going on. This unrest was crucially in response to the government's counter-insurgency policies and not predating them. The protests in 2009 also showed that the depth of feeling towards Beijing had not remotely dissipated, even after nigh on fifty years of counter-separatist policies.

The attacks in Xinjiang attributed to separatists clearly also accelerated only after the exceptionally harsh crackdown in 2009.[6] And while it is too early to judge the fruits of the even more extreme policies of mass sterilization, internment and removal of children, it is difficult to see how anyone subjected to these policies would ever forget or forgive them. China has, according to conservative figures, interned over a million Uyghurs – there were clearly not a million insurgents, real or potential, in Xinjiang. So China has likely detained nigh on a million people and taught them to fear and despise the Chinese government, where previously there was likely only acquiescence and ambivalence.

It is also difficult to see how China will 're-normalize' Xinjiang in the coming years. Will adult internees be allowed to leave their camps and reintegrate into society, or will Beijing be forced to keep them in labour camps for their whole lives? Will a generation of children traumatized by an upbringing in a state orphanage lead successful adult lives, or must they too be interned as they come of age? A counter-insurgency strategy with no end in sight is not an effective one.

Defeating insurgencies: Picking your partner

This example of states using illiberal ways to defeat insurgencies and subsequently failing is backed up elsewhere and for conciseness can only be summarized here. Sri Lanka achieved the unusual feat of militarily defeating the insurgency in the north of the country, the Tamil Tigers, who announced their surrender in May 2009. This campaign stands accused by the UN of multiple war crimes. As for the situation now, large parts of predominantly Tamil areas are still designated

---

[6] First Post, *Timeline: Unrest Connected with China's Restive Xinjiang Region*, 2014, https://www.firstpost.com/world/timeline-unrest-connected-with-chinas-restive-xinjiang-region-1731073.html. Accessed: 2022.

'security zones' by the government and many Tamils are still displaced. It is that 'desert called peace' again. The Sri Lankan government, having grown accustomed to illiberal tactics such as imprisonment without trial and violent suppression of protests, became increasingly comfortable with using these tactics on the Sinhalese population as well, leading to the deposition of the government by popular protest in 2022.[7] Insurgencies also drag on in numerous other places around the world, with Yemen, Mali and the Philippines just some examples where harsh efforts to bring security are failing.

If the case for conducting counter-insurgencies not in line with liberal-democratic values looks, at best, weak and, more likely, even more ineffective, what do we see from counter-insurgencies that have ended successfully for the state actor? Examination here may indicate that while tactics should not be compromised, there may yet be an aspect of counter-insurgency where liberal-democratic values are best compromised. That is to say, the choice of partner.

The majority of states wishing to defeat an insurgency will need partners. This could include 'proxy forces' of military organizations of varied professionalism, from the Afghan National Army (ANA) to the Kurdish Peshmerga. It could include supporting a government that is not liberal or democratic – the Government of the Islamic Republic of Afghanistan was not in practice or by design a liberal democracy, though it had some liberal and democratic aspects in theory.

Working with or supporting actors that do not espouse the same values is surely hypocritical. However, as we are finding out, a liberal democracy is difficult to build in just a few short years. If a liberal democracy waits for a liberal-democratic partner, it will be waiting for a very long time. In reality, a liberal-democratic state will have to compromise its ideals in order to work with partners. The question then becomes one of relativity: How do you judge who should be fought against, and who should be fought with?

Partnering within democracies: Northern Ireland

The case study of particular interest here is Northern Ireland. This is unusual in that it was an insurgency that occurred within a liberal democracy, rather than one that liberal democracies went abroad to intervene in. Where it was not

[7] Nithyani Anandakugan, *The Sri Lankan Civil War and Its History, Revisited in 2020*, 31 August 2020, https://hir.harvard.edu/sri-lankan-civil-war/.

unusual was that its direct roots were in discrimination, in this case of Catholics by the Protestant Stormont government. It is important to note that this regional government was certainly not liberal democratic – gerrymandering of districts to ensure a Unionist majority in many city councils, despite a Catholic majority in those areas, was a key cause of resentment. The Special Powers Act allowed for detention without trial and was used almost exclusively on Catholics.[8]

While there had been violence between republicans and loyalists since the creation of Northern Ireland in 1921, it had been quite limited and poorly supported by the wider communities. However, the civil rights movement had gained momentum by the 1960s, with protests frequently turning into riots between the two communities, forcing the British government to send in the army to maintain order on what was supposed to be its own territory rather than relying on the questionable local police. At first, the army was used to even-handedly maintain peace between Catholics and Protestants, but the 'Troubles' are commonly dated from when the army broke with LOAC and shot and unlawfully killed fourteen unarmed civilians on Bloody Sunday on 30 January 1972.

This event had the effect of turbocharging support for terrorist groups within Northern Ireland. Attempts to enforce security through more troop deployments, internment without trial and more aggressive operations by British special forces were all contraventions of what would be considered liberal-democratic values, and they led to a concomitant uplift in violence by the IRA (Irish Republican Army).

The Troubles were not ended through a military defeat of the IRA, but, rather, through the signing of the Good Friday Agreement (GFA). Did this represent a successful outcome for the British government? Certainly, subsequent administrations have thought so. Soon after it was signed, Tony Blair, then prime minister, stated that 'the Good Friday Agreement is the one chance Northern Ireland has got' and was seen 'as a symbol of hope round the whole world'.[9] More recently, in the Queen's Speech, given by Prince Charles in May 2022, support for the Agreement was to be 'prioritized'[10] with the then prime minister Boris Johnson repeating soon after that it was 'the most important' in a speech to media.[11]

---

[8] Laura Donohue, 'Regulating Northern Ireland: The Special Powers Acts, 1922–1972', *The Historical Journal*, 1998, pp. 1089–120.

[9] Tony Blair, *Keynote Speech by Mr. Tony Blair at Stranmillis University College Belfast, 15 June 1999*, 1999, https://cain.ulster.ac.uk/events/peace/docs/tb15699.htm.

[10] *Queen's Speech*, 2022, https://www.gov.uk/government/speeches/queens-speech-2022.

[11] *Good Friday Agreement 'Most Important' Ahead of Northern Ireland Protocol, Boris Johnson Says*, 2022, https://www.belfasttelegraph.co.uk/news/politics/good-friday-agreement-most-important-ahead-of-northern-ireland-protocol-boris-johnson-says-41640054.html.

However, there are others who question as to whether the GFA represented a success for the British state. The journalist Peter Hitchens often criticizes the Agreement, calling it 'an instrument of surrender'.[12] He notes that the British government agreed to a series of compromises that would have been unthinkable at the start of the Troubles in the late 1960s, which included the disbandment of the Royal Ulster Constabulary, the restriction of the flying of British flags on official buildings, the release of scores of convicted IRA terrorists and the promise to cease pursuing IRA suspects as yet unprosecuted for horrific terrorist acts. For him, the sight of the Queen shaking hands with Martin McGuinness, a member of the same organization that had assassinated her husband's uncle Lord Mountbatten, was a sign of humiliation rather than reconciliation.

What is clear about the GFA is that it was overwhelmingly the democratic choice of Northern Ireland. The referendum held to approve it saw 71 per cent of the Province vote to endorse it. Perhaps it is this that really provides the metric by which to measure its success. If we measure the conduct of a campaign by its adherence to liberal-democratic values, then we should apply the same test to how it is ended. Merely saying whether the British government achieved all or some of its goals set out at the beginning of the conflict is actually a test measured using authoritarianism, that is, how successful the application of the government's authority was.

What if we measure the success of the GFA using liberal-democratic values? The GFA provided for the establishment of a power-sharing government, the circumstances for a referendum on Irish unity and the establishment of a police and justice system that would represent both communities and therefore deliver truly fair justice. The commitment to equality of treatment of both Catholics and Protestants was a key tenet that ran throughout the whole of the document. So far, so liberal democratic.

Where the GFA scores noticeably less well is in who it was signed with. Although nominally signed by only political parties, these included both Unionist and nationalist parties with very close links to loyalist paramilitaries and the IRA, respectively. It was certainly understood that these parties were signing with the consent of the armed groups, otherwise what would have been the point of doing so?

Both loyalist and nationalist paramilitaries were decidedly grisly in their approach and certainly did not adhere to principles of LOAC. Indiscriminate

---

[12] Peter Hitchens, *Her Majesty's Pleasure?*, 2014, https://hitchensblog.mailonsunday.co.uk/2014/04/her-majestys-pleasure-.html.

bombing, assassinations and kidnapping were common tactics. And yet, the GFA could not have been achieved without their cooperation. So here perhaps is the principle that liberal democracies must be prepared to compromise on: any successful counter-insurgency will require a peace agreement with the insurgents, and their likely subsequent involvement in government.

The wrong partners? Afghanistan

That is not to say that partnering any old terrorist group at any time will lead to resolution. A key hallmark of Western interventionism has been to partner with 'acceptable' host nation forces and militias, be that the ANA or the Peshmerga. The partnering of the ANA is widely likely to have contributed to defeat – their corruption and predilections made them very unpopular in the communities they were supposed to be protecting. Even the Kabul administration was a poor partner. It openly did not seek to bring good governance to Helmand and other remote provinces, leaving a power vacuum that the Taliban were only too happy to exploit.

As for the Taliban, the United States avoided entering talks with them for years, strongly counselling President Karzai to rebuff the Taliban's offer of talks in 2002 and doing nothing to support tentative dialogue between Kabul and the Taliban in ensuing years even as Pakistan directly thwarted them.[13] By 2010, however, the Obama administration began to encourage dialogue with the Taliban; this initiative, however, failed in early 2012 over Washington's naive insistence that the Taliban negotiate with Kabul directly. With American and Allied pressure at its height in the Afghan campaign, with surges in multiple provinces, the United States's bargaining hand would never be stronger.

However, the United States turned away from seriously pursuing peace negotiations and, once it announced its withdrawal and the handing of the combat mission from ISAF (International Security Assistance Force) to Afghan government forces in 2013, the compulsion for the Taliban to compromise began to wither. As the United States accelerated its wish to leave Afghanistan almost at any cost, it signed the Doha Agreement with the Taliban in 2020, followed by a dramatic scaling down of its support to the Afghan forces, leading inevitably to the collapse of the Republic's government in August 2021. The Taliban had

---

[13] James Dobbins and Carter Malkasian, 'Time to Negotiate in Afghanistan: How to Talk to the Taliban', *Foreign Affairs*, 2015, 94(4), pp. 53–64.

achieved their full aim of re-establishing the Islamic Emirate with no place for any non-Taliban political parties or movements. Whether it will once again oversee an Afghanistan that acts as a haven for terrorist groups is now out of the hands of the West.

It is clear that agreeing to negotiate with the Taliban at their weakest in 2002, or their relative weakness in 2010, would have compromised the liberal-democratic values of not adopting partners who refute or contravene those principles. Nevertheless, it could have delivered a solution to the conflict that would have seen a government infinitely superior to that which is now in place in Kabul. Democratic rights such as equality of women could have been a key plank of a settlement. The conflict could also have ended at least a decade before it did, saving the lives and limbs of hundreds of ISAF soldiers and thousands of Afghans.

When to make peace

This would suggest that the challenge for liberal democracies is not whether to make peace agreements with particularly unsavoury partners, but when and under what circumstances. The application of force is an incontrovertible piece of that process. It is only this that will create the incentive for an opposing insurgency to compromise its own campaign ends and to agree to a solution that will end violence. As part of this, as with any negotiation, there will be concessions that the state party will need to make. This will involve recognizing the failures of their own side that perhaps led to the violence, whether that was corruption by Afghan security forces or discriminatory application of police powers in Northern Ireland. Not an easy thing to do, but quintessentially liberal-democratic, nevertheless.

Warfare is difficult. It is even more so when the enemy is hidden, allies are questionable and resources are scant. But it is clear to me that the values underpinning a liberal democracy are the same as those that underpin a successful military counter-insurgency campaign. Be in no doubt, warfare will always be necessary and, by definition, violent and hellish. The fog of war will also always lead to incidents of injustice and brutality, but these must never become the stated aim of the security forces. It is not naive or wishful thinking to adhere to LOAC; rather, LOAC is the bedrock of a successful military campaign. The campaign in Afghanistan should leave us reassured that whatever else it had in the way of deficiencies, and there were many, the commitment of the West to an ethical way of war was not one.

Where the question gets harder is on the subject of who you make peace with, and when. Here there is an unavoidable truth: that to make peace you must forgive the unforgivable. You must sit down with the grisliest of enemy combatants and shake their hand. The skill is to know when, with whom and how. But there is no escaping that, at some point, it will have to be done. It is no use pretending that peace can be made only with good guys. Instead, there must be recognition that the only truly ethical option available for liberal democracies ends in something very like the GFA, and the Queen shaking hands with Martin McGuinness.

The campaign in Afghanistan saw numerous points at which an acceptable settlement with the Taliban could have been achieved, even as far back as 2003. Among the arguments over whether Western forces were adequately equipped, funded or led, lies the central truth that Afghanistan could now be a decade into a power-sharing administration in Kabul, backed and recognized by the international community, with girls in school and women in the workplace, and not facing extensive poverty and even famine. Afghanistan did not have to be the graveyard of an empire. It could have been the cradle of a modern nation.

Part Four

Myths, stories and memory

10

The lonely death of Highlander Scott McLaren

Edward Burke[1]

Introduction

On 23 August 2021, Lance Corporal Ryan MacKenzie was found dead in his room at Catterick Garrison in North Yorkshire. MacKenzie, originally from the Scottish Hebrides and a soldier in 4th Battalion, The Royal Regiment of Scotland (4 SCOTS), had committed suicide a few days earlier. At his inquest his family revealed that Ryan MacKenzie had been haunted by the murder of his friend in Afghanistan. The Taliban had captured and killed twenty-year-old Highlander Scott McLaren on 4 July 2011 after he had walked alone into the Afghan countryside for unexplained reasons. Lance Corporal MacKenzie told his family that McLaren had been 'hanged from a tree and skinned'. MacKenzie's commanding officer in Afghanistan in 2011, Brigadier Alastair Aitken, said that the circumstances of Highlander McLaren's murder 'had a big impact on everyone'.[2]

Why did a Scottish soldier, located in one of the most dangerous districts in Afghanistan, pack up his belongings, leave a place of relative safety and set out on foot through an area he knew was full of Taliban insurgents? That question has never been answered. However, in 2013 Scott McLaren's parents, Ann and James McLaren, revealed that soldiers who served alongside their son told them that he was persistently bullied while in Afghanistan. The McLarens believed that their son's erratic behaviour may have been a direct consequence of this abuse.[3]

In 2011 the BBC reported that David Ridley – the Wiltshire coroner in charge of the inquest into the death of Scott McLaren – generally preferred 'not to go

[1] I am grateful to Dr Huw Bennett of Cardiff University for his helpful comments on an earlier draft of this chapter.
[2] Mark Branagan, 'Soldier Who Killed Himself "Traumatised By Friend's Murder in Afghanistan"', *Times*, 31 May 2022.
[3] Mark Nicol, 'Why was Our Weeping Son Allowed to Wander Off Base to be Killed by the Taliban?', *Daily Mail*, 10 August 2013; 'Deepcut Recruit Sean Benton "Assaulted and Bullied"', *BBC*, 7 March 2018.

into painful details again in open court', although he would make distressing reports available to the family for private consultation if they wished. That approach was appreciated by some families, for whom the circumstances of a soldier's death appeared clear.[4] For James McLaren, the inquest into his son's death appeared rushed and inadequate; he told a journalist from the *Daily Mail* that 'the conclusions that were reached [at the inquest] were just too neat and tidy, suspiciously so'.[5] Coroner David Ridley concluded that it was impossible to make sense of some apparent contradictions in the evidence presented at the inquest. Persistent allegations that McLaren had been subjected to prolonged and sadistic types of torture were publicly refuted by neither the coroner nor the Ministry of Defence (MOD), with serious and ongoing consequences for the British Army. After the inquest, the McLaren family did not know where to turn for answers.

Controversies over inquests into military deaths are not new. The failure of coroners to effectively gather evidence related to the deaths of four soldiers at Deepcut Barracks in Surrey in suspicious circumstances between 1995 and 2002 meant that new inquests had to be held more than a decade later.[6] Families of soldiers killed while serving overseas have also reported frustrations with the inquest process, especially when it came to acquiring detailed information on the circumstances in which their loves ones died. Individual coroners adopted differing approaches; some disclosed more public information than others.[7]

This chapter does not pretend to corroborate or refute allegations of bullying in the case of Highlander McLaren. Its conclusions are that the mechanisms of accountability in place when a soldier is unlawfully killed are inadequate. There was a clear lack of urgency and interest on the part of the MOD in responding to McLaren's parents' concerns that their son embarked on the journey that led to his death as a direct response to the abuse he suffered at the hands of people also serving in the British Army.

The killing of Highlander McLaren

At approximately 2.19 am on 4 July 2011, Highlander Scott McLaren packed his British Army bag or day kit, put on his body armour, picked up his SA80 rifle

---

[4] Lisa Mitchell, 'Ten Years of Inquests', *BBC News*, 4 October 2011.
[5] Nicol, 'Why was Our Weeping Son Allowed to Wander Off Base to be Killed by the Taliban?'.
[6] Richard Norton-Taylor, 'Fresh Inquest Ordered into Soldier's Death', *Guardian*, 18 July 2014.
[7] Nicola Lester, 'Reflecting on the Experiences of Bereaved Military Families in the Coroner's Court', *RUSI Journal*, 2019, 164(4), p. 30. See also for context, Anthony Forster, 'British Judicial Engagement and the Juridification of the Armed Forces', *International Affairs*, 2012, 88(2), 283–300.

and walked alone out of Checkpoint (CP) Salaang into the surrounding Nahr-e Saraj district of Helmand Province. McLaren was part of a multiple made up of nine soldiers from D Company, 4 SCOTS. The highlanders were at CP Salaang together with a multiple of Royal Marines from 45 Commando to reinforce an operation led by 1st Battalion, The Rifles (1 RIFLES), to secure the southern part of Nahr-e Saraj district – an area just to the north of Lashkar Gah, the provincial capital of Helmand. CP Salaang also served as the headquarters (HQ) of Major Paul Kyte, Officer Commanding Support Company, 1 RIFLES.[8]

At approximately 3.30 am Captain Callum MacLeod, the officer in command of the 4 SCOTS multiple, became aware of McLaren's absence. After a search of CP Salaang, MacLeod reported McLaren's absence to Major Kyte at 4.30 am. Kyte had been preparing for an imminent operation against suspected Taliban positions a kilometre to the north. Now he turned his attention to locating McLaren instead.[9] After an unsuccessful search of the immediate perimeter, a report was sent to Task Force Helmand HQ at Lashkar Gah that McLaren could not be found. Prime Minister David Cameron, who was visiting Helmand at the time, was also informed. Cameron told the military to 'throw everything you have got at trying to pick up this young man'. Reinforcements, including British special forces based in Helmand, were despatched to locate McLaren.[10]

At around midday, an Afghan man on a motorbike approached Lieutenant Daniel Bedford, a Royal Marines officer attached to the 1 RIFLES Battlegroup, who was in command of a vehicle checkpoint (VCP – Route Pluto, Trident Junction) a few miles south of Salaang. The man appeared nervous. But he had important information; he told Lt Bedford that there was a body of an International Security Assistance Force (ISAF) soldier in the Nahr-e Bughra canal. Bedford accompanied the man to the canal, but there was no sign of a body.[11]

At 5.00 pm the same Afghan man returned to Bedford's VCP and told him that the body had been moved and was now closer to a location the British called 'Culvert 12' on the Bughra canal. Bedford returned to the canal where he saw a group of children clustered around the bank. Highlander McLaren's body was lying face down in the water. There were no signs of life; the young soldier had sustained multiple gunshot wounds to his head and neck. Bedford immediately

[8] Wiltshire Coroner's Office, United Kingdom [hereafter WCO]: Recording of an Inquest into the Death of Highlander Scott McLaren, held in Trowbridge, 9 December 2011.
[9] Ibid.
[10] Steven Morris, 'Taliban Killed Soldier Who Left Camp at Night, Inquest Told', *Guardian*, 9 December 2011.
[11] WCO: McLaren Inquest Recording.

radioed to K Company, 42 Commando HQ, at nearby Patrol Base 5 for a quick reaction force to secure the area. At 6.00 pm a Royal Marines medical officer confirmed McLaren's death; his body was then removed to Camp Bastion for repatriation to the United Kingdom.[12]

A Home Office pathologist, Dr Nicholas Hunt, subsequently reported that McLaren had been shot five times by a high-velocity assault rifle, not his own weapon. All the wounds were on the right side of his head and neck. Scott McLaren died almost instantly after being shot – and certainly before his body was thrown into the canal sometime in the early afternoon of 4 July 2011. Dr Hunt also concluded that McLaren had been assaulted before his murder. Further wounds were also inflicted on his body after death.[13]

The inquest

Coroner David Ridley opened the inquest into Scott McLaren's death in the Wiltshire town of Trowbridge on the morning of 9 December 2011. Like most experienced coroners, he adopted an appropriately hushed tone, sympathizing with the family and explaining the purpose of proceedings – to attempt to find out how, when and where Highlander McLaren died. Since Wiltshire was the first location for the repatriation of the body into the United Kingdom, through RAF Lyneham, under British law that was where the inquest should be held.

The first witness was Captain Callum MacLeod. He told the court that he knew Scott McLaren since the latter first joined the British Army in 2009. MacLeod described his new recruit as 'very self-enclosed, he didn't usually talk to people, and he didn't express himself easily'. However, he was a competent infantry soldier – MacLeod ranked him as 'a middle third' soldier among the forty-eight new recruits under his command.[14]

McLaren deployed to Afghanistan as part of 7 Platoon, D Company, 4 SCOTS, in early April 2011. He was a newcomer to D Company, having been moved from B Company just before the deployment. 7 Platoon's commander, Lieutenant Simon Taylor, recalled a happy soldier, 'I will always remember the time when I was sat next to him on a hill in the pouring rain and he couldn't stop talking about how much he was looking forward to the future, the pinnacle being his upcoming deployment to Afghanistan.' This account of an outwardly happy

12 Ibid.
13 Ibid.
14 Ibid.

McLaren, a soldier with a 'dry sense of humour', is quite different to Captain MacLeod's recollection and that of other members of the 4 SCOTS multiple at Camp Salaang. One of these, Sergeant Finn Beary, described MacLeod as 'the grey man' in the background.[15]

MacLeod told the inquest that McLaren and another soldier from 7 Platoon, Highlander Mark Purves, were moved to his command in order to replace two men who were going on leave. CP Salaang was a difficult place to get to; 4 SCOTS HQ in Lashkar Gah wanted to minimize movements in and out of the area. A few days after the move to CP Salaang, MacLeod himself went on three weeks' leave and did not return until shortly before McLaren's death. Sergeant Beary took command of the multiple for two weeks; he then handed over to Corporal Douglas Young until MacLeod returned.[16]

MacLeod's evidence indicated that the mostly likely trigger for Highlander McLaren's disappearance from CP Salaang was the loss of a Head Mounted Night Vision System (HMNVS) sometime during the evening of 2 July. The main purpose of CP Salaang was control of a nearby road, dirt tracks and a bridge on the Nahr-e Bughra canal. As well as 'punching out' patrols in the immediate area, MacLeod's multiple also spent long periods observing and searching traffic at a VCP a hundred yards or so from their camp, including in darkness. An Afghan National Army (ANA) position was also located close to ISAF's VCP. The night vision 'goggles' were shared between the men on duty. MacLeod was annoyed by the loss of the HMNVS; he ordered his men to search for them throughout the day of 3 July, including doing a full kit check to see if they had been packed away in the wrong place. Corporal Young and the other soldiers in the multiple – with the exception of Captain MacLeod – searched for them until last light. A patrol was also sent back to the location where the HMNVS was lost but without success.[17]

At 8.00 pm on the night of 3 July, MacLeod gathered his men together and told them that everything they had done to date would be overshadowed by the loss of a piece of kit of value to the enemy. He believed that Highlander McLaren was the last person to see the goggles. But his criticism, he told the inquest, was directed at the entire group, not at a single person. He then issued his orders for the following day. He did not detect anybody being 'treated unfairly' later

[15] 'Highlander Scott McLaren Killed in Afghanistan', Ministry of Defence, 5 July 2011.
[16] WCO: McLaren Inquest recording.
[17] Ibid.

that night, just the ordinary 'hustle and bustle getting ready for the next day's operation'.[18]

Corporal Douglas Young was the next witness to give evidence. He corroborated MacLeod's account of the missing night vision goggles and said that he had given the group a 'bollocking' using plainer language than his officer. He did not see anything about McLaren that caused him any concern during his time at CP Salaang. Nothing was ever highlighted to him; if it was he 'would have sorted it'.[19]

Sergeant Finn Beary had noted behaviour of concern at CP Salaang. On one occasion in June, the multiple had 'crashed out' with an ANA unit in response to an incident. A soldier had left behind electronic countermeasures (ECM) equipment. Beary gave the group a 'bollocking' but claimed that it was probably another soldier who left the equipment behind, not McLaren, even though McLaren was often responsible for carrying ECM on patrol. Nonetheless, McLaren took it personally. Later Beary found him 'welling up' while sitting on his bed in the accommodation tent, saying, 'I keep messing up.' McLaren later seemed 'back to his old self'.[20]

Three highlanders who were on 'stag' during the hours between 11.00 pm and 2.00 am – the hours immediately preceding McLaren's disappearance from CP Salaang – gave accounts of Scott McLaren acting 'oddly'. He was packing his 'day kit', dressed in his combat uniform and boots, and was agitated or upset about the goggles. Highlander Ross claimed that McLaren told him he was going to go out and look for the goggles and that he saw him looking at a map outside at 11.30 pm.[21]

In the early hours of 4 July, soldiers from 1 RIFLES were on duty at the same VCP where the goggles were lost. Highlander McLaren did not go there. Instead, evidence given by an ANA soldier, corroborated by CCTV near the camp, revealed that he went in the opposite direction, due south instead of north. Scott McLaren's body was found four and a half kilometres to the south of CP Salaang. In summing up, Coroner David Ridley said that it was not his job to try to find out why Scott may have been going south in contradiction of his purported concern to go back to find the HMNVS. According to Ridley, 'the only person [McLaren] that could help us is no longer with us.'[22]

---

[18] Ibid.
[19] Ibid.
[20] Ibid.
[21] Ibid.
[22] Ibid.

Not 'a court of blame'

Coroner David Ridley stressed at Scott McLaren's inquest that his role was very different to that of a police officer or a criminal court. His was not 'a court of blame'. He repeatedly thanked the witnesses for their help and guidance. At times Ridley asked leading questions. During his questioning of Highlander Owen Moir about the fallout over the loss of the HMNVS, Ridley enquired, 'as the evidence suggests, was it a general bollocking?' He then began another question with, 'As Corporal Young has said, you draw a line under it', inviting assent on the part of Moir.[23]

Coroner David Ridley invited the parents of Scott McLaren – whom he addressed as 'Mum and Dad' – to put questions to the witnesses. They made sparing interventions, which were always polite and calmly delivered. However, their questions revealed important information, such as the fact that Scott McLaren packed his laptop in his daysack in the early hours of 4 July – a strange thing for him to do, since the evidence provided by 4 SCOTS witnesses suggested that McLaren was only intending on walking a few hundred yards away to look for a set of night vision goggles.[24]

James McLaren asked Captain MacLeod whether he had given a full account of his 'bollocking' on the night of 3 July, suggesting that the two 7 Platoon newcomers to the multiple, his son and Highlander Purves, were singled out and humiliated. James McLaren wanted to know about accounts he had heard about his son crying in the hours before he left CP Salaang. Coroner David Ridley interrupted proceedings before Captain MacLeod could respond, saying that James McLaren was referring to an earlier incident (that described by Sergeant Beary). Ridley went on to tell the court that in the hours before his death, 'there is nothing from what I have read to date that suggests that Scott was emotionally crying'. James McLaren pushed back at this suggestion by the coroner, 'No. No. Some says [sic] that and some don't say that. I'm just trying to work it out, that's all.' Captain MacLeod made no further response; the next witness was called. Instead of simply relying upon what he had 'read' in advance of the inquest, the coroner could have facilitated James McLaren's pertinent question to Captain MacLeod.[25]

A number of other anomalies in the evidence provided to the inquest were not explored. The account of Sergeant Beary – that Scott McLaren cried and

---

[23] Ibid.
[24] Ibid.
[25] Ibid.

said he kept 'messing up' after the ECM incident, even though another soldier was apparently the culprit – could have been probed further, especially since Corporal Young claimed he was unaware that there were any issues at all with McLaren before his murder. For such a small group of soldiers, it is striking that Sergeant Beary did not pass on information about McLaren's behaviour to Corporal Young. Why not? Other pertinent questions were also never posed. If the HMNVS was lost, the alleged incident that prompted McLaren to leave CP Salaang, what was its serial number and when was its loss reported? A witness from 1 RIFLES was also present at the inquest. He was one of the soldiers who had replaced 4 SCOTS at the VCP where the HMNVS was lost. This witness spent a few short minutes giving evidence, but the coroner did not ask him or other riflemen to confirm that the 4 SCOTS witnesses returned to the VCP to look for the HMNVS as they claimed.[26]

What about the Royal Military Police (RMP) investigation? Captain Stephen Robbins, a RMP Special Investigation Branch (SIB) officer, was also called as a witness at the inquest. He gave some basic information in response to the coroner's questions, such as confirming the times on the CCTV recordings, which showed Scott McLaren leaving CP Salaang on the morning of 4 July. But he was not asked whether the information provided by the 4 SCOTS witnesses could be corroborated by other evidence or whether he had come across any accounts of the bullying of Highlander McLaren during his investigation. Nor did he volunteer such information.[27]

Towards the end of the inquest David Ridley turned to Ann McLaren, telling her that, since he was now going to read out details of how her son died, she may wish to leave the room. She declined. Ridley then summarized parts of Dr Hunt's report on the cause of death. He also said that there was evidence that Scott McLaren was tortured before his death. Initially the McLaren family told the coroner that they had no questions to ask. James McLaren had already spoken to Captain Robbins. A minute later he changed his mind. He wanted to know more about his son's torture.

'James McLaren: "Was he tortured before he was shot or was he shot and then tortured?"'

'Coroner David Ridley: "The injuries seem to be consistent with when he was still alive. There is no evidence of restraining. What Dr Hunt suggests to me is

---

[26] Ibid.
[27] Ibid.

the possibility the assault and other acts were to make him . . . to get him into a more submissive position prior to execution.'"[28]

What David Ridley eventually confirmed during the public hearing – and only after pressing by James McLaren – about the violence inflicted on Scott McLaren before his death was somewhat vague, but nonetheless sounded less extreme than the horrific accounts that were circulating within the British military at the time and since.

More information about the final hours of Scott McLaren's life – including specific intelligence on his time and whereabouts as a prisoner of the Taliban – than was made available at the inquest appears to have been passed by military sources to the media. (Indeed, Captain Robbins gave evidence that the SIB did not know the location where McLaren was killed.) The *Daily Mail* reported that the search for McLaren was led by teams from 42 Commando, backed up by 30 Commando's Information Exploitation Group. The Taliban who captured Highlander McLaren had destroyed the infrared tracker in his helmet. They then dressed their prisoner in a *shalwar kameez* and some form of head covering. This suggests that they may have intended to keep McLaren as a prisoner for some time. However, the deployment of hundreds of British soldiers searching for McLaren prompted the Taliban to change their plans and shoot him instead. The article also added that, before his departure from CP Salaang, another soldier saw Scott McLaren crying while examining a map of Babaji. Babaji is a rural suburb of Lashkar Gah, close to where 4 SCOTS HQ was located.[29]

The campaign to free 'Marine A': Collateral damage for the McLaren family

On 15 September 2011, Royal Marine Colour Sergeant Alexander Blackman stood over a wounded Taliban insurgent and shot him. Blackman later claimed that he believed that the insurgent was already dead and that he shot a corpse. The footage produced at his court martial comprehensively contradicted that account. (See also Chapter 11 in this volume.) Blackman was based at Nad-e Ali, a district in Helmand to the south-west of Nahr-e Saraj, where he had been in command of sixteen marines at CP Omar, part of J Company, 42 Commando. Juliet Company had taken a number of casualties. When a Taliban insurgent was

---

[28] Ibid.
[29] Nicol, 'Why was Our Weeping Son Allowed to Wander Off Base to be Killed by the Taliban?'.

wounded by an Apache helicopter gunship, an angry and frustrated Blackman took revenge.

The war crime was caught on a marine's body camera. Blackman moved the badly wounded man out of sight of the Apache, then shot him in the chest from a foot away. The insurgent, clearly still alive in the film footage, then lifted up his hands to his chest and moved his leg. Blackman then stood over him, watched him for a few seconds and, quoting Shakespeare, said, 'Shuffle off this mortal coil, you cunt.' The footage then shows Blackman telling the other marines present that he had just broken the Geneva Conventions and that they should keep what happened between themselves.[30]

In the course of an investigation into another crime, police in England came across footage of the killing and passed it to the SIB. Blackman was arrested, charged and convicted of murder (later reduced to manslaughter on the grounds of diminished responsibility upon appeal). The death of Scott McLaren was raised during Sergeant Blackman's court martial to illustrate the barbarity of the Taliban and the pressures the accused was under. Blackman declined to provide information on the nature of McLaren's death, stating that he did not want to cause further pain to the family. However, Blackman's barrister drew the court's attention to a *Daily Telegraph* article written by Chris Terrill, a journalist who had been embedded with the Royal Marines in Afghanistan. Terrill wrote that around the time of Blackman's deployment, the capture of any marine or soldier by the Taliban was 'a guarantee of torture – probably skinning followed by beheading'.[31] The *Daily Mail* reported that Blackman was involved in the search for Highlander McLaren who had been 'horribly tortured, executed'.[32]

Ann McLaren made her views on Blackman's veiled reference to her son's death clear in an interview with Scotland's *Daily Record*, 'I'm not glad that he kept back details of what he saw. I wish it had all come out into the open. I wish he had gone into greater detail. I want to know exactly what happened to Scott. I'd like to know any detail he could give me.'[33] Blackman's barrister during his appeal hearing, Jonathan Goldman QC, passed on the McLaren family's request for Blackman to reveal details he had withheld at his court martial about her

[30] Testimony by Jeff Blackett, Judge-Advocate General of the UK Armed Forces (2004–2020), *Channel 4*, 'War and Justice: The Case of Marine A', first broadcast on 31 July 2022, https://www.channel4 .com/programmes/war-and-justice-the-case-of-marine-a. Accessed: 25 September 2022.

[31] Chris Terrill, 'Marine A: Criminal or Casualty?', *Daily Telegraph*, 1 December 2013.

[32] Richard Pendlebury, 'A Fall Guy For A Fiasco', *Daily Mail*, 15 September 2015.

[33] Lauren Crooks, 'Heartbroken Family Demand Truth About Tragic Soldier's Death At Hands of Taliban', *Daily Record*, 20 September 2015.

son's death. Ann McLaren told the media she was now 'hopeful he'll be able to help answer some of the unanswered questions I have'.[34]

In reality Blackman remained at CP Omar, some miles away from where Highlander McLaren's remains were recovered. In his memoir Alexander Blackman wrongly described McLaren as a soldier in the Scots Guards and that his body had been found in a 'ditch'. Blackman then wrote, 'I never saw that body, but I heard the stories. Another young man flagellated and mutilated before they snubbed out his life'.[35]

Fuelling the rumour mill

Accounts – real, exaggerated or imagined – of prisoners of war suffering horrific acts of torture are often a topic of discussion among soldiers.[36] Some militaries, paramilitaries and insurgents have used torture as a means to attempt to undermine the will of an enemy or as a form of extreme revenge. Pro-Russian Chechen fighters filmed the castration and murder of a Ukrainian prisoner of war in the summer of 2022 for these reasons.[37]

Stories of extreme torture by the Provisional Irish Republican Army (IRA) in Northern Ireland also shaped the conduct of soldiers. False rumours spread in 1971 that suggested that three young soldiers in the Royal Highland Fusiliers (RHF) who were abducted by the IRA from a pub in Belfast had been castrated before being shot dead. Although the RHF's officers and non-commissioned officers (NCOs) worked hard to prevent acts of revenge, their soldiers' shock and disgust found expression in a generally punitive approach towards the local population in the months afterwards.[38]

Similar rumours of extreme torture also spread in the aftermath of the kidnapping and brutal murder of Private James Elliott, a part-time Ulster Defence Regiment (UDR) soldier, by the IRA near the Irish border in 1972. In the latter case the Royal Ulster Constabulary (RUC) were concerned that,

---

[34] Lauren Crooks, 'Lawyer Vow on Soldier Murder; New Hope for Mum', *Daily Record*, 24 September 2015.

[35] Alexander Blackman, *Marine A: My Toughest Battle* (London: Mirror, 2019), 133.

[36] See John Horne and Alan Kramer, *German Atrocities, 1914: A History of Denial* (New Haven: Yale University Press, 2001), 107; Edward Burke, *An Army of Tribes: British Cohesion, Deviancy and Murder in Northern Ireland* (Liverpool: Liverpool University Press, 2018), 164–7.

[37] Bellingcat, 'Tracking the Faceless Killers Who Mutilated a Ukrainian POW', 6 August 2022, https://www.bellingcat.com/news/2022/08/05/tracking-the-faceless-killers-who-mutilated-and-executed-a-ukrainian-pow/. Accessed: 26 September 2022.

[38] Richard English, *Armed Struggle: A History of the IRA* (London: Pan, 2004), 115–16.

although explosives had been placed near the body to target recovery teams, accounts of Corporal Elliott's treatment by the IRA were becoming dangerously exaggerated and issued a statement to that effect. Real and imagined accounts of the murder of Elliott and other UDR soldiers had a significant radicalizing effect on a few within the UDR who joined loyalist terrorist groups.[39] Fears over the possible capture and torture of a missing soldier from D Company, 1st Battalion, Argyll and Sutherland Highlanders, in October 1972, prompted a group of Argylls to violently interrogate and stab to death a farmer called Michael Naan in County Fermanagh who they wrongly believed to be a leading member of the IRA. (The missing soldier later turned up unharmed; he had got lost. See also Chapter 11 in this volume.)[40]

Conclusion

During a parliamentary debate on the treatment of Alexander Blackman in 2015, Johnny Mercer MP, a former army officer who later served as Minister for Veterans' Affairs, referred to the killing of Scott McLaren. Mercer told MPs that Colour Sergeant Blackman had tried to locate McLaren; however, he was too late – the search for the 4 SCOTS soldier had 'ended in such bad circumstances that to this day they rightly remain unreported'.[41] Mercer believed that a mercy had been extended to the McLaren family by not making publicly available the full circumstances of Highlander McLaren's death. Ann and James McLaren did not see it that way. For years after the inquest into their son's death, they desperately sought to have the accounts of the torture and murder of their son confirmed or refuted. The same rumours have also exacted a toll beyond Scott McLaren's family. His murder continues to haunt the British Army.

Exaggerated or false rumours can also lead to acts of retribution. Stories of the treatment of McLaren and other Taliban atrocities against British soldiers fuelled Sergeant Blackman's mental decline and led ultimately to his killing of a prisoner.[42] It was suggested that Blackman knew what really happened

[39] The National Archives: WO 305/4209: 3rd Infantry Brigade: Records of the Meeting of the South Eastern Security Committee Meeting, 10 May 1972.

[40] Burke, *An Army of Tribes*, 227–332.

[41] Hansard: Sgt Alexander Blackman, debate at Westminster Hall, 16 September 2015, https://hansard .parliament.uk/Commons/2015-09-16/debates/15091640000001/SgtAlexanderBlackman(Marine A)?highlight=alexander%20blackman%23contribution-15091640000006. Accessed 25 September 2022.

[42] Sean O'Neill, 'Mental State and Change of Character Are the Key', *Times*, 16 March 2017.

to Highlander McLaren. Did he? In the days after McLaren's death, the MOD denied that he had been tortured. (The first allegations of torture reported by the media came from Afghan sources.)[43] Since then the British government has not responded to shocking assertions about McLaren's torture, such as that reported by the media in May 2022 at the inquest into the death of Lance Corporal MacKenzie. (A request made by this author to the Wiltshire Coroner's Office to view the pathologist's report submitted in advance of Highlander McLaren's inquest was refused in September 2022.)

The events at CP Salaang immediately preceding Scott McLaren's death should have been fully explained, including probing claims by Captain MacLeod, those of other soldiers and the behaviour of Highlander McLaren. Accounts received by the family, that Scott McLaren had been badly bullied and that this prompted his desperate decision to undertake the journey that led to his death, should have been followed up. Instead, the McLarens were left with nowhere to go.

---

[43] *The Times*, 31 May 2022; Martin Fricker, 'Soldier Snatched, Tortured and Killed', *Daily Mirror*, 6 July 2011.

11

Military myths

John Wilson

Introduction

In the autumn of 1972 in Fermanagh, Northern Ireland, Michael Naan and Andrew Murray were murdered in cold blood by two soldiers (a staff sergeant and a sergeant at the time of their arrest) from the Argyll and Sutherland Highlanders, using the bowie knife of another soldier from their patrol of four. The case came to light in 1979 as part of the 'Yorkshire Ripper' investigation. The pathologist said Naan's wounds were 'consistent with an attack by someone who had gone berserk'. During an interview with the Royal Ulster Constabulary (RUC), the staff sergeant said, 'I did it. I did the killings. I killed them and they just wouldn't stop screaming. Oh my God, I have been having bloody nightmares about it. The bloody dog at the farm must have found the bodies and kept howling . . . I have been hearing that dog ever since.'

A young subaltern, the platoon commander, Lieutenant Andrew Snowball, was not present but withheld the story: 'I mulled the whole thing over in my mind and decided that for the good of the army and the regiment it must never go any further.'

He received a one-year suspended jail sentence.

The case became known as the 'Pitchfork Murders' and you can find a full account in *An Army of Tribes* by Ed Burke. For seven years it was thought to have been the work of loyalist terrorists, so the case did not resonate with soldiers. Had it been known at the time that it was murder by regular soldiers, the British Army might have paid more attention to the horror of it and drawn some conclusions.

The origins of the behaviour can be traced back to the Argylls in Aden (Crater) in 1967. Much has been written about Lieutenant Colonel Colin

Mitchell[1] and the 're-taking' of Crater. Separating fact from fiction is nigh on impossible, but the battalion record shows that thirty-eight people were killed and eight wounded in that one operation, a statistic that suggests a major battle. We don't know how many weapons were recovered from bodies, so at this remove justification for the deaths has to remain open-ended. But there is no doubt that the battalion acted very robustly in comparison to other units, which conformed to the orders of the day. The events in Aden created a culture that engendered an attitude that taking life was a less serious matter than it should have been. And the murders in Fermanagh were just five years later. At one simple level, how could the carriage of a bowie knife be permitted within the battalion/company? We know stories get around and lose little in the telling. Events in Aden were allowed to affect the behaviour in this rifle platoon to the extent of murder and covering it up.

In some ways, the covering-up by the platoon commander was almost as bad as the murders themselves. His failure to report the murders gave rise to false stories and the subsequent revelations besmirched the reputation of the army as an institution trying to uphold law and order. That an officer can condone murder shows how far the toxic culture within the battalion had spread. And it also raises indirectly the nature of loyalty. Mitchell had demanded and got total loyalty from his battalion in Aden and gave his loyalty to his soldiers. But he did not give his loyalty to his brigade commander.

Loyalty is a difficult subject, for a commander has to be loyal upwards as well as downwards. It is easy to say that no commander can go far wrong by giving total loyalty to his soldiers. But soldiering in conflict is not a simple business and loyalties have to be balanced. Although the platoon commander had not served with Mitchell, the Argylls was his family regiment and he would have been well aware of the Aden culture and Mitchell's style. A healthier regimental culture would have made clear the responsibilities of its officers to the regiment, and that covering up murder was not one of them – there are limits to an officer's loyalty to his soldiers.

Myths of this kind are dangerous because their very nature is usually lurid and attractive in its simplicity. They tell a story that is appealing, otherwise they would not gain currency. And they appeal to soldiers especially because they seem to offer a solution and, with it, legitimacy. That's what they did then, so we can do it now. And we can gain the approval of our forebears and peers because we are taking heed of past practices.

---

[1] See *Mad Mitch's Tribal Law* by Aaron Edwards.

Omerta in the British Army

The myth can also deliberately conceal and become a code of silence or 'omerta'. An incident does not turn out as desired, indeed it might even have been an embarrassment. A story is concocted to deceive and avoid unwanted consequences. An example is the case of Karen Reilly and Martin Peake, who were killed in Belfast by a patrol from 3rd Battalion, The Parachute Regiment on 30 September 1990. The then Private Lee Clegg was found guilty of the murder of Karen Reilly but acquitted at a retrial, although he was found guilty of the attempted murder of Martin Peake. At a later appeal, that conviction, too, was overturned.

In brief, the patrol had fired on a joyriding car. The patrol had not been under threat from the car and it was decided to injure one soldier's leg in an attempt to claim that the car had hit him and so justify the firing of thirty-six rounds. The patrol was led by a lieutenant and was accompanied by a policeman. The policeman subsequently retracted his statement and his new version was corroborated by a traveller who saw the incident – hence the court cases. The appeal court judge described Clegg's evidence as 'untruthful and incapable of belief'. It was the forensic evidence that led to the overturning of the convictions – in effect the soldiers displayed a culture of omerta within the unit and the wider regiment. A myth was already in the making: in the canteen at Palace Barracks, soldiers from the unit had made a model of the car complete with a blood-stained head and a notice that read 'Vauxhall Astra. Built by Robots. Driven by joyriders. Stopped by A Company'.

Two young people had died in highly disputed circumstances, but such was the culture within the unit that they thought it appropriate to make it a joke, to lie and to try to pervert the course of justice. Yet, this patrol was led by an officer, who conspired in this deceit. What action was taken by the army against him? I do not know. Indeed, the myth of total army loyalty to its soldiers was so strong that all the soldiers convicted of murder in Northern Ireland have been released under licence and permitted to rejoin the army. A soldier convicted of theft and jailed would not be permitted to rejoin the army, yet four murderers were. Such is the power of myth. And the myth of the rightness of an omerta was further strengthened in this case.

Collusion

Sometimes myths are thrust upon us. The Ulster Defence Regiment (UDR) did not seek to be tarred with the brush of collusion, yet in the mind of many who pay even a passing interest in the affairs of Northern Ireland, the UDR is a murderous sectarian organization serving, and paid for by, a brutal British government.

In the decades since the last locally recruited soldiers and police officers were murdered behind their shop counters or delivering mail or putting milk bottles on the doorstep, a fiction has been carefully created that there was a retributive aspect to these killings by the Irish Republican Army (IRA), which morally validated them.[2]

There was no such aspect nor any such validation. This was a campaign of unprovoked homicide that constituted a serial war crime that in any other jurisdiction would have merited the equivalent of a Nuremberg trial.

The most striking evidence against the collusion thesis comes from the loyalist paramilitaries themselves. Their conduct achieved levels of cowardice, brutality and sheer incompetence that remain without peer in any conflict that I know of. For far from attacking the IRA, which they would have done had they been controlled by the British, loyalist paramilitaries were, instead, usually content to kill harmless Catholics, often drunks on their way home. As a general rule, they left the IRA alone, even when they knew the names and addresses of republican leaders. Such knowledge came via criminal leaks from army or police intelligence or from open-source outlets such as media reports on court cases. By 1973, both the Ulster Volunteer Force (UVF) and the Ulster Defence Association (UDA) had vast amounts of material on the IRA, but seldom did loyalist killers use such information.

The reality is that thousands of UDR soldiers knew the names and addresses of IRA terrorists in their areas, their movements, their associates, their places of work and where they drank. Yet, these obvious targets were seldom touched by loyalist paramilitaries, who preferred to attack blameless families such as the Devlins.

In May 1974, James and Gertrude Devlin were ambushed as they arrived at their home in Tyrone. Each was shot eight times, while their teenage daughter Patricia, quite incredibly, survived being shot nine times. As it happens, the Devlins were not 'republicans' but supporters of the SDLP (Social Democratic and Labour Party), which detested and repeatedly condemned the IRA. One of the perpetrators of these utterly foul murders was a part-time UDR man, William Leonard, who was also a neighbour in Moygashel Park in Dungannon

---

[2] I am indebted to Kevin Myers for his deep knowledge of Northern Irish matters for much of this material on collusion. https://kevinmyers.ie.

of the loyalist terrorist Wesley Somerville. Another gunman was Harris Boyle who, like Leonard, was a post office engineer.

They also went for the politically obvious like Austin Currie, a SDLP politician, whose opposition to, and loathing of, the IRA was vocal and undeniable. He and his family were the repeated targets of loyalist paramilitary attacks on their home in Co Tyrone. In November 1972, his wife Anita suffered a brutal attack when two armed and masked men burst into her home looking to attack her husband, who happened to be away at a political speaking engagement in County Cork that evening. Speaking about it in a TV interview two days later, Anita Currie spoke of how she was punched, cut with a blade and kicked unconscious on the floor, while her two young daughters looked on helplessly.

A few statistics are an equally eloquent rebuttal of the charge of collusion. By November 1975, 1,888 applications for UDR membership had already been rejected and 108 serving UDR soldiers had been expelled on security grounds. Far stronger evidence is seen from the casualty figures: UDR/RIR (Royal Irish Regiment) deaths totalled 182, killings for which they were responsible totalled 8, and one of these was a Protestant paramilitary. These are not figures that remotely support a charge of collusion.

Ambush? What ambush?

According to the 1st Battalion, The King's Own Royal Border Regiment (1 KORBR), probably four PIRA (Provisional Irish Republican Army) members were killed on 8 February 1973 on the border near Strabane:

> 8 Feb – Return with platoon – overnight someone had constructed a brick wall with firing ports in front of the caravan. Ten minutes later shots fired from the firing ports and from two trenches beside the main road. 'All hell broke out. Six Brownings on the Saracens, the Ferrets and the troop leader's Saladin [heavy armoured car] were firing, plus the three GPMGs. Sgt H tried to grip the fire discipline but they couldn't hear him; I watched transfixed at the impact of this weight of fire on a hurriedly constructed brick wall. Within seconds it was gone and the poor sods who had taken us on.'[3]

There is no record of any PIRA gunmen killed on 8 February 1973 or around that date in the Strabane area – certainly not four. There were only two

---

[3] From the platoon commander's diary quoted in *The Making of the British Army* by Allan Mallinson.

occasions when PIRA lost four men or more in one go, so it would have been a memorable event; and in keeping with PIRA's usual stance there would have been a strident campaign on 'shoot to kill' lines. Also, in accordance with PIRA practice, the deaths would have been acknowledged. PIRA considered itself as an army and conducted some of the common military practices, which included acknowledging casualties. Nor did any local papers or television carry the story of a major gun battle. In other words, there was no such ambush. Yet, the story was constructed and no doubt believed by many to this day.

Does it matter? Yes, because, firstly, if we are to base our operations on events, as will be done to some extent, it is important that the facts are observed. Otherwise intelligence is faulty and wrong conclusions are drawn. Why trust a unit that makes up stories? And what was the motive for this fabrication? So in this instance, PIRA's records are more credible than the army's – and in counter-insurgency that matters. The army's reputation is important, local people will know much of the truth and lies like this diminish trust in the security forces. So, yes, it does matter, very much.

This example is a particularly egregious one, but the pattern is like many, many other similar stories told by soldiers or former soldiers to each other and their gullible companions. An engagement is entirely imagined or wildly exaggerated, typically there is a major gun battle, hundreds of rounds are exchanged, usually no soldiers are wounded but hits are claimed. The absence of bodies is explained by PIRA spiriting them away to the Republic – these stories are especially common on the border. Over time, the narrator may actually come to believe his own fiction. His (it is, of course, always a 'he') listeners don't have to fully believe the stories but a standard or pattern is introduced that lowers thresholds of behaviour. We cannot police such stories, and nor would we wish to, but we can encourage a healthy scepticism.

A breakdown in battlefield discipline

A patrol from 42 Commando operating from Checkpoint Omar in the Upper Sangin Valley on 15 September 2011 was tasked to search a nearby compound. On their way back, some fighters engaged another checkpoint, Fallander. An Apache AH helicopter was ordered to find and destroy those fighters. It saw one fighter and fired 139 rounds of 30mm cannon. The man was seen to fall, apparently wounded. The patrol was re-tasked to conduct battlefield damage assessment. It was afternoon on a hot (50°C) day.

Marine C[4] (the Vallon man) accompanying the patrol commander (an acting colour-sergeant), Marine A, spotted the wounded man. He was alive and moving slightly; C had him in the rifle (Sharpshooter) sight and so informed Marine A. Marine A approached the man, and searched him. He had an AK with two magazines and a grenade in a pocket. He was badly wounded and unconscious. They called for assistance and he was dragged to the corner of the field into cover.

A dressing was applied and the patrol debated whether he was still alive. Eventually, Marine A told his command post over the radio that the man was dead. Bio-metrics were taken, and the patrol started to pack up. Marine C, who had been covering the man, walked away to take up a position prior to moving off. Marine A then leant over the man and fired a round from his 9mm pistol into his chest. The man writhed, showing that he was clearly alive; he died shortly after.

Those are the bare details. Marines A, B and C were charged with murder, B and C were acquitted, Marine A was found guilty. In his case, it turned on whether he believed that the wounded man was dead or alive at the point of the shooting. The Board decided he knew the man was alive. It is fair to say that signs of life were fleeting and feeble.

We know all this because Marine B wore a helmet camera (privately owned) and recorded it. The videos were found a year later when civil police arrested another marine on an unrelated case and came across them on his laptop. Other witnesses to part of the activities were the Apache crew, and by omission the sensors on the tethered balloon at the checkpoint. The allegation was that the patrol deliberately moved out of sight of both potential witnesses because they intended to kill the fighter.

I attended the trial (see also Chapter 10 in this volume) and was the only member of the public who had no link to the case. The others present were family, journalists and interested police and lawyers. As in the earlier examples given, some units seem to exhibit a more 'macho' or aggressive style than others. Yet, all units undergo very similar preparation for operations, so that variation must be down to the culture within them. And that culture is created over time. Occasionally, a unit might behave more aggressively than was usual, and those occasions can be put down to an individual commander or a clique within the unit, but such behaviour rarely lasts. In some units, however, it is endemic. Stories circulate and gain credence by the failure of the chain of command to suppress or refute them. Some may be true, but the myth that attaches to them is that the behaviour was effective and therefore justified. British counter-insurgency practice is littered with such examples ranging from actions in Palestine, Malaya,

---

[4] The Court of Appeal withdrew anonymity from Marine A – Sergeant Alexander Blackman RM.

Cyprus, Aden and, more latterly, Northern Ireland, Iraq and Afghanistan. And the case of Marine A is one such illustration.

The unit had a reputation for being 'robust'. This is a common term and has been used by senior officers in Northern Ireland to refer to the policy of 'teaching hooligans a lesson'. It is a simple idea and attractive because it seems to offer a straightforward and effective way of dealing with trouble. In practice, it is literally a blunt instrument, which metes out a collective punishment. It generates resentment, which does nothing to shorten the campaign.

Of course, when an army is called upon to deal with disorder and, more seriously, an insurgency, there will be over-reactions, errors, misconceptions and those seeking to pour blame on the army. Such military operations are inevitably somewhat indiscriminate and crude, and there will often be an unfavourable reaction to military force. Most units in Northern Ireland and elsewhere knew the limits and kept within them. But some did not, and seemed to be able to call upon an unhealthy regimental culture to justify their actions. The myth that they were effective was shared by some senior commanders. And the consequences of that were seen on Bloody Sunday on 30 January 1972. As to the effectiveness, in the twelve months prior to Bloody Sunday, 45 soldiers were killed, and in the following twelve months this number reached 127. Effective? Yes, for PIRA in their campaign to gain public support and kill British soldiers.

Yet, despite this clear failure of the 'robust' approach, a few units still seemed determined to show that this aggressive approach was the right one. 42 Commando had not learnt that lesson. In many ways, Marine A was the victim of his unit's culture – a better-led unit would not have let him believe that such actions could be in any way acceptable. That soldiers (Royal Marines in this case) were obviously wearing private head cameras, banned in theatre, suggests a poorly disciplined unit. It would have been better if the unit had viewed lapses in standards as breakdowns in battlefield discipline. Such an approach would have made it clearer to all that the operating concept of restrained behaviour was in part a disciplinary matter. In more general war, such as the Falklands War, being willing to stand up and go forward under fire was also a matter of battlefield discipline. The point of pre-deployment training is to define the nature of battlefield discipline in that theatre, and part of the role of the chain of command in theatre is to monitor and enforce it.

The 'Big One'

Perhaps the strongest myth prevalent in British defence circles since the Second World War is that we, the British, are especially good at counter-insurgency (COIN).

This is a big question for just part of a chapter, but there is a simple truth that seems to have eluded many and permitted this myth to develop. This is that the British experience of COIN was always in regions that 'were under British administration'. In other words, Britain controlled all the levers of power: government (law-making), the courts, the police, the local militias, the army (British and regional, for example, the Indian Army), so that any measure could be made legal. Collective punishments, the punitive destruction of houses, internment, forcible relocation, control of food, curfews were all legal in administrations from Malaya to Palestine.

From that experience, the British Army deduced that it was good at COIN and, under those conditions, so it was. The record of colonial withdrawal – leaving a working administration under some form of democratic government with a reasonable economy within a functioning infrastructure – is a model that those powers who have quit Iraq and Afghanistan would be more than delighted to have on their CV.

However, nobody ascribed the 'success' of British-style COIN to its control over the levers of power. Even the searing experience of the US Army in Vietnam was not enough to reveal the full truth. It was not just that the scale of the Vietnam conflict was hugely greater than that of Malaya under the British, it was also that there was a Vietnamese government – however puppet-like others thought that it was.

To take just one aspect, arrest and trial or detention. If the COIN strategy is based on the forensic-judicial approach (as today it must be), then captured insurgents are treated as criminals and put before local courts and tried and sentenced. But if local courts are influenced by non-judicial aspects such as sectarianism, tribalism or corruption, then the forensic-judicial approach collapses.

Here is an example of how a flawed concept works its way down to the unit level. A court martial at Bulford in March 2010 tried an officer and NCO (non-commissioned officer) from 45 Commando who beat up a detainee in Helmand Province on 19 March 2009.

> The trial heard that Mr Ekhlas was apprehended on suspicion of planting an IED. He was subjected to violence and transported to a nearby base where he was assaulted by Sergeant Leader and Captain Wheelhouse. The trial heard that Leader was seen hitting Mr Ekhlas with a boot. He needed four stitches to his lip and two of his teeth were loose.
>
> Leader claimed he used lawful violence against Mr Ekhlas in self-defence. But the court heard that Leader said of Mr Ekhlas: 'I don't know why they brought him back. They should have killed him.'[5]

[5] *BBC News*, 26 March 2010.

Almost certainly, the suspect would have to have been released because British legal requirements would not have permitted Ekhlas to be put before an Afghan court, and the British Army would only be allowed to detain him without trial for a short period. In other words, what is the point of capturing an insurgent if he is likely to be released shortly thereafter to continue attacking coalition forces?

A swift look at the Iraq Revolt of 1920 would show that modern COIN cannot work. On one day in 1920 over a hundred soldiers of the Manchester Regiment were killed by Iraqis rebelling against the British mandate. Over the course of the following months, reinforcements, largely from the Indian Army, restored order. They used well-tried colonial methods ranging from collective punishments to bribery, coercion and violence in a series of messy little deals, some of which might last just a few days and others more enduring. Most of these methods would not be acceptable today, thereby contributing to the myth of British success at COIN. It can work, but you cannot do it that way now. It is unfortunate that this example was not more deeply studied before 2003.

Countering myths

The COIN example is instructive. As in so many military events, it is as important to know what you cannot do as to know what you can. The British Army, and other armies as well as many academic departments, started with the assumption that the British record on COIN was good. Indeed, one of the more recent examples, the insurrection in Oman in the 1960s and 1970s, had been handled in an exemplary way and seemed to validate the assumption. A closer look would have shown that the relationship between the Sultan of Oman and the COIN forces was unusual. There was an almost complete alignment of thought on how to proceed. The Omani forces were largely indigenous and the British support was small, subtle, skilled and highly influential. The conflict was also small by the standards of other examples. But it was successful and it has endured, thanks largely to a set of unrepeated elements.

The failure to conduct COIN by proxy is the failure to study closely enough why it worked when it did, and why it failed when it failed. It depends in the first instance on this alignment between the ruler/host government and the COIN forces, and yet in the context of so many examples, the COIN forces are a mix of local forces, those from outside plus external advisers at all levels. When that link is 'colonial' in nature, then close alignment can be expected. Does the host state have a functioning administration? Are its laws and procedures acceptable to the external force's government? In other words, are the levers of power available and effective? None of these needs were met in Iraq or Afghanistan. Thus, the chances of conducting successful COIN were low.

So, even at a high level, a myth can be countered if the background to it is studied and the deductions followed. And the same applies at the lower levels. Assumptions should be regularly challenged. It is why Western armies have staff colleges, courses of instruction, study days and, in good units, frequent informal discussions among and between soldiers and officers. 'What works?' should be a routine refrain.

Myths have an emotional appeal: they simplify, they justify, they are props for the lazy. They are also useful for the overbearing, an easy way of imposing a way or a method – tell a story to justify the dubious path. The counter here is good unit discipline and a listening culture by officers and junior leaders. What is going on in the unit, is the taught approach (doctrine) understood and accepted? Is the culture in the unit a healthy one based on sound training, competent leadership and good administration? Are junior officers aware of their responsibilities to the commanding officer and the unit generally as well as the soldiers under their command? A good unit can spot an emerging toxic culture early and deal with it.

Perhaps, most importantly, myths should be identified and put into context. Some have value: the sterling behaviour of the regiment at Waterloo, the gallant defence at Sidi Rezegh or the fine assault of Darwin/Goose Green – military history kept alive through stories. It is when these stories turn rancid that intervention is needed. Turning a blind eye is behind so many military horror stories from Baha Mousa in Iraq to Deepcut in Surrey (the poor regime at the Royal Logistic Corps recruit training centre where four young trainees took their own lives). As so often, we can turn to Field Marshal Slim[6] for guidance:

> There is another kind of courage you must have as an officer. You must have moral courage. Moral courage is a much rarer thing than physical courage. Moral courage means you do what you think is right without bothering very much what happens to you when you are doing it. It is not often a question of great issues. It is a small thing of everyday life. A young officer passes an untidy soldier on the road who does not salute him, and the officer does nothing about it and pretends he does not see. He does that because if he calls after him, 'Why didn't you salute?' he may get a bit of lip back at him and it may be a bit

---

[6] Address by Field Marshal the Viscount Slim on 14 October 1952 to officer cadets of the Royal Military Academy, Sandhurst.

unpleasant and there may be a scene. It is much easier to take no notice and walk on. Every time that you do that you are losing your stock of moral courage. Every time that you check a man for something that is wrong you add to your stock of moral courage and you build it up. Do not think you can dodge the little issues – the little everyday things of duty – and then when the great test comes you will be alright. You won't because you will have undermined the foundation. That is the courage that makes him do what is right because he believes it to be right.

Field Marshal Slim's test was a soldier who failed to salute, Lieutenant Snowball's test was two soldiers who had committed murder: a spectacular chasm of morality.

12

Remembering the British soldier in Iraq and Afghanistan

Helen Parr

On 28 June 2004, Private Gordon Gentle of the Royal Highland Fusiliers died when a roadside bomb exploded in Basra next to his Snatch Land Rover. He was only a few weeks out of basic training. His mother, Rose, spent the night before his funeral by his body in the bedroom of their Glasgow home.[1] Later that year Mrs Gentle established the campaign group Military Families Against the War, with Reginald Keys, the father of Lance Corporal Tom Keys, a member of the Royal Military Police killed by a mob in June 2003. They felt that Labour prime minister Tony Blair had taken Britain into Iraq against international law. There had been no weapons of mass destruction (WMD), as he had claimed. Bereaved families could never have the comfort of knowing their sons died in a just war. Gentle and Keys campaigned for a public inquiry into the decisions that led up to the war and Gentle also pursued an inquiry into the use of Snatch Land Rovers, which were deemed inadequate to protect troops against explosive devices. Their campaigning led ultimately to the government's agreement in 2009 to establish the Chilcot Inquiry to consider Britain's involvement in Iraq.

On 14 September 2003, Baha Mousa, a twenty-six-year-old hotel receptionist was arrested along with six other men in Basra and taken to a British military base. Mousa and nine other civilian detainees 'had their heads encased in sandbags and their wrists bound by plastic handcuffs and were kicked and punched with sustained cruelty'.[2] The next day, Mousa was dead on the floor of a latrine, a knee in his back and his throat possibly constricted by the rough hem of his hood. He had 93 injuries, including fractured ribs and a broken nose,

---

[1] Deborah Anderson, 'Grieving Mother of Glasgow Soldier will Fight to Stop Tony Blair Knighthood', *The Herald*.
[2] Andrew T. Williams, *A Very British Killing: The Death of Baha Mousa* (London: Jonathan Cape, 2013), p. 1.

and the pathologist flown from London to examine him judged he had died of 'positional asphyxia.'[3] His father, Daoud Mousa, campaigned for a public inquiry into the circumstances of his death. Mousa's campaigning led to a court martial of four British soldiers in 2005 and a public inquiry in 2008.

On 14 July 2009, people lined the streets of Wootton Bassett in Wiltshire to pay their respects at the procession of eight hearses containing the bodies of soldiers killed in Helmand Province, in the deadliest twenty-four hours of the conflict in Afghanistan. Five of the dead were killed rescuing comrades from a roadside bomb when a second device exploded. Three of the men were eighteen years old. The brother of one of the soldiers pushed through the crowds at the roadside to tie a rose to the rack of his brother's carriage and hammered on the window, and the crowd started to clap.[4]

Two years later, on 15 September 2011, a Taliban fighter in Afghanistan, already wounded, probably fatally so, died as a Royal Marine shot him, turned to his men and said, 'I've just broken the Geneva Convention'. The action was caught on headcam, and in September 2013 Marine A was sentenced to life imprisonment and told he would serve ten years. His wife campaigned to reduce his sentence and, at the appeal hearing in 2017, his sentence was lessened to manslaughter on grounds of serious psychological stress and he was released from jail.

These deaths, some of which have been referred to in other chapters in this book, came to define how the public viewed British soldiers during the wars in Iraq and Afghanistan. The period from the entry into Iraq in March 2003, until the winding-down of operations in Afghanistan in 2014, was one of unprecedented visibility for the armed services. The days of restrained wartime mourning that characterized the Second World War, and the days of the MOD's 'unassailable supremacy and secrecy', in the words of one of the solicitors who brought charges against it, had largely disappeared. Instead, politicians, press and public paid far greater attention to the deaths of individual soldiers and to the feelings of their families. Further, although it was often slow, difficult and opaque, individuals could and did use the legal process to contest the decisions and actions of the state. These deaths brought the British soldier into the public mind in new ways and shaped political and public reactions to these contemporary conflicts.

This chapter explores, firstly, the politics of sending Britain to war in Iraq and families' demands for a public inquiry; secondly, the repatriation ceremonies at

---

[3] Ibid., p. 3.
[4] 'From All Corners, Britain Turns Out for its Dead', *The Times*, p. 1.

Wootton Bassett; and, thirdly, allegations of criminality committed by British troops and their impact. By focusing on reactions to these particular deaths, the chapter traces the evolution of public attitudes towards British soldiers during this time and suggests that the wars in Iraq and Afghanistan were a watershed in civil-military relations. In a more individualized society, where fewer people had personal experience of military life, the collective values of the military were poorly understood. Further, the traditional view that the armed services served the state, as represented by the elected government in Parliament with legislative authority over military deployment, was questioned. The public came to display sympathy with individual soldiers but suspicion of the politicians who had ordered the war and, over time, even hostility towards an anonymous bureaucratic 'establishment' that sought to obstruct 'ordinary' people doing their best in difficult circumstances. The extent to which these changes were a specific response to the politics of the wars in Iraq and Afghanistan, or whether they denoted a deeper social or political shift, is still uncertain.

The politics of deployment in Iraq

On 24 September 2002, the government published a dossier, based partly on intelligence, with a foreword from Prime Minister Tony Blair. This said: 'The document discloses that his [Saddam Hussein's] military planning allows for some of the Weapons of Mass Destruction (WMD) to be ready within 45 minutes of an order to use them.'[5] The dossier prompted some of the press to report that Britain, or at least, British military bases in Cyprus, were 'just 45 minutes from attack'.[6] A year later, the *Sunday Times* correspondent Andrew Gilligan reported on the BBC Radio 4 *Today* programme that the so-called '45-minute claim' was included in the dossier at the insistence of Alastair Campbell, Blair's director of communications. Gilligan's source might have been Dr David Kelly, one of the chief weapons inspectors at the United Nations (UN). Kelly committed suicide shortly afterwards and, at the Hutton Inquiry into his death, the chair of the Joint Intelligence Committee, John Scarlett, said that the report could have made clearer that the 45-minute claim referred to battlefield munitions and not to longer-range strategic weapons.[7] The intelligence community did not

---

[5] 'Labour MPs Split Over Iraq Dossier', *The Times*, 25 September 2002.
[6] For instance, this was the headline in the *London Evening Standard*, and The *Sun* said 'Brits 45 Minutes from Doom'.
[7] Mary Ann Sieghart, 'There was No Crime, but Hoon is Guilty of it', *The Times*, 12 September 2003.

consider Saddam Hussein to be an 'imminent' threat to the United Kingdom.[8] Neither Defence Secretary Geoff Hoon nor Scarlett corrected the reporting of the '45-minute claim', although Hoon recognized that its rendering was 'more dramatic than the material upon which it is based'.[9]

The 45-minute claim, and the emphasis on Iraq's WMD, demonstrated the significance of national defence to the political and public legitimization of committing British forces to war. In fact, the government's motives for entering Iraq were not primarily to do with defending the British nation from immediate attack by another state. Rather, Blair was motivated in several ways: partly by the ideal of pursuing New Labour's 'ethical' or 'humanitarian' foreign policy and therefore of using British forces to protect people from 'evil' dictatorship; partly by his world view, influenced by President Bush, especially after the 9/11 attacks in the United States, that 'rogue states' or the 'axis of evil' threatened British interests everywhere because such states might undermine the spread of liberal democracy and globalization, or might sponsor terrorist attack on a massive scale, particularly if WMD were available to them; and partly by his conception of Britain's historic role of standing 'shoulder to shoulder' with the United States, strengthening Britain's international influence by forming a lynchpin or a pivot in the American–European relationship and the Atlantic Alliance.[10]

The deployment of British military forces to a pre-emptive attempt to depose Saddam Hussein, without a second UN resolution specifically authorizing the action, was therefore unprecedented. It indicated that Britain would use its armed forces ostensibly to protect people in another country from the iniquity of their president, rather than in a narrow conception of national defence. That said, the action was driven by the US administration, and Britain's choice was the extent to which it backed this. Bush told Blair that Britain could stand outside the combat phase of the war but, as Blair noted in his diary at Christmas 2002, he felt that if Britain was 'in', it was better to go in fully.[11] In a vote in the House of Commons on 18 March 2003, the Conservatives voted with the Labour Party in favour of using armed force to enter Iraq. The former foreign secretary Robin Cook, one of the architects of New Labour's 'ethical' foreign policy, resigned the previous day, and a quarter of Labour MPs voted against the proposal. Blair

---

[8] Report of the Inquiry into the Circumstances surrounding the death of Dr David Kelly C. M. G., by Lord Hutton, 28 January 2004, HMSO. (Hutton Inquiry), paragraph 221, 920173PAG1 (fas.org)
[9] Report of Hutton Inquiry, paragraph 225, reporting Hoon's evidence on 22 September 2003. 920173PAG1 (fas.org)
[10] See, for instance, David Coates and Joel Krieger, *Blair's War* (Cambridge: Polity Press, 2004).
[11] Tony Blair, *A Journey* (London: Arrow Books, 2011).

made the vote into a *de facto* vote of confidence in his prime ministership and it passed easily by 412 votes to 149.[12]

By the summer of 2003, the fact that weapons of mass destruction had not been found in Iraq intensified questions about the basis under which the government had taken Britain to war. On 29 May, Gilligan reported that the government had 'sexed up' the September document, specifically regarding the claim that Iraq's weapons would be ready in 45 minutes.[13] After Kelly's suicide on 17 July, the government established an inquiry led by Lord Hutton, which reported in January 2004. He concluded that Gilligan's claims could not be substantiated. There was not enough evidence that the government had deliberately embellished the case for war. Nevertheless, although the Inquiry did not adjudicate on whether the government had a sufficient case to go to war, it focused attention on the issue of Iraq's WMD. In the debate after Hutton reported, Blair said that when he asked the Commons to vote on 18 March on whether to go to war, he did not know that the '45-minute claim' referred only to battlefield munitions. Robin Cook said he found this unlikely: 'I find it difficult to reconcile what I knew and what I am sure the Prime Minister knew at the time we had the vote in March.'[14]

Later that year, in November 2004, doubts about the legality of the war encouraged bereaved parents Rose Gentle and Reg Keys to create the group Military Families Against the War. In March 2005, a Freedom of Information request led the Foreign and Commonwealth Office (FCO) to release the resignation letter of Elizabeth Wilmshurst, the erstwhile deputy legal adviser to the FCO, who had resigned in March 2003. Her letter showed that she did not believe the war with Iraq was legal without a second UN Security Council resolution. It suggested that the FCO agreed with her and that Attorney General Lord Goldsmith had changed his mind.[15] In April, political speculation forced Blair to release in full Goldsmith's legal advice. Although Goldsmith had said there was a reasonable legal justification for the war, the publication showed that on 7 March he had given advice that was full of 'clarifications and warnings', as leader of the opposition Michael Howard put it in the Commons. Contrary to Blair's assurances, Goldsmith's legal advice had changed, and there was no apparent basis on which it had done so.[16]

[12] Coates and Krieger, *Blair's War*, p. 60.
[13] Transcript of *Today* programme, 29 May 2003. bbc_1_0004to0017.pdf (guardian.co.uk).
[14] Philip Webster, David Charter, and Gabriel Rozenberg, 'Blair Admits Dossier Confusion', *The Times*, 5 February 2004.
[15] Frances Gibb, 'Attorney Changed Mind Twice', *The Times*, 24 March 2005; 'The Attorney General's Advice on the Iraq War', *The Independent*, 24 April 2005. The Attorney General's advice on the Iraq war | The Independent | The Independent
[16] David Charter and Rosemary Bennett, 'After Iraq Advice u-turn', *The Times*, 29 April 2005.

This evidence galvanized Military Families Against the War to press for a public inquiry. To draw attention to their cause, Keys stood against Blair in his Sedgefield constituency in the May 2005 general election and Gentle against the armed forces minister Adam Ingram in East Kilbride, Strathaven and Lesmahagow. Gentle said that they had been told that Britain was fighting a war justified in international law. Now they knew that 'their military orders were unlawful and the war was illegal'. As time went on, she indicated, the military families believed that Blair had lied. If the government did not announce a public inquiry within fourteen days they would make an immediate application for judicial review.[17] Bringing their case to the High Court, Gentle and Keys stressed that they would not be there if WMD had been found and if the Attorney General had not changed his advice.[18]

The families lost that legal challenge in December 2005 but, in July 2006, won the right to bring a judicial review to the Court of Appeal. On 10 April 2008, that challenge again failed. Led by Rabinder Singh QC, the case was that under the European Convention of Human Rights, if the state was involved in the use of lethal force, an inquiry was mandatory. However, the nine Supreme Court judges ruled that this could not apply: '[T]he proud sovereign states of Europe [would not have] bound themselves legally to establish an independent public inquiry into the process by which a decision might have been made to commit the state's armed forces to war.'[19]

Despite this, the challenges to the legality of the war in Iraq weakened Blair and, on 27 June 2007, he stepped down and Gordon Brown took over as prime minister. Two years later, Brown bowed to public and political pressure and agreed to an inquiry. Initially he wanted this to be in private, but he rapidly backtracked and Sir John Chilcot, chosen to lead it, stated that it should take place in public.[20] Parts of the press criticized the Chilcot Inquiry for taking too long. The inquiry stopped taking evidence in 2011, but the report was not published until July 2016, partly because of 'Maxwellization', which allowed anyone criticized to have a chance to respond, but also because of the time it took to declassify, gather and analyse the large volume of written evidence.[21]

When Chilcot did report, however, the results were damning. The Inquiry found that the decision to commit British forces was made on the 'basis of

[17] Michael Evans, 'Families of Dead Soldiers Challenge the Legality of the War', *The Times*, 4 May 2005.
[18] Michael Horsnell, 'Families in High Court Fight for Iraq War Inquiry', *The Times*, 18 August 2005.
[19] Frances Gibb, 'Dead Soldiers' Mothers Fail to Force Inquiry into Legality of Iraq Invasion', *The Times*, 10 April 2008.
[20] 'Iraq Inquiry Must be Public, Says Chairman', *The Times*, 23 June 2009.
[21] 'Damaging Delay', *The Times*, 21 August 2015.

flawed intelligence assessments', because nobody seriously considered that Saddam Hussein might have destroyed his weapons stocks.[22] Intelligence 'was not challenged and should have been' and therefore the threat posed by Saddam Hussein had been overstated. Blair committed himself to the American president – 'I'm with you whatever' – before the case for war had been made and there was no basis for Goldsmith's change of heart when he advised the war was lawful. Further, there was inadequate planning for the aftermath of the invasion.[23] Blair apologized to the families of the dead but repeated that he believed the moral cause for going to war was justified and therefore he had done the right thing.[24]

Remembering the dead: Wootton Bassett

Military Families Against the War focused on the politics of deployment in Iraq. However, it was the dead of Helmand Province in Afghanistan who stimulated a transformation in the conventions of remembering British war dead. That transformation was most visible as people came to the town of Wootton Bassett in the summer of 2009 to line the route of the hearses containing repatriated bodies of service personnel. Initially, following the tradition established after the 1982 Falklands War, when bodies were repatriated for the first time, there was little political or public ceremony. On arrival in the United Kingdom, there would be a military ceremony to which the family was invited. A coroner would then hold an inquest, the body would be conveyed to the family's funeral director and the funeral arranged as per the family's wishes.

The journey of the hearses through the town of Wootton Bassett had begun in 2007 when flights started to land at RAF Lyneham because of a problem with the runway at RAF Brize Norton, and Wootton Bassett found itself on the route from the airfield to the mortuary. Three members of the British Legion spotted the carriages and asked the airbase to notify them in advance. On a subsequent occasion, the hearse's journey coincided with a bell-ringing practice at the local church and a custom developed of tolling the bells for the dead.[25] On 15 July 2009, as eight hearses passed through, Wootton Bassett made front page news

[22] Sean O'Neill, 'Spy Chiefs were Too Eager to Please with Flawed Weapons Intelligence', *The Times*, 7 July 2016.
[23] 'Catalogue of Failure', *The Times*, 7 July 2016.
[24] Lucy Fisher, 'I'm Deeply Sorry but I did the Right Thing', *The Times*, 7 July 2016.
[25] Will Pavia, 'Town that Paid Respects with Dignity Becomes Grief Tourism's Front Line', *The Times*, 29 July 2009.

with increasing numbers of people going to the town to pay their respects or show their grief.[26]

The practice of crowds lining the route in Wootton Bassett probably then grew because of the growing number of dead. Following deployment of British forces to Helmand in 2006, and the increase in their number in spring 2008, deaths in Afghanistan peaked at more than 100 in 2009 and 2010, and reduced again to just over 40 in 2011, before beginning to tail off from 2013. Further, as deaths mounted, the unpopularity of the campaign in Afghanistan increased. The British were accustomed to understanding death in war in terms of eventual victory, but forces in Afghanistan seemed to be facing defeat.[27] Challenged about its policies, the government might have welcomed this public display of support for the armed forces.[28] By 2009, one poll showed that the conflict's unpopularity had grown from 31 per cent to 'somewhere between 51 and 56 per cent' of respondents.[29] Some people maintained that British forces were redeployed to Helmand to compensate for failure in Basra and therefore some of the unpopularity of the Iraq War transferred to the campaign in Afghanistan. Others saw Helmand in terms of British overstretch. The House of Commons Defence Select Committee suggested in July 2011 that 'given the demanding nature of the situation in Iraq, we do not consider that the implications of the decision to move UK armed forces into the South of Afghanistan in early 2006 were fully thought through, in particular, the potential risk to UK armed forces personnel'.[30] Some relatives of the dead believed that their sons or husbands had been under-equipped. Margaret Evison's son Lieutenant Mark Evison died on 12 May 2009 from wounds sustained on patrol in Helmand. She suggested that poor radio equipment and delays in helicopter evacuation contributed to Mark's death.[31] One reporter attending a repatriation ceremony in November reported that the crowd favoured British retreat from Afghanistan.[32] Some have suggested that soldiers were now seen as victims, and repatriation ceremonies 'a silent protest to a war that most ordinary people did not support nor want'.[33]

---

[26] *The Times*, From all corners, Britain turns out for its dead, p. 1.
[27] Hew Strachan and Susan Schulman, 'The Town that Weeps: Commemorating Life and Loss in Wootton Bassett', *The RUSI Journal*, December 2010, 155, p. 6.
[28] K. Neil Jenkings, Nick Megoran, Rachel Woodward, and Daniel Bos, 'Wootton Bassett and the Political Spaces of Remembrance and Mourning', *Area*, 2012, 44(3), pp. 356–63, 361.
[29] Cited in Michael Clarke, 'The Helmand Decision', *Whitehall Papers*, 2011, 77(1), p. 5.
[30] House of Commons, Defence Select Committee, Operations in Helmand 2006, paragraph 28, 11 July 2011. House of Commons – Operations in Afghanistan – Defence Committee (parliament.uk).
[31] Margaret Evison, *Death of a Soldier: A Mother's Story* (London: Biteback, 2012), pp. 171–209.
[32] Valentine Low, 'More sad Homecomings but Public Mood is Changing', *The Times*, 11 November 2009.
[33] Sandra Walklate, Gabe Mythen, and Ross McGarry, 'Witnessing Wootton Bassett: An Exploration in Cultural Victimology', *Crime, Media, Culture*, 2011, 7(2), p. 163.

However, people did not line the streets in Wootton Bassett to protest against the war. Rather, following traditions of war commemoration, they wanted to pay their respects to the dead. But the new practice showed the public viewed soldiers in a new way. Soldiers came to be remembered increasingly as individuals, killed less for Queen and country or campaign, but doing a job at which they excelled, mourned by loving families. That professionalization and domestication of their memories muted criticism of soldiers and of the armed services. Anthony King called this 'postmodern memory'. Soldiers were no longer regarded as purveyors of state-sanctioned violence, as they might have been in the 1970s and early 1980s. Instead, the public could support the armed services and show sympathy and respect for soldiers but criticize the government who had sent them to war.[34]

This postmodern memory reflected social change. Fewer people had personal experience of armed service, and hence the experience, particularly of combat, came to be more revered. Traditional class structures had eroded, leading to less public distaste towards infantry soldiers, particularly those in the ranks. Society had become more individualized and confessional, making public expression of emotion, particularly by men, more acceptable.[35] But postmodern memory also derived from the specific political circumstances of these conflicts and of twenty-first-century Britain. If the soldiers were victims, then they were victims not of war. Rather, they were victims of a government that did not have to pay its own personal price for the conflicts it authorized; and they were victims of government decisions that put the army in a position where it could not triumph, and of government resourcing that did not prioritize its troops sufficiently. In that sense, remembrance at Wootton Bassett looked back to a previous era, in which the armed services had greater influence and more resources, and in which Britain had more global presence.

War crimes inquiries and trials

The conflicts in Iraq and Afghanistan drew attention to issues of ethics in the armed services as never before. In previous conflicts, reports of atrocity had usually been suppressed or handled by inquiries that shielded the institution from scrutiny. By contrast, in Iraq, investigations into allegations of abuse by British soldiers began early in the campaign. First, in May 2003, a British soldier

---

[34] Anthony King, 'The Afghan War and Postmodern Memory: Commemoration and the Dead of Helmand', *The British Journal of Sociology*, 2010, 61(1), pp. 1–25.
[35] Helen Parr, *Our Boys: The Story of a Paratrooper* (London: Allen Lane, 2018), pp. 287–93.

from the 1st Battalion, The Royal Regiment of Fusiliers, took his photographs of British troops abusing Iraqis in a detention centre – 'Camp Breadbasket' – to be developed in the English town of Tamworth. A shop worker, on seeing the photographs, reported him to the police. In February 2005, a court martial found three soldiers guilty and all were jailed, for eighteen months, two years and five months, respectively. The soldier whose photographs were discovered was tried in a separate court martial a month earlier. He pleaded guilty, had the charges dropped and was sentenced to eighteen months in a young offenders' unit, which was reduced to nine months because he gave evidence against others.[36] At this point, there seemed to be little sympathy for the accused. The photographs of Iraqi prisoners being forced to simulate sex acts were shocking and echoed the scandal of the humiliation by American troops of detainees at Abu Ghraib prison, which broke in April 2004.[37] However, although the major in charge of the facility had given an order to round up and 'work hard' looters, no officers were charged, prompting comment from the defence counsel that the prosecuted soldiers were 'scapegoats'.[38] Further, in May 2004, the editor of the *Daily Mirror*, Piers Morgan, was sacked after publishing photographs of abuse that were subsequently shown to be fake. His sacking illustrated that the *Daily Mirror* had been willing to expose such abuse, but also that subsequent evidence might lose its shock factor, find its authenticity called into question, or be embellished or fabricated.[39]

As more allegations emerged, contestations about who, how and whether to prosecute also became more intense. First, in July 2004, a young private soldier with the King's Own Scottish Borderers was charged with wounding a thirteen-year-old Iraqi at a checkpoint. His mother was angered: 'Tony Blair makes the bullets and my boy fires them. The politicians sit in Westminster twiddling their thumbs while my son is out there risking his life.'[40] She spearheaded a campaign that reduced the charges to negligent discharge, although the MOD paid compensation to the victim.[41] Second, following the death of Hassan Said during an attempted arrest in Basra, the investigating commanding officer of the 2nd Battalion, Royal Tank Regiment, found that no offence had been committed. In September 2004, Attorney General Lord Goldsmith overturned this judgement,

---

[36] 'Four Soldiers Charged with Abusing Iraqis', *The Times*, 15 June 2004; 'Eighteen More Troops Face Iraq Abuse Trials', *The Times*, 4 February 2005.

[37] 'Abuse Pictures that Shame the British Army', *The Scotsman*, 19 January 2005.

[38] 'Eighteen More Troops Face Iraq Abuse Trials'; 'Iraq Abuse Case Soldiers Jailed', *BBC News*, 25 February 2005.

[39] 'Piers Morgan Sacked from Daily Mirror', *The Guardian*, 14 May 2004.

[40] 'Soldier Charged with Wounding 13 Year Old Iraqi', *The Times*, 3 July 2004.

[41] 'Record Damages for Iraqi Victim of Gunfire Incident', *Daily Record*, 16 April 2008.

and Trooper Williams was charged with the murder.[42] Subsequently, in April 2005, charges against Trooper Williams were dropped because, following evidence from senior commanders in Iraq, Mrs Justice Hallett judged that the legal test was the soldier's 'actual perception of danger'. Williams believed his life, and the life of his colleague, to be at risk, and therefore there was no chance of a prosecution.[43] Third, in February 2005, seven paratroopers were charged with the murder of an Iraqi civilian in a fatal roadside beating in May 2003.[44] In November 2005, charges against the paratroopers were also dropped, as the judge ruled that the evidence from Iraqi witnesses was unreliable, and one or more had been paid to lie in their witness testimony.[45] Fourth, three further soldiers, two from the Irish Guards and one from the Coldstream Guards, were also acquitted of manslaughter after an Iraqi boy they detained drowned in a canal.

The persistence of the father of Baha Mousa, the hotel receptionist killed in detention in Basra in September 2003, ensured that his son's case came to dominate attention. In December 2004, Rabinder Singh QC, representing Iraqi families, won a case at the High Court that the Human Rights Act could be extended to British prisons abroad. This meant that Defence Secretary Geoff Hoon was in breach of the Human Rights Act by failing to conduct an independent inquiry into Mousa's death.[46] Subsequently, the Attorney General Lord Goldsmith judged that three men from the Queen's Lancashire Regiment would be the first Britons to be tried under the International Criminal Court Act of 2001, as this was the most up-to-date legislation. The soldiers charged included their commanding officer (CO), Lieutenant Colonel Jorge Mendonca. The regiment felt the prosecution of the CO was unfair because no officers had been charged in the 'Breadbasket' case referred to earlier. Mendonca was cleared at court martial in 2007. The judge argued that as his superiors had condoned the use of hooding and placing detainees in stress positions, he did not have a case to answer.[47] One soldier, Corporal Donald Payne, pleaded guilty to a charge of inhumane treatment and received a sentence, but he was acquitted of manslaughter and perverting the course of justice. Two other soldiers, and two intelligence officers, were also acquitted. The judge, Mr Justice McKinnon, said that some soldiers had not been charged 'because there is no evidence against

[42] Michael Evans Horsnell, 'Army on Trial Over Murder Charge Soldier', *The Times*, 8 September 2004.
[43] Richard Norton-Taylor, 'Trooper's Murder Charge is Dropped', *The Guardian*, 8 April 2005.
[44] 'Soldiers Face Death Charge', *The Times*, 3 February 2005.
[45] 'Iraq Murder Trial Charges Dropped', *BBC*, 3 November 2005.
[46] 'Iraqi Wins Court Battle Over Death in British Jail', *The Times*, 14 December 2004.
[47] 'Judge Reveals Why he Acquitted Officer', *The Times*, 13 March 2007.

them as a result of a more or less obvious closing of ranks'.[48] Subsequently, the head of the British Army, General Sir Richard Dannatt, said that the prosecuting authority and the Royal Military Police would consider whether a further investigation was appropriate as Mousa had died of asphyxiation and 93 injuries and this could not be considered misjudgement in the heat of the moment.[49] On 15 May 2008, the MOD bowed to pressure and agreed to hold a public inquiry.

That inquiry, led by the Rt Hon Sir William Gage, reported in September 2011. His verdict was damning. One *Times* reporter called it 'Britain's Abu Ghraib moment'.[50] The report showed widespread abuse by soldiers and looking away by superiors and criticised the CO either for not knowing that the abuse was happening or for turning a blind eye to it. In the House of Lords, the Conservative hereditary peer and Parliamentary Under-Secretary of State at the MOD, Lord Astor of Hever, called the events leading up to Mousa's death 'deplorable, shocking and shameful', and pointed to the failures of British command in not knowing that abusive techniques were banned and the lack of moral courage in not reporting what was happening.[51] The Iraq Historical Allegations Team (IHAT) was to undertake further investigation. IHAT had begun work in November 2010 to ensure Britain's compliance with the European Convention of Human Rights (ECHR). Its role was to investigate allegations of unlawful killings and ill-treatment and to assess if they were credible. According to IHAT's website, about 70 per cent of claims were sifted out and never reached full investigation. If IHAT found credible evidence of potential criminal acts, they referred the case to the Director of Service Prosecutions in accordance with the Armed Forces Act 2006. If they did not find credible evidence but were still concerned, they could pass the case back to the MOD who could then refer it to the Iraq Fatality Investigations (IFI).[52] The existence of IHAT and IFI prevented claims from being taken to the International Criminal Court (ICC) because it could not investigate if the national authority was doing so.

However, after this point, public and, to an extent, political opinion began to turn against the investigation of alleged abuse by British soldiers. In 2009, the government set up the al-Sweady Inquiry under Sir Thayne Forbes, because

[48] CM79/22/19-23, cited in The Report of the Baha Mousa Inquiry, The Rt Hon Sir William Gage, 8 September 2011. The Baha Mouse Public Inquiry Report HC 1452-I (publishing.service.gov.uk).

[49] Michael Evans, 'Acquitted Soldiers Face Army Inquiry into Prisoner Abuse', *The Times*, 2 May 2007.

[50] Deborah Haynes, 'Baha Mousa "Shame"', *The Times*, and Editorial, 'A Chastening Verdict: Baha Mousa's Death in Cold Blood, Not the Heat of Battle, is a Terrible Indictment of the British Armed Forces', 9 September 2011.

[51] Hansard, House of Lords, vol.730, 8 September 2011, Baha Mousa Inquiry – Hansard – UK Parliament.

[52] Iraq Historic Allegations Team (IHAT) – GOV.UK (www.gov.uk).

the MOD had not properly investigated claims that British soldiers murdered twenty Iraqis and abused nine others at the Camp Abu Naji base. In 2014 the Inquiry reported that soldiers were guilty of mistreating detainees, but that the murder allegations were 'wholly without foundation and entirely the product of deliberate lies, reckless speculation and ingrained hostility'.[53] Two years later, Phil Shiner, the human rights lawyer who had brought most of the cases to the ICC admitted using and paying intermediaries and changing some evidence about how the clients had been identified.[54] Shortly afterwards, Shiner was struck off.[55]

Shiner's misconduct gave force to a reaction in elements of the press against investigating soldiers. For instance, IFI had considered again the cases of Trooper Williams and the seven paratroopers who had been cleared of murder charges in 2005.[56] The *Daily Mail* reported that while Williams was 'penniless and jobless after being repeatedly hounded by ambulance chasing lawyers', the victim's family could receive a large payout in compensation.[57] The newspaper also reported: 'Cleared UK troops could face a war crimes trial: prosecutors in The Hague refuse to grant soldiers immunity from fresh charges'. The presiding judge at IFI, Sir George Newman, commented that the article was substantially incorrect. The United Kingdom had a legal obligation to carry out the investigations just as the ICC, which was a court of last resort, had a legal obligation to examine claims lodged with them.[58] However, the idea that human rights legislation originating in Europe was making it impossible for soldiers to fight, and that opponents of Britain could use the courts to bring sometimes egregious claims, began to gain wider purchase.[59] In February 2017, Defence Secretary Michael Fallon closed IHAT. In June 2019, Jeremy Hunt and Boris Johnson, both contending for leadership of the Conservative Party, backed a

---

[53] Richard Norton-Taylor and Ian Cobain, 'Al-Sweady Inqiry: Iraqis Mistreated but UK Troops did not Murder Insurgents', *The Guardian*, 14 December 2014.

[54] 'I was Wrong, Says Lawyer in Torture Cases Against the Army', *The Times*, 9 December 2016.

[55] 'Phil Shiner: Iraq Human Rights Lawyer Struck Off Over Misconduct', *The Guardian*, 2 February 2017.

[56] 'Soldiers were Still at war When Iraqi Died at Checkpoint', *The Times*, 11 November 2014.

[57] 'Betrayal of a Hero: Sgt Kevin Williams went Through 12 Years of Hell Before Being Cleared of Killing an Iraqi. Now he's Jobless and broke . . . While the Dead Man's Family are in Line for a Big Payout', *Daily Mail*, 23 March 2015.

[58] Ian Drury and Larisa Brown, *Daily Mail*, 21 January 2015, https://www.dailymail.co.uk/news/article-2919225/Cleared-UK-troops-face-war-crimes-trial-Prosecutors-Hague-refuse-grant-soldiers-immunity-fresh-charges.html; Iraq Fatality Investigations, Consolidated report into the death of Nadheem Abdullah and Hassan Abbas Said, CM9023, March 2015. Iraq Fatalities Investigations: consolidated report into the death of Nadheem Abdullah and the death of Hassan Abbas Said (publishing.service.gov.uk).

[59] Tom Tugendhat, 'Our Enemies are Using the Courts as a Weapon of War', *The Times*, 19 December 2014; Melanie Philips, 'Soldiers are Facing a Human Rights Minefield', *The Times*, 27 September 2016.

report by the Policy Exchange think tank to amend the Human Rights Act to protect veterans from prosecution for anything that happened before the act took force in 2000. They also wanted specific legislation to protect soldiers who had served in Northern Ireland during the 'Troubles' after the prosecution of Soldier F for murder and attempted murder during Bloody Sunday in January 1972.[60]

Public support also crystallized around 'Marine A', Sergeant Alexander Blackman.[61] Blackman was charged with murder after headcam footage that surfaced in an unrelated investigation revealed him shooting a mortally wounded Taliban fighter in Afghanistan. He said: 'shuffle off this mortal coil, you c***', turned to his men and said 'this goes no further. I've just broken the Geneva Convention'. In December 2013, at court martial, Blackman was given a life sentence, told he would serve at least ten years, reduced to the ranks and dismissed with disgrace. The judge said he had brought the armed services into disrepute. He was the first serviceman in modern times to be convicted of murder.[62]

The campaign to reduce his sentence began immediately. His wife said the troops in Afghanistan were under strain unimaginable to civilians and that Blackman had believed the Afghan was already dead.[63] She maintained he had been let down by the chain of command and commented that he should be tried by a civilian jury, where he would be likely to receive more lenient treatment. Admiral Lord West, formerly First Sea Lord and Chief of Naval Staff, wrote to the *Times* to agree. At Blackman's court martial, the 5-2 verdict was sufficient for conviction but in a civilian jury it would result in a retrial.[64] The author Frederick Forsyth and the brigadier who commanded 3 Commando Brigade during the Falklands War, Major General Julian Thompson, joined the campaign to reduce his sentence. Blackman told the *Daily Mail*: 'I had been sent to a brutal battlefield to fight for my country in an unpopular war. And yet at the end of my trial, the establishment lined up to portray me as an evil scumbag.'[65] Forsyth, Richard Drax MP, Major General John Holmes and former Royal Marine John Davies each contributed £50,000 to the campaign, arguing that the court martial judge had failed to offer a manslaughter conviction. In March 2017, Blackman was

---

[60] Lucy Fisher, 'Backing for New Law to Protect Soldiers', *The Times*, 29 June 2019.
[61] See also Chapter 11 in this volume.
[62] 'Sorry Says Marine Jailed for Ten Years Over Afghan Killing', *The Times*, 7 December 2013.
[63] Danielle Sheridan, 'My Husband is No Murderer', *The Times*, 14 December 2013.
[64] Richard Vinen, 'We are Too Sentimental About Our Armed Forces', *The Times*, 29 August 2014; Admiral Lord West, letter to the *Times*, 31 October 2015.
[65] 'Campaign to Review Murder Sentence of Marine', *The Times*, 12 September 2015.

released. His sentence was reduced to manslaughter and five appeal judges accepted he was suffering from a mental health disorder at the time of the killing, exacerbated by the dreadful conditions in which his patrol operated.[66]

These examples illustrate the complexity of the legal and political environment in which allegations of abuse were brought to court martial and public inquiry. They suggest an evolution of public opinion, from an early horror at the treatment of Iraqi detainees and readiness to prosecute soldiers, to a growth in sympathy for soldiers who were cleared at court martial and re-questioned in inquiry. This was often a reaction to the form that inquiries took. Arguments were made that human rights legislation originating in the European Convention on Human Rights, which had been incorporated into British law in 1998 as part of New Labour's reforms of foreign policy, made the job of a soldier harder.

As the wars continued, the public response to Marine A's case began to suggest public views had evolved from 'postmodern memory' of support for the troops but disdain for the government as displayed at Wootton Bassett. The headcam evidence meant nobody could dispute Blackman had shot his adversary. During the campaign to reduce his sentence, he was portrayed as a courageous soldier who had been let down by his military superiors and was suffering under the psychological stresses of battle. It was wrong to single him out because, as a sergeant, his role in the army was limited and because civilians could not understand the daily dangers faced by service personnel. Public support developed at least in part because he was perceived as relatively powerless in the context of a military hierarchy, government decision-making machine and legal bureaucracy. If this is correct, it indicates a perception on the part of the public of a division between 'the establishment' – which might include senior military as well as politicians, lawyers and academics – and ordinary people, doing their best in the difficult circumstances in which they found themselves.

Conclusion

The wars in Iraq and Afghanistan were fought in a new era. Britain did not face an existential threat as it had done in the Second World War and the Cold War, although Tony Blair's argument that Saddam Hussein possessed WMD illustrated his awareness that such a defence mattered in the legitimization of war.[67] Rather,

---

[66] 'Marine A will Get Police Protection Once Released', *The Times*, 29 March 2017.
[67] Alan Doig and Mark Phythian, 'The National Interest and the Politics of Threat Exaggeration: The Blair Government's Case for War Against Iraq', *The Political Quarterly*, 2005, 76(3), pp. 368–76.

Blair sought to use British forces for what he saw as the greater international good, deposing a dictator and diminishing threats to a stable international order by promoting democracy overseas. The connection with the 9/11 terrorist attacks in the United States gave legitimacy to Britain's engagement in Afghanistan, at least in the early stages, and the wars were often framed in terms of defence against terrorists. However, the fact that WMD were not found in Iraq meant many service families questioned the legitimacy of the war when their relatives were killed, and this contributed to weakening support for Blair and the Labour government and to growing public sympathy for service personnel as the wars continued without meeting Britain's goals and as more of them died.

Responses to the death of service personnel also led to a change in commemorative practices, as they were understood less as representatives of a collective and more as individuals and professionals who died doing jobs they loved. The spontaneous repatriation ceremonies at Wootton Bassett suggested a tendency for the public to support the military and to sympathize with the individuals in it, but to blame the government for the fact that Britain was at war. The treatment of soldiers after allegations of abuse or criminality indicated a slightly different public attitude, as soldiers were seen not only as victims of government policy but also as pawns toyed with by a wider legal, military and political 'establishment'. The British Army and MOD's long-standing tendency towards 'put up, shut up, cover up' when it came to allegations contributed to the length and intensity of some of the inquiries. Social media and headcam technology meant the behaviour of soldiers was sometimes brought into public view and the new legal apparatus of the Human Rights Act 1998 and the International Criminal Court Act meant the MOD and armed services operated in a new environment. This stimulated a political, as well as public, reaction against the idea of 'hauling soldiers through the courts', particularly for alleged crimes committed before 1998.

The extent to which changes in commemorative practices might become permanent remains to be seen. The sympathy expressed for individual service personnel could add to the difficulties of committing British forces to high-profile operations, although different politics of deployment or outcomes on operation could change that. It is also uncertain how the armed services and government will respond to any future allegations of abuse. The armed services' reputation would surely be better served, however, by working to prevent abuses taking place at all and to address proficiently allegations of criminality in order to avoid them being drawn into the everyday politics of British national life.

Bibliography

Afghanistan Inquiry, Report of; (Australia 'Brereton Report' November 2020). https://www.defence.gov.au/about/reviews-inquiries/afghanistan-inquiry.

Afghanistan Inquiry; UK Inquiry Investigating Matters Arising from the Deployment of British Armed Forces into Afghanistan from 2010. Website of the Inquiry is available at https://www.iia.independent-inquiry.uk/.

Akam, Simon. *The Changing of the Guard – The British Army Since 9/11*, London: Scribe Publications, 2021.

Anandakugan, Nithyani. *The Sri Lankan Civil War and Its History, Revisited in 2020*, 31 August 2020. https://hir.harvard.edu/sri-lankan-civil-war/.

Anderson, David. *Histories of the Hanged: The Dirty War in Kenya and the End of Empire*, New York: W.W. Norton, 2005.

Aspinall-Oglander, C. F. *History of the Great War: Military Operations Gallipoli (Vol. II) May 1915 to the Evacuation*, London: William Heinemann, 1932.

Bandura, Albert. 'Moral Disengagement in the Perpetration of Inhumanities'. *Personality and Social Psychology Review*, 1999, 3, pp. 193–209.

Barry, Ben. *Blood, Metal and Dust – How Victory Turned Into Defeat in Afghanistan and Iraq*, Oxford: Osprey Publishing, 2021.

Bartlett, F. C. *Remembering: A Study in Experimental and Social Psychology*, Cambridge: Cambridge University Press, 1932.

BBC Panorama. *SAS Death Squads Exposed; A British War Crime*. BBC, 2022. https://www.bbc.co.uk/programmes/m0019707.

BBC Panorama Investigation into Repeated Killings by an SAS Unit in Afghanistan. 2019. https://www.bbc.co.uk/news/uk-62083196.

Bellingcat. 'Tracking the Faceless Killers Who Mutilated a Ukrainian POW'. 6 August 2022. https://www.bellingcat.com/news/2022/08/05/tracking-the-faceless-killers-who-mutilated-and-executed-a-ukrainian-pow/

Benest, David. 'A Liberal Democratic State and COIN: The Case of Britain, or Why Atrocities Can Still Happen'. *Civil Wars*, 2012, 14(1), pp. 29–48.

Benest, David. 'Atrocities in Britain's Counter-Insurgencies'. *The RUSI Journal*, 2011, 156(3), pp. 80–7.

Benest, David. 'British Atrocities in Counter Insurgency'. *Encyclopedia of Military Ethics*, 10 April 2011, https://www.militaryethics.org/British-Atrocities-in-Counter-Insurgency/10/.

Benest, David. 'British Leaders and Irregular Warfare'. In *The Moral Dimensions of Asymmetrical Warfare*, edited by Th. A. van Barda and D. E. M. Verweij, Leiden: Brill, 2009, 169–78.

Benest, David. 'Review of Aaron Edwards, *Mad Mitch's Tribal Law: Aden and the End of Empire* (Edinburgh: Mainstream 2014)'. *RUSI Journal*, June 2014, 159(3), pp. 101–2.

Benest, David. 'Review of *An Army of Tribes* by Ed Burke'. *British Army Review*, Summer 2019, 175, pp. 175–9.

Benest, David. '*Review of Morality and War: Can War be Just in the Twenty-first Century?* By David Fisher'. *RUSI Journal*, 2011, 156(4), pp. 80–7.

Benest, David. 'Review of *Secret Victory: The Intelligence War That Beat the IRA* by William Matchett'. *British Army Review*, Winter 2018, 171, p. 138.

Bennett, Hew. *Fighting the Mau Mau: The British Army and Counter-Insurgency in the Kenya Emergency*, Cambridge: Cambridge University Press, 2012.

Blackman, Alexander. *Marine A: My Toughest Battle*, London: Mirror, 2019.

Blair, Tony. *A Journey*, London: Arrow Books, 2011.

Blair, Tony. *Keynote Speech by Mr. Tony Blair at Stranmillis University College Belfast*, 15 June 1999. https://cain.ulster.ac.uk/events/peace/docs/tb15699.htm.

Bloody Sunday Inquiry (Saville Report; Proceedings and Report). January 1998. https://www.bloody-sunday-inquiry.org.uk/.

Boff, Jonathan. *Haig's Enemy: Crown Prince Ruprecht and Germany's War on the Western Front*, Oxford: Oxford University Press, 2018.

Brown, Sand A. Hoskins. 'Terrorism in the New Memory Ecology: Mediating and Remembering the 2005 London Bombings'. *Behavioral Sciences of Terrorism and Political Aggression*, 2010, 2(2), pp. 87–107.

Burke, Edward. *An Army of Tribes: British Cohesion, Deviancy and Murder in Northern Ireland*, Liverpool: Liverpool University Press, 2018.

Burton, James. 'Culture; Addressing Apathy and Dishonesty Within the British Army'. 4 April 2021. https://wavellroom.com/2021/04/13/addressing-culture-apathy-dishonesty-british-army-part-2/.

Catignani, Sergio. '"Getting COIN" at the Tactical Level in Afghanistan: Reassessing Counter-insurgency Adaptation in the British Army'. *Journal of Strategic Studies*, 2012, 35(4), pp. 513–39.

Centre for Military Justice Guide. https://centreformilitaryjustice.org.uk/guide/service-complaints/.

Chandrasakaran, Rajiv. *Little America*, London: Bloomsbury, 2012.

Channel 4, 'War and Justice: The Case of Marine A'. First broadcast on 31 July 2022. https://www.channel4.com/programmes/war-and-justice-the-case-of-marine-a.

Charters, David. *Whose Mission, Whose Orders? British Civil-Military Command and Control in Northern Ireland, 1968–1974*, Montreal and Kingston: McGill-Queen's University Press, 2017.

Clarke, Michael, ed. 'The Helmand Decision'. *Whitehall Papers*, 2011, 77(1), pp. 6–31.

Cohen, Stan. *States of Denial: Knowing About Atrocities and Suffering*, Cambridge: Polity Press, 2001.

Connerton, Paul. 'Seven Types of Forgetting'. *Memory Studies*, 2008, 1(1), pp. 59–71.

Crompvoerts, Samantha. 'Special Operations Command (SOCOMD) Culture and Interactions: Perceptions, Reputation and Risk'. February 2016. https://www.defence .gov.au/about/reviews-inquiries/afghanistan-inquiry/resources.

Dewar, Michael. *The British Army in Northern Ireland*, London: Arms and Armour Press, 1985.

Dobbins, James and Carter Malkasian. 'Time to Negotiate in Afghanistan: How to Talk to the Taliban'. *Foreign Affairs*, 2015, pp. 53–64.

Doig, Alan and Mark Phythian. 'The National Interest and the Politics of Threat Exaggeration: The Blair Government's Case for War Against Iraq'. *The Political Quarterly*, 2005, 76(3), pp. 368–76.

Donohue, Laura. 'Regulating Northern Ireland: The Special Powers Acts, 1922–1972'. *The Historical Journal*, 1998, 41(4), pp. 1089–1120.

Downie, Richard. *Learning From Conflict: The US Military in Vietnam, El Salvador and That Drug War*, Westport: Praeger, 1998.

Edwards, Aaron. *Mad Mitch's Tribal Law; Aden and the End of Empire*, Edinburgh: Mainstream Publishing, 2015.

Elkins, Caroline. *Britain's Gulag – The Brutal End of Empire in Kenya*, London: Pimlico, 2005.

English, Richard. *Armed Struggle: A History of the IRA*, London: Pan, 2004.

European Court of Human Rights Judgement. *Al-Skeini and Others v. the United Kingdom*, Application no. 55721/07, 7 July 2011.

European Court of Human Rights Judgement. 'Osman v United Kingdom'. *E.H.R.R.*, 1998, 29, p. 245 at [116].

Evison, Margaret. *Death of a Soldier: A Mother's Story*, Hull: Biteback, 2012.

Farrell, Theo. 'Improving in War: Military Adaptation and the British in Helmand Province, Afghanistan, 2006–2009'. *Journal of Strategic Studies*, 2010, 33(4), pp. 567–94.

First Post. *Timeline: Unrest Connected with China's Restive Xinjiang Region*, 2014. https://www.firstpost.com/world/timeline-unrest-connected-with-chinas-restive -xinjiang-region-1731073.html. Accessed: 2022.

Fisher, David. *Morality and War: Can War be Just in the Twenty-First Century*, Oxford: Oxford University Press, 2011.

Fitz-Gibbon, Spencer, *Not Mentioned in Dispatches: The History and Mythology of the Battle of Goose Green*, Cambridge: James Clarke, 2001.

Forster, Anthony. 'British Judicial Engagement and the Juridification of the Armed Forces'. *International Affairs*, 2012, 88(2), pp. 283–300.

Fox, Aimee. *Learning to Fight: Military Innovation and Change in the British Army, 1914–1918*, Cambridge: Cambridge University Press, 2019.

Freedman, Sir Lawrence. *Command: The Politics of Military Operations From Korea to Ukraine*, London: Allen Lane, 2022.

French, David. 'Nasty Not Nice: British Counter-Insurgency Doctrine and Practice, 1945–1967'. *Small Wars & Insurgencies*, 2012, 23(4–5), pp. 744–61.

Frese, Michael and Andreus Bausch. 'Explaining the Heterogeneity of the Leadership-innovation Relationship: Ambidextrous Leadership'. *The Leadership Quarterly*, 11 August 2011.

Good Friday Agreement 'Most Important' Ahead of Northern Ireland Protocol, Boris Johnson Says, 2022. https://www.belfasttelegraph.co.uk/news/politics/good-friday -agreement-most-important-ahead-of-northern-ireland-protocol-boris-johnson -says-41640054.html.

Grossman, Lieutenant Colonel Dave. *On Killing: The Psychological Cost of Learning to Kill in War and Society*, New York: Little, Brown, 1995.

Gwynn, Major General Sir Charles. *Imperial Policing*, London: Macmillan and Co, 1934.

Hack, Karl, *Defense and Decolonization in Southeast Asia: Britain, Malaya and Singapore, 1941–68*, Richmond: Curzon, 2001.

Hale, Christopher. *Massacre in Malaya: Exposing Britain's My Lai*, Stroud: The History Press, 2013.

Hansard; Debates on the Overseas Operations (Service and Veterans) Bill (Fourth Sitting). October 2020. https://hansard.parliament.uk/commons/2020-10-08/debates /f7a00940-5c69-4b9d-9c03-dbc31feadc8d/OverseasOperations(ServicePersonnelAn dVeterans)Bill(FourthSitting).

Hansard, House of Lords, vol. 730, 8 September 2011, Baha Mousa Inquiry - Hansard - UK Parliament.

Hansard: Sgt Alexander Blackman, debate at Westminster Hall. 16 September 2015. https://hansard.parliament.uk/Commons/2015-09-16/debates/15091640000001/ SgtAlexanderBlackman(MarineA)?highlight=alexander%20blackman%23contribut ion-15091640000006.

Hansen, Thomas Obel. 'The Multiple Aspects of "Time" Rendering Justice for War Crimes in Iraq'. *International Criminal Law Review*, 2021, 21(5), pp. 1–27.

Hardt, H. 'How NATO Remembers: Explaining Institutional Memory in NATO Crisis Management'. *European Security*, 2017, 26(1), pp. 120–48.

Higham, R. D. S., ed. *Official Histories: Essays and Bibliographies From Around the World*, Kansas State University Library Bibliography Series, Manhattan: Kansas State University Library, 1970.

Hitchens, Peter. *Her Majesty's Pleasure?*, 2014. https://hitchensblog.mailonsunday.co.uk /2014/04/her-majestys-pleasure-.html.

Horne, John and Alan Kramer. *German Atrocities, 1914: A History of Denial*, New Haven: Yale University Press, 2001.

House of Commons Debates (Hansard), 8 July 1920, Vol. 131, 1705–819.

House of Commons Defence Committee. 'Obsolescent and Outgunned; The British Army's Armoured Vehicle Capability'. March 2021. https://committees.parliament .uk/publications/5081/documents/50325/default/.

House of Commons Defence Committee. 'We're Going to Need a Bigger Navy'. 2022. https://committees.parliament.uk/work/1209/the-navy-purpose-and-procurement/ news/159793/were-going-to-need-a-bigger-navy/.

House of Commons, Defence Select Committee. *Operations in Helmand 2006.* House of Commons - Operations in Afghanistan - Defence Committee (parliament.uk).

House of Commons and House of Lords Joint Committee on Human Rights. 'Legislative Scrutiny on the Overseas Operations Act (Service Personnel and Veterans) Bill Session 2019–1020'. 29 October 2020. https://committees.parliament .uk/publications/3191/documents/39059/default/.

Hughes, Matthew. *Britain's Pacification of Palestine: The British Army, the Colonial State, and the Arab Revolt, 1936–1939,* Cambridge: Cambridge University Press, 2019.

Hutton Inquiry: Report of the Inquiry into the Circumstances Surrounding the Death of Dr David Kelly C.M.G., by Lord Hutton, 28 January 2004, HMSO. (Hutton Inquiry), para 221, 920173PAG1 (fas.org).

Imperial War Museum Sound Archive, Interview with Michael Gray. Reel 28/52. https://www.iwm.org.uk/collections/item/object/80030368.

International Committee of the Red Cross. 'Customary International Humanitarian Law'. Volume 1; Rules (ICRC 2005 - Regularly updated). https://ihl-databases.icrc .org/customary-ihl/eng/docs/home?opendocument.

International Committee of the Red Cross. 'Evidence Submitted to UK Parliament Public Bill Committee on the Overseas Operations (Service Personnel and Veterans) Bill'. October 2020. https://publications.parliament.uk/pa/cm5801/cmpublic/ OverseasOperations/memo/OOB04.htm.

International Committee of the Red Cross. 'Guidelines on Investigating Violations of International Humanitarian Law: Law, Policy, and Good Practice'. 2019, para 8. https://www.icrc.org/en/document/guidelines-investigating-violations-ihl-law -policy-and-good-practice.

International Criminal Court. 'Office of the Prosecutor's Final Report on the UK/ Iraq Situation'. December 2020. https://www.icc-cpi.int/sites/default/files/ itemsDocuments/201209-otp-final-report-iraq-uk-eng.pdf.

International Criminal Court. 'Statement of the Prosecutor, Fatou Bensouda, on the Conclusion of the Preliminary Examination of the Situation in Iraq/United Kingdom Para 4'. https://www.icc-cpi.int/Pages/item.aspx?name=201209-otp -statement-iraq-uk.

International Criminal Tribunal for Rwanda (ICTR). 'The Prosecutor v. Ignace Bagilishema (Trial Judgement), ICTR-95-1A-T'. 7 June 2001, para 37. https://www .refworld.org/cases,ICTR,48abd5170.html. Accessed: 4 August 2022.

International Criminal Tribunal for Rwanda (ICTR). 'The Prosecutor v. Ignace Bagilishema (Trial Judgement), ICTR-95-1A-T'. 7 June 2001, para 38. https://www .refworld.org/cases,ICTR,48abd5170.html. Accessed: 4 August 2022.

Iraq Fatality Investigations. 'Consolidated Report Into the Death of Nadheem Abdullah and Hassan Abbas Said, CM9023'. March 2015. Iraq Fatalities Investigations: Consolidated report into the death of Nadheem Abdullah and the death of Hassan Abbas Said (publishing.service.gov.uk).

Iraq Historic Allegations Team. Iraq Historic Allegations Team (IHAT) - GOV.UK (www.gov.uk).

Jenkings, K. Neil, Nick Megoran, Rachel Woodward, and Daniel Bos. 'Wootton Bassett and the Political Spaces of Remembrance and Mourning'. *Area*, 2012, 44(3), pp. 356–63.

Judiciary NI, In the Matter of a Series of Deaths that Occurred in August 1971 at Ballymurphy, West Belfast – Incident 4, delivered 11 May 2021. https://www .judiciaryni.uk/judicial-decisions/2021-nicoroner-6.

King, Anthony. 'The Afghan War and Postmodern Memory: Commemoration and the Dead of Helmand'. *The British Journal of Sociology*, 2010, 61(1), pp. 1–25.

Kitson, General Sir Frank. 'Statement to the Bloody Sunday Inquiry, Dated 18 February 2000'. https://webarchive.nationalarchives.gov.uk/ukgwa/20101017060841/http:// report.bloody-sunday-inquiry.org/evidence/CK/CK_0001.pdf.

Krulak, General Charles C. 'Responsibility, Accountability and the Zero-Defects Mentality'. *Marine Corps Gazette*, May 1997.

Ledwidge, Frank. *Losing Small Wars*, London: Yale, 2011.

Leibold, Dr James and Nathan Ruser. *Family De-planning: The Coercive Campaign to Drive Down Indigenous Birth-rates in Xinjiang*, Barton, Canberra: Australian Strategic Policy Institute, 2021.

Lester, Nicola. 'Reflecting on the Experiences of Bereaved Military Families in the Coroner's Court'. *RUSI Journal*, 2019, 164(4), p. 30.

Liddell Hart Centre for Military Archives. King's College London, Sir Frank Cooper Papers, 4/1/2, Interview With Sir Frank Cooper, 2 April 1998.

Loden, Colonel Edward. 'Statement to the Bloody Sunday Inquiry, Dated 28 September 2000'. https://webarchive.nationalarchives.gov.uk/ukgwa/20101017060841/http:// report.bloody-sunday-inquiry.org/evidence/B/B2212.pdf.

Mallinson, Alan. *The Making of the British Army*, London: Bantam, 2011.

Mitchell, Lisa. 'Ten Years of Inquests'. *BBC News*, 4 October 2011.

Mockaitis, Thomas R. *British Counterinsurgency in the Post-Imperial Era*, Manchester: Manchester University Press, 1995.

Murray, Williamson and Peter Mansour, eds. *The Culture of Military Organisations*, Cambridge: Cambridge University Press, 2019.

Nagl, John. *Learning to Eat Soup With a Knife: Counterinsurgency Lessons From Malaya to Vietnam*, Chicago: The University of Chicago Press, 2005.

Office of the Prosecutor, International Criminal Court. 'Situation in Iraq/UK'. 2020, para 2. https://www.icc-cpi.int/sites/default/files/itemsDocuments/201209-otp-final -report-iraq-uk-eng.pdf.

Orwell, George. 'Looking Back on the Spanish Civil War'. 1942, Made available by the Orwell Foundation. https://www.orwellfoundation.com/the-orwell-foundation /orwell/essays-and-other-works/looking-back-on-the-spanish-war/#:~:text =Everyone%20believes%20in%20the%20atrocities,bothering%20to%20examine %20the%20evidence.

Parr, Helen. *Our Boys: The Story of a Paratrooper*, London: Allen Lane, 2018.

Porch, Douglas. *Counterinsurgency: Exposing the Myths of the New Way of War*, Cambridge: Cambridge University Press, 2013.

Queen's Speech, 2022. https://www.gov.uk/government/speeches/queens-speech-2022.

Report of the Inquiry Into the Circumstances Surrounding the Death of Dr David Kelly C.M.G., by Lord Hutton, 28 January 2004, HMSO. (Hutton Inquiry).

Ricketts, Peter. *Hard Choices: The Making and Unbreaking of Global Britain*, London: Atlantic 2021.

Roark, Michael; Deputy Inspector General for Evaluations. 'Evaluation of U.S. Central Command and U.S. Special Operations Command Implementation of the DoD's Law of War Program'. (Project No. D2021-DEV0PD-0045.000), 25 January 2021.

Rodger, N. A. M. *Command of the Ocean; a Naval History of Britain 1649-181'5*, New York: Penguin, 2006.

Saferworld. *Britain's Shadow Army; Policy Options for External Oversight of Britain's Special Forces*, ORG 2018, pp. 19–26. https://www.saferworld.org.uk/resources/publications/1278-britainas-shadow-army-policy-options-for-external-oversight-of-uk-special-forces.

Sanders, Andrew. 'Principles of Minimum Force and the Parachute Regiment in Northern Ireland, 1969–1972'. *Journal of Strategic Studies*, 2018, 41(5), pp. 659–83.

Shanks, Pauline Kaurin. 'Questioning Military Professionalism'. In *Redefining the Modern Military*, edited by Nathan Finney and Ty Mayfield, Annapolis, MD: Naval Institute Press, 2018.

Shaw, Kang Hwa, Na Tang, and Hung-Ye Liao. 'Authoritarian-Benevolent Leadership, Moral Disengagement, and Follower Unethical Pro-organizational Behavior: An Investigation of the Effects of Ambidextrous Leadership'. *Frontiers in Psychology*, 21 April 2020.

Sheffield, Gary. *Forgotten Victory: The First World War: Myths and Realities*, London: Headline, 2001.

Simson, H. J. *British Rule, and Rebellion*, London: William Blackwood & Sons, 1937.

Smith, General Sir Rupert. *The Utility of Force: The Art of War in the Modern World*, London: Allen Lane, 2005.

Smith, M. L. R. and Peter R. Neumann. 'Motorman's Long Journey: Changing the Strategic Setting in Northern Ireland'. *Contemporary British History*, 2005, 19(4), pp. 413–35.

Strachan, Hew. 'British Counter-Insurgency From Malaya to Iraq'. *RUSI Journal*, December 2007, 152(6), pp. 8–11.

Strachan, Hew. *The Politics of the British Army*, Oxford: Oxford University Press, 1997.

Strachan, Hew and Susan Schulman. 'The Town That Weeps: Commemorating Life and Loss in Wootton Bassett'. *The RUSI Journal*, December 2010, 155, p. 6.

Stubbins Bates, Elizabeth. 'The British Army's Training in International Humanitarian Law'. *Journal of Conflict & Security Law*, 2020, 291–315, pp. 1–25.

Stubbins Bates, Elizabeth. 'Impossible or Disproportionate Burden': The UK's Approach to the Investigatory Obligation Under Articles 2 and 3 ECHR'. *E.H.R.L.R.*, 2020, 5, pp. 499–511.

Thornton, Rod. 'The British Army and the Origins of its Minimum Force Philosophy'. *Small Wars & Insurgencies*, 2004, 15(1), p. 83.

TNA: WO 305/4209, 3rd Infantry Brigade: Records of the Meeting of the South Eastern Security Committee Meeting, 10 May 1972.

TNA, WO 305/4411, Regimental History, 2nd Battalion the Parachute Regiment for the Period 1 April 1971 to 31 March 1972.

TNA, WO 305/7876, Unit Historical Record, 2 Para Commanding Officer's Directive (96/97), dated 14 February 1996.

TNA, WO 373/138/55, Citation for the Military Cross awarded to Edward Charles Loden, 7 August 1967.

TNA, WO 373/181/310, Recommendation for the Award of the MBE to Major David Gareth Benest, 11 November 1988.

Tobin, Dr David. *The 'Xinjiang Papers': How Xi Jinping Commands Policy in the People's Republic of China*, Sheffield, England: University of Sheffield, 2022.

Transcript of Sentencing of Corporal Donald Payne. https://www.asser.nl/upload/documents/DomCLIC/Docs/NLP/UK/PaineSentencingtranscript.pdf.

Tsouras, Peter, ed. *Greenhill Dictionary of Military Quotations*, Mechanicsburg, PA: Stackpole Books, 2002.

United Kingdom Ministry of Defence. *Armed Forces Covenant*. https://assets.publishing.service.gov.uk/government/uploads/system/uploads/attachment_data/file/578212/20161215-The-Armed-Forces-Covenant.pdf.

United Kingdom Ministry of Defence. 'The Army Leadership Code; an Introductory Guide'. 2016. https://www.army.mod.uk/media/2698/ac72021_the_army_leadership_code_an_introductory_guide.pdf.

United Kingdom Ministry of Defence. 'Values and Standards of the British Army'. https://www.army.mod.uk/media/5219/20180910-values_standards_2018_final.pdf.

United Kingdom Ministry of Defence Army Doctrine. *Publication: Land Operations*, updated 31 March 2017.

United Kingdom Ministry of Justice Press Release. *UK Provides Lawyers and Police to Support ICC War Crimes Investigation*, 6 June 2022. https://www.gov.uk/government/news/uk-provides-lawyers-and-police-to-support-icc-war-crimes-investigation.

United Nations Human Rights Council. 'Report of the Special Rapporteur on Extrajudicial, Summary or Arbitrary Executions. Addendum: Study on Targeted Killings'. *Philip Alston*, 28 May 2010.

Walklate, Sandra, Gabe Mythen, and Ross McGarry. 'Witnessing Wootton Bassett: An Exploration in Cultural Victimology'. *Crime, Media, Culture*, 2011, 7(2), pp. 149–65.

Walpole, Liam. 'The US Congress Understands the Importance of Special Forces Oversight Why Doesn't the UK Parliament?'. 23 March 2019. https://blogs.lse.ac.uk/usappblog/2019/03/23/the-us-congress-understands-the-importance-of-special-forces-oversight-why-doesnt-the-uk-parliament/.

Ward, Ian and Norma Miraflor. *Slaughter and Deception at Batang Kali*, Singaport: Media Masters, 2009.

Weatherburn Dr Michael. *Project Hindsight*. https://projecthindsight.co.uk/current -projects/.

Wilford, Lt Col Derek. 'Statement to the Bloody Sunday Inquiry, Dated 18 September 2002'. https://webarchive.nationalarchives.gov.uk/ukgwa/20101017060841/http:// report.

Williams, Andrew. *A Very British Killing: The Death of Baha Mousa*, New York: Vintage, 2013.

Williams, Andrew. 'The Iraq Abuse Allegations and the Limits of UK Law'. *Public Law*, July 2018, 2018(3), pp. 461–81.

Williams, Andrew. 'War Crimes Allegations and the UK: Towards a Fairer Investigative Process'. *Legal Studies*, 2020, 40, pp. 301–20.

Williamson Victoria, Neil Greenberg, and Dominic Murphy. 'Moral Injury in UK Armed Forces Veterans: A Qualitative Survey'. *European Journal of Psychotraumatology*, 14 January 2019, https://www.kcl.ac.uk/kcmhr/publications/ assetfiles/2019/williamson2019.pdf.

Williamson, Victoria, Dominic Murphy, Andrea Phelps, David Forbes, and Neil Greenberg, 'Moral Injury: The Effect on Mental Health and Implications for Treatment'. *The Lancet*, 17 March 2021, https://www.thelancet.com/journals/lanpsy/ article/PIIS2215-0366(21)00113-9/fulltext.

Wiltshire Coroner's Office, United Kingdom. Recording of an Inquest into the Death of Highlander Scott McLaren, held in Trowbridge, 9 December 2011.

Winograd Commission Final Report (Israel 2008). http://www.mfa.gov.il/mfa/mfa -archive/2008/pages/winograd%20committee%20submits%20final%20report%2030 -jan-2008.aspx.

Winter, Jay. *War Beyond Words: Languages of Remembrance From the Great War to the Present*, Cambridge: Cambridge University Press, 2017.

Yingling, John A. 'Failure in Generalship'. *Armed Forces Journal*, May 2007. http:// armedforcesjournal.com/a-failure-in-generalship/.

Authors' biographies

Colonel David Benest OBE

Born on 29 April 1954 in north London, David Benest attended the Royal Grammar School, Guildford, where he played rugby for the first XV and was a keen member of the Combined Cadet Force. Commissioned into The Parachute Regiment in 1973, his first tour was with the 2nd Battalion in Northern Ireland, to which he was to return many times, finally in 1996 as Commanding Officer in South Armagh for which he gained his OBE. He also had several tours in the Ministry of Defence from 1986 onwards where he played a key part in the provision of equipment and communication systems for use in Northern Ireland and enjoyed the stimulus of working with scientists on the application of technology in counterterrorist operations.

David won the respect of fellow officers and soldiers for his fairness, generosity and intelligent approach to military life. He took an in-service degree in international relations at Keele University, graduating with first-class honours in 1981. The following year he was Regimental Signals Officer with 2nd Battalion, The Parachute Regiment, during the Falklands Conflict, after which he was tasked by his Commanding Officer, then Lieutenant Colonel David Chaundler, with writing an account of the battalion's campaign. This formed the basis of *2 Para Falklands: The Battalion at War* by Major General John Frost, published in 1983. David's determination to pin down the truth led him to rework the original manuscript in recent years, with the support of his sister Jacquetta, and to entrust it to the National Army Museum for safe keeping.

A soldier-scholar, David was able to combine his military and academic interests in more senior Army roles, notably as Colonel Defence Studies (Army). He was never afraid to challenge conventional wisdom, but recurring strain led to a diagnosis of PTSD (post-traumatic stress disorder), which troubled him in later years. In retirement from 2009, he reviewed numerous books for the British Army Review and pursued his arguments for a better ethical education for all ranks in the national media, military publications and discussion with military and academic colleagues. Drawing on his military experiences, he was keen to tell the truth about war and to encourage honest reflection for lessons to be learnt. A committed humanist, he believed that soldiers should be fully accountable for their actions but that they need clear ethical guidance on the responsibility they hold.

David raised more than £10,000 for The Ulysses Trust, a national charity that funds expeditions for young cadets, through a local newspaper round in Wiltshire, his home from 2001 onwards. He died of heart disease on 10 August 2020, at the age of sixty-six.

Authors

Aaron Edwards is a Senior Lecturer in Defence and International Affairs at the Royal Military Academy Sandhurst, UK, and an Honorary Research Fellow in the School of History, Politics and International Relations at the University of Leicester. He is the author of several books, including *Agents of Influence: Britain's Secret Intelligence War Against the IRA* (2021).

Dr Simon Anglim is a military historian who teaches in the Department of War Studies at King's College London. His research interests include insurgency and counter-insurgency, the strategy and history of special forces and unconventional warfare from the Second World War to the present, the life and military career of Major General Orde Wingate, the British Army in the Middle East since the 1930s, with special reference to their presence in the Oman Djebel War of the 1950s, and the Dhofar Insurgency of the 1960s to the 1970s.

Lieutenant Colonel the Reverend Nicholas Mercer was educated at St Andrews and Oxford University, admitted as a solicitor in 1990 and commissioned into the Army Legal Service in 1991. He served in Northern Ireland, Bosnia Herzegovina, Cyprus and Germany and was the Command Legal Adviser for the Iraq War, 2003. He was Liberty Human Rights Lawyer of the Year 2011–2012. Ordained in 2011, he was formerly the Rector of the Falkland Islands, South Georgia, South Sandwich Islands and British Antarctica. He has been Rector of Bolton Abbey in North Yorkshire since 2019.

Professor Andrew Williams teaches law and creative writing at the University of Warwick. Williams qualified as a solicitor in 1986. After commercial practice in London, he joined Warwick Law School in 1996. He is the author of *A Very British Killing: the Death of Baha Mousa* (2013), which won the George Orwell Prize for Political Writing. His latest book, *A Passing Fury: Searching for Justice* *at the end of WWII* (2016), examines the British investigations and trials of Nazi war criminals after 1945 and was shortlisted for the 2017 CWA Daggers Non-Fiction Award. He is currently co-director of the Centre for Human Rights in Practice and editor-in-chief of *Lacuna Magazine*.

Dr Matthew Ford came to academia after a career in business consulting. After completing his doctorate in 2008, he joined the UK civil service as a strategic analyst with DSTL. He joined the University of Sussex as a lecturer in international relations in 2013 and has worked in many military and civilian academic institutions worldwide. He is a former West Point Fellow and is currently an Associate Professor at the Swedish Defence University. Dr Ford has published widely and is the founding editor of the *British Journal of Military History*.

Dr Frank Ledwidge is a senior lecturer in military strategy and law at the University of Portsmouth. He is a former practising barrister and author of several books including *Losing Small Wars* (2011/2017) and *Aerial Warfare* (2018). He also served in the reserve forces completing several operational tours as a military intelligence officer.

Colonel Oliver Lee OBE joined the Royal Marines on graduation from Jesus College, Cambridge, in 1996. He won the Sword of Honour in training and served for eighteen years, including in Bosnia, Northern Ireland, Iraq and Afghanistan. He became the youngest full colonel since the Second World War and his senior roles included Commanding Officer of 45 Commando Group on operations in Helmand and working on the personal staff of defence ministers in Whitehall. He left the Royal Marines in 2014 and has since pursued a career as a civilian chief executive. In 2022, he became chief executive of Places Leisure, a non-dividend organization dedicated to community fitness, health and well-being.

Chris Green commissioned from the Royal Military Academy, Sandhurst, in 1989 and served in Gulf War 1, South Armagh and the Balkans, where he was awarded a Queen's Commendation for Valuable Service, before retiring in 1996. In 2010 he re-commissioned into a reserve infantry battalion and deployed to Afghanistan in 2012 with 1st Battalion Grenadier Guards, retiring a second and final time in 2016. Today he divides his time between the French Alps, where he is a founder of The Freeride Republic, and Bristol, where he occasionally drives the Bristol Harbour Ferry.

Louise Jones is a former British military intelligence officer whose service included covering a wide range of military strategic issues as well as operational deployment to Afghanistan. Louise currently works for an intelligence firm specializing in using remote sensing and geospatial data. She is regularly invited to speak on national and international media on military affairs and conflict including the war in Ukraine. She holds an MA in Chinese from the University of Edinburgh and is a fluent speaker of Mandarin.

Dr Edward Burke is an assistant professor in the history of war at University College Dublin (UCD). Prior to joining UCD, he was an assistant/associate professor in international relations at the University of Nottingham (2017–2022). From 2015 to 2017 he was a lecturer in strategic studies at the University of Portsmouth, attached to the Royal Air Force College from 2015 to 2017. He received his PhD in International Relations in 2016 from the University of St Andrews. From 2020 to 2011 he served as the Deputy Head of the International Police Coordination Board in Kabul, Afghanistan. His most recent book is *An Army of Tribes: British Army Cohesion, Deviancy and Murder in Northern Ireland* (2018).

Colonel John Wilson served for more than three decades in the Royal Artillery prior to his retirement in 2001. From 2002 to 2011, he held the post of editor of the *British Army Review*. He is the editor of *The British Army Campaign Guide to the Forgotten Fronts of the First World War* (2017).

Helen Parr is a professor of history at Keele University and author of *Our Boys: The Story of a Paratrooper* (2018). She has published on Britain's relations with Europe and British nuclear weapons policies. *Our Boys* was awarded the Templer Medal Book Prize, the Wellington Medal for Military History, the Longman-History Today Book Prize, and was longlisted for the Orwell Prize for Political Writing.

Index

Note: Page numbers followed by "n" refer to notes.